SPIRITUAL HANDBOOK FOR THE TWENTY-FIRST CENTURY

Wes Penre

Copyright © 2013 by Wes Penre
All rights reserved. This book or any portion thereof may not be reproduced or used in any manner whatsoever without the expressed written permission of the publisher, except for the use of brief quotations in a book review or scholarly journal.
Second Edition: 2021

(This book was first published as an e-book in 2013. A second edition was published as a paperback and in Kindle in 2021. Only small changes in the Introduction section was made in this Second Edition).

CONTENTS

INTRODUCTION: LOST IN A LABYRINTH OF INFORMATION 1

CHAPTER 1: THE UNIVERSE INSIDE 15
- Power of Thoughts 15
- Your Own Version of the Multiverse 19
- The Genetically Modified Food Industry and the Machine Kingdom 33
- Beliefs and Belief Systems 49
- Our DNA: A Corridor of Light Switches 55
- Exercises 58
  - Power of Thought 58
  - Create Your Own Local Universe 59
  - Maintain a Healthy Body 60
  - Practice How to Activate and Deactivate Your Own DNA 61

CHAPTER 2: PROGRAMMING FOR THE SECOND GOLDEN AGE 63
- How the Alien Invader Forces Counteract the Awakening 63
- How to View Reality 72
- Foods and Diets 82
- The Tree of Life Found? 85
- The Human Body as a Divine Vessel 88
- Our Current Life Situation 91
- What to Do About It 95
- Exercises 96
  - Train Your Intuition 96
  - Pay Attention 96

Look for Learning Lessons..97
Learn to Become More Compassionate....................97

CHAPTER 3: ATTRIBUTES OF SOUL AND MIND...........99
Language versus Telepathy...99
The Ego and the Multidimensional Mind 101
What is Consciousness? 105
3-D Versus Higher Dimensions.................................107
Images, Imagination, and Projection—an Exercise in Nano-Traveling..111
Where Do You Want To Go After Death?...................118
Exercises 141
Visualization..141
Separating Your Own Thoughts From Your Environment...142
Travel in Your Mind...142

CHAPTER 4: DREAM MUSINGS....................................145
Brainwave States 145
Phone Calls from the Other Side 149
Aliens and Dreaming...151
Has Dream Research Become Militarized?................152
Living in a Dream...154

CHAPTER 5: CONSCIOUS DREAMING—HOW TO CONNECT WITH YOUR MULTIDIMENSIONAL SELF........156
The Illusion of Being Disconnected 156
How to Prepare Yourself and Your Environment for Conscious Dreaming..159
Step #1: Learn How to Recall Your Dreams.............163
Step #2: Learn How to Be Aware of That You Are Dreaming..169
Step #3: Learn How to Consciously Interact with Your Dreams (Become a Conscious Dreamer) 173

CHAPTER 6: THE INNER JOURNEY................................182

Forgive Yourself and Others 182
Entity Possession and How to Get Rid of It 188
Symbols and their Meanings 190
The Language of Light 193
Using the Language of Light to Travel Within 200
Disclosure of the ET Phenomenon from a
Multidimensional Perspective 206
The Feminine Side of Men 211
A Comparison between Physical and Non-Physical
Beings 213
Sacred Sex and the Divine Blood of the Goddess ... 226
The Six Heart Virtues—Making Use of the Fourth
Body Chakra 237
Our Breath—The Physical Body's Connection with
the Quantum Field 241

CHAPTER 7: HOMO NOVA—THE NEW GUARDIANS OF
THE LIVING LIBRARY 245
A Voluntary Mission and the Year 1 AN 245
The Three Important Post-Nano Phases Discussed
.... 253
    Phase 1 (Anno 1-5, or 2013-2017) 254
    Phase 2 (Anno 6-15 or 2018-2027) 260
    Phase 3 (Anno 16 and onward or 2028 and on) 261
Living in the Living Library—Guardians of the New
World 261

Your love and your knowledge will protect you—
always! 267

INTRODUCTION:
LOST IN A LABYRINTH OF INFORMATION

First, I want to thank you for reading this! You would probably not even have found this book and been curious about it if you hadn't already done a lot of spiritual research and some work on yourself. How you found it is irrelevant, but this book will probably change your way of looking at life. You have heard that about many books, but I truly mean it. How would I know? I know because that's what it's done to me—and yet, I was the one who wrote it!

I envision this book as a sequel, of sorts, to a series of papers I wrote between the years 2011 and 2013 called *The Wes Penre Papers* (WPP), and for those who have read them, this book comes as a natural next read. However, it's not a prerequisite to read the papers first, but if you *do* want to start with the papers, as there are some references back to them in this book, you can find them for free at wespenre.com.

The *WPP* are divided into three *levels of learning*[1], which will take the reader on a mind-blowing journey through the history of the universe and our human origins. The *WPP* will also, in detail, bring up the reason behind why we are so trapped within a societal structure, or system, with no obvious way of

---

[1] As of 2021, when this Second Edition is published, there are six levels of learning on the website.

breaking out in the sense of being able to live the life *we* want to live without interference. The papers will show evidence that there is an extraterrestrial force behind the suppressive control system, which includes, more or less, the entire world. In this book, I will call this force the *Alien Invader Forces* (AIF). The *WPP* also discuss channeling and whom these entities are who are contacting us in these times and what they want. In the middle of many different agendas is mankind, and most of us are absolutely ignorant of what is going on in secret, way above our heads—literally.

A big part of the *WPP* is unique—you will not find this information anywhere else—at least not in a coherent form. I have been very lucky to find extremely good sources and have been in contact with those who are *in the know*—both those from here and *elsewhere*. People who have read the papers have been enthusiastic, and many, many readers have told me that the papers have changed their lives completely, which makes me very happy.

The papers also suggest a soulution (yes, a <u>soul</u>ution) to an otherwise overwhelming situation we have been living in for thousands of years—in fact, since Homo sapiens were created by a part of the AIF. There actually is a soulution to this dilemma, and to understand it well enough, I advise you to read the papers. A short synopsis here won't give the *WPP* justice.

How I found out about this is a long story, and parts of it are told in the papers, but readers can *feel* that it's true, and although it's quite a dark and sometimes terrifying story, people who otherwise prefer more "light" material have still been praising it because they believe it should be studied, or we stand little to no chance to make it out in the cosmos and survive the experience. It's that crucial. However, it's not only that it's presenting an accurate version of our multidimensional past—

more important is the imperative necessity to meet and confront our personal inner darkness.

It's easier to see darkness and evil in someone else than it is to confront that we all carry those traits inside, alongside our human friendliness and benevolence. I would go so far as to say that the incapability to see our own faults and shortcomings have led to the situation we are facing today with authoritarian governments, a failed economy, war, famine, manufactured diseases, incest in high places, rape of women and children, and so on. It's become a very solid trap, and ever since that time in the ancient past when it all started, mankind has done very little to free themselves from the master-slave situation that is still prominent on this planet. Instead, we have accepted that we are slaves and a working force for a small clique of super-wealthy people—an unelected power elite who runs the show behind the scenes. We have also forgotten that above this level of manipulation are the cosmic visitors themselves, pulling the strings on those who are selected by *them* to control the rest of us. We can't see these visitors unless they make themselves visible to us because they are not third-dimensional (3-D) beings. Hence, they exist outside the small, visible spectrum, which is all that we humans, from our 3-D perspective, are able to perceive. What we can see and perceive, however, are the huge corporations and what they do to us and our planet. We can also see (if we choose to) the international bankers who keep us on a tightrope with great help from the moneymaking multimillion dollar corporations that benefit the few and make billionaires, while most of the population is on the brink of starvation and poverty. We can also see (again, if we choose to) how we are all used in a system where we have to work ourselves to illness and exhaustion in order to make the owners of the big corporations wealthier and even more powerful. We can see how governments, for their own personal, often financial, gains start wars in other countries, killing thousands, even millions of innocent people, while the super-rich again become wealthier by creating this giant war machine. We can see the unfairness in all this—nevertheless, we agree to play their game. Why is that? Why are we putting up with it when statistics show that even here in America we are a million to one against a small clique of powerful super-rich families?

It is because the families in power, and the AIF above them, keep the population in fear and terror. People are afraid to look outside the box because they are scared that they will be punished for it in one way or the other by the *authorities* and maybe become unable to survive on their own. Ultimately, they are afraid of death, something the Elite knows and, therefore, keep us in the dark when it comes to what happens after we die.

Only by confronting the darkness inside of us can we free ourselves from such an immense, negative power. After all, the AIF and its minions, the Illuminati or the Global Elite (whatever we want to call them), are not the real problem. They wouldn't even be able to do what they are doing without our consent, so the responsibility comes back on us. If we want a change, we have to create it because no one else will. This is way too much for most people to comprehend and deal with—therefore, the majority of the population gives away their power to others, who they hope will fix the situation—be it cults, religions, alien saviors coming down from the sky, or the next door neighbor. We may outnumber the slave masters by a million to one, but fighting them is still not an option. If the reader doesn't believe me, take a look at our history. People have tried many times to stand up against the *Beast*, only to have been defeated, resulting in the death of many good people. No, the actual solution is to look at the *Inner Universe*, which this book will not only show, but also prove. There is no other way to achieve real inner peace and freedom from oppression.

People who read the *WPP* often told me that afterward they were able to separate themselves from this global, oppressive force, and it felt like a huge burden had been lifted from their shoulders. They now had the freedom to step outside the situation and look at it from a whole new angle, and for the first time they could see that there is a way out. This book will show you the tools so that you *can* find your way out. You are already well on your way, whether you realize it or not!

The earthly dramas are still going on all around us, but I have the same feeling as many of my readers—I am now able to create my own reality in the midst of all this, and very little of the bad things happening in the world affect me personally. It's not that I don't care anymore—it's like it is happening *over there* and is no longer part of my personal universe. In other words, the fear is gone, and when people no longer fear the Powers That Be, these powers no longer have any effect on us. From hereon, we will continue our journey into the great unknown, where freedom from control and suppression will be an everyday thing. Eventually, as I will show, these *earthly dramas* will cease to exist all together in our reality and become something of the past. We are regaining the feeling that we are sovereign beings and that no one has the right to control and manipulate us. We will more and more come to the insight that we no longer need authorities in order to survive. We will realize that this is an illusion we have lived in for thousands of years, and we survive so much better if we don't have those authorities in our lives at all.

One problem I am very well aware of is what I call *the human factor*. What I mean is that when we read about a person who has a darker side to him or herself than we have, the tendency is that we get interested in the information because it makes *us* feel good, thinking of ourselves as being better than the person we are reading about. Then, when we're done reading, we forget what we learned and just go on with our lives. In this case, however, the "dark person" is a whole alien agenda, which won't go away because we stop reading.

The following information requires that we do more than just reading, and hopefully, I have composed something that can be both useful and fun at the same time.

There is a lot of stigma in the 2012 number combination, and the ideas of what was going to happen that year were many. If people thought anything at all would happen, it usually had to do with old prophecies and the different ways they have been interpreted. When this book was first written, it's almost the middle of 2013, and we know what happened and what didn't happen in 2012. Or do we??? Well, we know that the world is still orbiting the Sun as usual and most people are still alive, although many of us had a rough time—especially around 2011-2012. However, there was no end-of-the-world scenario, at least. The world is still here. Therefore, did anything explosive happen then? Most people would probably laugh it all off and say that nothing did happen out of the ordinary, but I disagree with that.

The ones who were closest to predicting what happened around 2012 were those who talked about the *Return of the Gods*—although, those who were supposed to return are not Gods, but extraterrestrials presenting themselves as Gods in our ancient past. I usually call them *gods* with a small "g" to emphasize that they are not divine, but a technologically very advanced species from other dimensions. In this book, they will generally go under the term AIF. Although these gods from the past never left our planet—they left a skeleton crew here, and they now have company from their buddies from the stars. Evidence that I provided in my papers indicates that a large amount of these star beings came back in 2012 and occupied bodies here on Earth or hybridized bodies left in storage on other planets in the solar system. This was something that had been planned for maybe a thousand years or more and has been the reason for a lot of alien abductions. The AIF can't use their own original bodies here on Earth because our atmosphere and other circumstances prevent them from landing here. Therefore, the AIF have created a lot of human hybrids over the centuries, which they now have let their souls occupy and sent down to our planet to mingle with us. Most of these invaders must certainly have put themselves in leading positions, but I wouldn't be surprised if some of them also are mingling with ordinary people to have their agents *everywhere.*

This can only be proven by connecting the dots from evidence that is available to us (which I did)—hence, the future will tell what all this will lead us to. I have a few suggestions, which I included in the papers. However, this is what I mean when I say that 2012 certainly didn't pass by like any other year.

Another thing I discussed frequently in my papers was the term *nano-travel.* It is important that the reader of this book has at least a basic understanding of what that term means because we're going to go deeper into it here.

When we think of space travel, we often think of nuts-and-bolts ships traveling from one star system to another, or they use stargates, wormholes, or black holes to travel long distances. In the part of the universe where we are trapped (which I call the 4% universe), star races are more often than not technologically oriented, so they do use space craft and some of the above methods to overcome long distances. However, the most efficient way to travel from one point to another is instant travel, which we call nano-travel, and it is done in our minds and with our thoughts. In simple words, we split our soul unit into a smaller faction and send that out to the destination. That soul unit is riding an *Avatar,* which is a light-body. Having reached the destination, the traveler can either experience as a spirit/light-body, or *shapeshift* into something that looks just as material as you and I would look. We can all do this, and in the future, this will be our way of traveling, unless we stay with the gods, who are in charge of this planet. I suggest you read the *WPP* for more information.

This *handbook* is preparing the reader for the future, where many of us will become our true multidimensional selves again. I will suggest what to do next so that as fast as possible we can regain our old multidimensional abilities, and it includes exercises that will bring us toward that goal. Once you're done reading this material, I am convinced you will feel much more multidimensional than you did before you started.

There is a great awakening taking place in the world today. An incredible number of people, compared to the number from just 25 years ago, are waking up every week and every day to the fact that they are spiritual beings in a physical body, and life doesn't end when our body dies. Eager to find out more, the most curious and courageous of these people start searching for more information. Full of enthusiasm, they start meditating, reading about the subject, and in their own personal way begin to improve themselves and raise their consciousness. They may also realize that their health is very important and, therefore, start eating healthier. Hopefully, most of them, eventually, will come to the insight that they also need to balance it out with their dark side or vice versa.

In the *WPP,* I talked a lot about the *nano-second.* "This is a term that was coined by the Pleiadians and channeled by the medium Barbara Marciniak from North Carolina. The nano-second was basically the term they used for the time period between 1987 and 2012, when the mass awakening on the planet occurred due to our solar system's alignment with the Galactic Center of the Milky Way Galaxy of which the Sun and the Earth are a part. Enormous quantities of energies were released, particularly in the gamma ray spectrum, hitting the Sun and the Earth with full force. This was gradually happening as these cosmic bodies came more and more in alignment—the results from a process that has affected us since approximately 1987.

The alignment with the Central Sun of the Galaxy had a lot of consequences for us here on Earth. Time literally sped up a million-fold, and people could, if they put their minds to it, learn and progress more during these 25 years than they would in a million years otherwise. Parts of our DNA were lit up and energized parts that had previously laid dormant in our body system but now started to operate as they are supposed to. This led to an increase in awareness and consciousness in a short amount of time. A fast cosmic process like this could occasionally be hard on the neurological system, and people sometimes ended up with all kinds of neurological problems that the doctors couldn't explain. Those who understood the process, however, went with the flow, and in many cases, their physical problems resolved after a while, or if they still haven't as of this date, there is still a chance that they will soon, as the solar system is now slowly moving out of alignment again. No one on this planet was unaffected by the galactic alignment. However, not everybody took the opportunity to learn and progress on this *free ride* toward a higher consciousness. In fact, the majority of people did not care to educate themselves and acknowledge what happened. Instead, they tried to stay within their old norms as much as they could, such as watching reality shows on TV or cheering for their favorite football team on the weekend with a six-pack of beer. Many people got very ill, and some even went insane because they did not understand what was happening. The suicide rate increased quite dramatically during this period as well.

One may wonder why so many people who had this one-chance-in-a-million-years to educate themselves and take advantage of the information from those who had *awakened* didn't care to do so. You, who read this book right now, are *awakened*, relatively speaking, and both you and I have experienced how hard it can be to convince somebody how important it is to learn more about what's going on and about whom we are and where we come from. We may even have been given a wonderful example of how things work, backed up with evidence. The other people seemed to grasp what we were saying and might even have agreed, but nothing seemed to trigger an interest to find out more. This is very unfortunate because those who didn't take the opportunity to wake up will not get another chance like this for, perhaps, another million years. Even if an alignment with the galactic center is not extremely rare, nano-seconds are! The problem with humanity is that many have lost their curiosity. No one can say that the information is not there for everyone to see—the entire Internet is full of it, and anyone can learn something by only using a search engine. Instead, they use search engines to google products they wish to buy, such as new smart phones and other high-tech devices. That, to them, is a more interesting and important than learning about themselves and the situation they are in. This is how dumbed-down humanity has become from the manipulation we've been subjected to for a very long time. I am not putting any judgment behind it—I am merely stating a fact. Sadly enough, the consequences for ignorance are severe, which people will realize in the future when it may be too late to do anything significant about it.

The year 2012 was also like a *fork in the road*, where people finally decided which route they want to take from here on. People's timelines came together, and for some, it was overwhelming, and they couldn't handle it—whereas, others who were more prepared had an easier time to adapt and instead used this as a springboard to get over the next threshold to higher consciousness. Basically, we can choose one of two paths for the future, and from these, an infinite number of versions of these paths will be created as humanity moves on. The main paths can be seen as two trees standing next to each other with their roots connected. The trunks signify the two main paths (or timelines), and the branches on the trees symbolize parallel timelines, slightly different, but on a similar theme as the *main* timeline. Eventually, the roots that connect the two trees will break, and each tree will grow independently from each other.

The two main timelines leading into the future are *The Machine Kingdom* and *The New Era of the Enhanced Humanity*, where the latter is the faction of mankind who evolves independently from technology and *help* from so-called gods who don't have our best interest in mind, even if it may seem as if they do. The truth of the matter is, which the reader will find out after having finished the *WPP*, that mankind is already multidimensional, but we have forgotten what it is, and we have to learn how to reconnect with our inner selves, and that's one of the major themes in this book.

Those who spiritually awakened during the nano-second and also learned about what is happening here on our own planet will distinctively choose *The New Era of the Enhanced Humanity* and become increasingly less interested in all the high-tech and nano-technology and the way they are applied by our scientists.

The splitting of the worlds does not mean that the Earth will literally break in the middle and create two worlds—the term is a metaphor. In fact, there are, and has always been, more than one version of Earth. In reality, there are as many versions of Earth as there are humans on the planet, and much more—each human is living on an individualized version of the planet, which is slightly different from everybody else's, but humans share commonalities because we vibrate within the same range of frequency. This is why we all can see and interact with each other even though our worldviews are sometimes very different. Now, the majority of the world population is choosing to opt for the Machine Kingdom, although they have no idea what they're doing—they are simply on autopilot and *going with the flow* because they are literally asleep and can be led in any direction the manipulators choose for them. The consequences of this are explained in detail in my papers, so I won't go into that here, other than to say that the consequences are, in the long term, devastating for anybody who chooses that path.

The other path will be chosen by those who are spiritually awake and who feel the urge to connect with nature and live a simpler lifestyle. However, even those of us who are aware are in danger because the manipulation is very convincing and the propaganda easy to fall for unless we have done our homework. The Machine Kingdom is creeping up on us all, and it's easy to stay in that timeline without realizing it—we buy more and more technology because we think it will enhance our lives and make it easier, when, in fact, it eventually will do the exact opposite. You may think that if you just buy one more device, you'll be fine and don't have to buy more technology, but then another product hits the market, and it's very tempting to go and get that one too, even if you resist in the beginning. Therefore, be aware!

In the beginning, the Machine Kingdom and the New Era, or the Second Golden Age, will coexist. However, after a few generations, the enhanced human who is evolving without technology, the new species I call *Homo Nova*, will start vibrating within a higher frequency range than that of the Machine Kingdom, and the latter will cease to exist in Homo Nova's reality. When that happens, the *Splitting of the Worlds* is a fact! Homo Nova is then *literally* living on a different version of

Earth. The Machine Kingdom will still exist as a parallel reality, or better yet, in a lower dimension.

My papers were written in an attempt to wake up as many people as possible without forcing any dogma or religion upon anybody. All I wanted to do was to tell the true story about the Earth to the best of my ability and let the readers make up their own minds. The information can be taken literally, as a guideline, or an overall picture—it's up to the reader to decide. My project was also an attempt to write in such a manner that people who started waking up late during the nano-second (and afterward as well) would have a reference or a guideline so that it, hopefully, won't be too late for these people to reach the point where they can make conscious decisions about their future. Hence, the papers are always going to be available to be downloaded for free, so long as the Internet is available, and I can pay the annual fee for the domain and the web location. I know that more and more people will find the papers when they are ready for them, and that will, in turn, lead to this book. Of course, for those whom the papers don't communicate to will rather quickly abandon them and look for truth somewhere else, but in the near future, many people will find them, read them, and consider them very helpful.

Now, I think the reader is ready for the next step where we can learn how to develop our multidimensionality and how we can obtain that by working with our bodies. Still grounded here on Earth, our bodies will be our best friend and the main tool we will use when exploring the Multiverse.

I hope this book will be helpful on your never-ending experiences as a multidimensional being!

Happy Journey!

CHAPTER 1: THE UNIVERSE INSIDE

Power of Thoughts

You must be the change you want to see in the world – *Mahatma Gandhi (1869-1948)*

I don't know how many times I have used the quote above, but it's one of my absolute favorites, so the reader must excuse me for using it again. Gandhi was actually telling us the entire path to freedom in just one sentence, and I am going to start this book by discussing exactly what he meant by this quote.

Life is not always easy to live. We get up in the morning and think we are doing just fine. We take a shower, perhaps, eat our breakfast, and get ready for work, and we're still in quite a good mood. Then, when we come home in the evening and sit down at the table, we think, "What a terrible day!" Everything just seemed to go wrong—the boss yelled at us, we tried to talk nicely to our coworkers, but they misunderstood our communication and took offense, and with all that, we made one or two embarrassing mistakes. Therefore, we ask ourselves, how come? After all, we were in a good mood in the morning and didn't expect all this to happen. Don't we create our own reality?

Yes, we do! The trick is that we need to put the right energies behind our thoughts. We woke up in the morning and were in a good mood, and that's a very good start. However, maybe we didn't think more about it than that we were feeling good and that's it? Sometimes that's not enough—we need to be specific with what we want. Few people are aware of how many thoughts are going through their heads every day, and in fact, for most people, the majority of these thoughts are what I call *sloppy thoughts* or *junk thoughts*. How many times during a day have we thought something like, "I can't do this," "this is a pain in the butt," or even worse: "This particular task will kill me," or "I am always messing up." All these thoughts are typical examples of thoughts that go through most people's heads during a normal day, and I'll tell you—these thoughts are very powerful—especially if they become a pattern in people, which is very often the case. I had a coworker once who always used the expression, "It's a pain in the neck" because she thought it was better and more polite than to use the word "butt," I guess. More polite, perhaps, but certainly not better because what do you know—she developed neck problems and had no idea where they came from. I told her how this all works, but who knows if she believed me—she left for another job eventually. Anyway, it's important that we are aware of what we think because we may end up getting what we're thinking and saying, and it's not always what we want. The body has a tendency to take you literally. Whatever you do, *never* think or say that something is going to kill you—you understand why now!

Negative thoughts like these can make our days a living hell, and we don't understand why. I do now, and it's interesting because I hear people saying these phrases all day long to each other, and no one is reacting because they have no idea about the consequences of using such repetitive phrases. We need to change these patterns, and now when you are becoming aware of it, I can't stress enough how helpful it is to tell others who use these automated phrases how this all works. Be prepared that most of the time you will be met by skepticism and even laughter because they won't believe you, but do your best not to be effected by that. Even if people seem to laugh it off, they may very well think about it afterward without telling you about it because they don't want to admit that they were doing something destructive to themselves. Remember that anything you're saying, if there is truth in it, will at least remain in the thoughts of the other person, and one day, he or she may actually start taking your advice.

Instead, if you want to have a good day, there is a formula I can suggest for you. When you wake up in the morning, whether you feel good or not, tell yourself, "This is going to be a fantastic day! Everything is going to go my way, and my day will be better than fine!" If you're in a bad mood already when you wake up, repeat it a few times to make sure you are putting some energy behind it. If you notice that junk thoughts, such as "I don't believe that" or "Yea, we'll see about that" when you're saying your formula, add a "Cancel that!" after you've thought it, not to put any power to the negative. Then repeat the formula. Right there, you're setting the guidelines for your day. By doing this every morning when you get up, it will change your days dramatically. Don't linger on the phrase, though—just give it a light thought and let it go. Even better would be if you also can say it with a smile—that puts some extra positive energies to the intention. Then just forget about it and go on with your day. Repeat this every morning and you will notice a difference.

Step two will be to become aware of your negative thoughts and your automatic thought patterns. For many people who read this book, it is the first time they have even heard about junk thoughts, but there is no doubt that being aware of our patterns and changing them will make a huge difference. If this were the only thing I wrote about in this book, it would still be well worth reading. Don't be surprised if you find yourself having many thoughts such as this. If you do, so much more powerful the change will be. Every time you come upon a thought, such as "I'm like a magnet to negative people," "I always have bad luck," "I always choose the wrong partner," "I never get what I want," "I look awful," "I'm not good enough," and so on, immediately think, "Cancel that!" afterward. This is all you need to do, but the important thing is to continue finding these thoughts within yourself. Of course, you need to be aware of when you're saying things like this as well, not just thinking them, but anything you say is preceded by a thought anyway. Eventually, you will get better and better in spotting these patterns, but you need to be persistent and never stop or give up. If you're lucky, you don't have too many of these thoughts (although I think we all have them to a certain degree), and this will not be too much of a process, but most people are quite loaded with them. In the beginning, you will probably find yourself forgetting to do this, so a good idea is to put sticky notes in good places, reminding you to be aware of your thoughts. The notes don't need to say exactly what you need to do if you don't want others to know what you're doing, but just write something down that will remind you. In addition, it's a very good idea to actually let others know what you're up to because it may inspire them to do the same thing—especially if they see results in you. At first, you may have to say "Cancel that!" to the same pattern over and over again, but eventually you will notice that the thought is not coming up anymore! Then, after having done this process x amount of days/weeks/months, you will be very conscious about what you're thinking, and your thought process will be much more positive and to the point. You will notice that negative things that may have happened to you earlier stop happening because you are no longer creating that reality with your thoughts.

Why are we creating all these negative thoughts in the first place? Even otherwise positive individuals have them, so why are we doing this to ourselves? Well, it's usually due to failures and disappointments in the past, which, in turn, happened because we created them by making bad decisions, either from lack of knowledge or earlier junk thoughts. It's often repetitive failures that create the automated patterns, so this is something to be aware of. If something unpredicted happens that we think is not in our favor, be conscious of your thoughts after the incident, and if something similar to what I gave an example of above happens, such as a voice in your head telling you something negative about yourself, be sure to cancel it. It is okay to make mistakes—that's how we learn, but we save ourselves a lot of hardship and unnecessary suffering by just changing our thinking patterns. Moreover, this is absolutely necessary in order to become multidimensional—therefore, let's start practicing! I am suggesting that this is the first step to take toward multidimensionality if you've come to the point in your spiritual development that it's time to read a book like this. Being multidimensional means, as one of its basic tenets, that we are steadfast, have clear thoughts, and know what we want and where we're heading. It's a difficult task, but a whole lot of fun. However, failure is not an option! We all need to practice what I am suggesting in this book, or we will be stuck where we are for a much longer time than we need to. Even if some of these practices will take some time, it's still a very effective shortcut to become multidimensional.

Your Own Version of the Multiverse

All of us live in our own, personal Multiverse. Your Multiverse is quite different from your neighbor's, but there are also a lot of similarities. I know that this is something that is quite difficult for many people to understand, especially for those who think we all live in only one universe. However, I think it's because no one has cared to explain this simple concept in simple terms. I have noticed that many writers and researchers want to add a lot of quantum physics and advanced metaphysics into their writing, and then the whole purpose for explaining it to the reader is lost—how many of us are educated in quantum physics and quantum mechanics? It's like one Elite member is communicating with another, leaving the majority of the population to hopelessly try to figure it out.

Therefore, let's keep it simple—as simple as we can ever keep it. As a starter, let's explain what the Universe is and what the difference is between the Universe and the Multiverse. The universe is basically the physical existence of galaxies, nebulae, stars, planets, moons, and asteroids—i.e. more or less, the universe we can perceive as human 3-D beings. It's a 3-D picture of the Creation as we know it—it's the version of space and time our scientist have decided is All There Is. It's a very physical view of the cosmos, where no spirits or souls are included in the equation—it's either pure matter or it doesn't exist. This is the version we all learn about in school. With the Multiverse, however, we add metaphysics into the picture, and it's getting much more interesting. Suddenly, the universe gets a soul, and there is so much more to explore than just the physical. We can see that the Multiverse is teeming with life, but not only physical life—life exists in all dimensions and on almost all planets—it's just that we can't perceive it because it operates outside the range of the electromagnetic spectrum we here on Earth normally operate in—i.e. other dimensions. It's just as simple as that—there is nothing magical or spooky with it. It all has to do with frequencies and how fast and how slow energy vibrates because in our essence, we are all just energy beings. A Pleiadian soul group, who dwells in the fifth-or sixth dimension, said through its *vehicle*[2] that if it looks at Mother Earth from above and watches us humans here on the ground, it sees a dance of energy moving back and forth—beings vibrating on slightly different frequencies, but usually within the small range of the electromagnetic spectrum we call the third dimension. Therefore, the main difference between the Universe and the Multiverse is that we add a new dimension to the equation—that of the spirit. In metaphysics, we prove that the whole universe is a living entity in itself and is aware and conscious—every part of it is aware. We claim that there is consciousness in everything, even planets, stars, nebulae, and galaxies. Even space is aware! In this Multiverse, billions upon billions of entities of all different types are living—each and every dimension is populated. All these beings have their own personality and their own thought patterns. Many believe that just because of the *multi* prefix in Multiverse, we mean many universes. This is not necessarily true—instead, we mean an almost endless different version of the *same* universe making up a Multiverse. Most of us agree that we all share the same universe with the same stars and galaxies, but more than that, we also have our own personal and very unique universe inside of us, which is built from our own thoughts, actions, and inactions. My Inner Universe is very different from your Inner Universe because I am not the same personality as you are, and I don't think exactly like you do on all subjects. Hence, both our Inner Universes are unique. Then, add another 7 billion people to that, who all have their unique Inner Universes. If we want to continue, we have all these star beings out there who also have their Inner Universes. As you can see, it's almost endless. Still, it is all living creatures combined that make up the ever-expanding Multiverse. The

---

[2] A "vehicle" is the human body through which channeled entities communicate with an audience on Earth. A medium has agreed to let certain entities use his or her body to spread the medium's message to those who want to hear.

scientists have noticed that the universe is expanding and retracting in some kind of cycles, as if some giant being were breathing in and breathing out (which in fact is the case), but that is different from the Multiverse, which also includes the spirit and the non-physical. As long as there are thinking souls in the universe, we are expanding the metaphysical part with our thoughts and creations and, therefore, making the Multiverse bigger. The Multiverse, in other words, is our own personal Inner Universes added to a Universe we all agree on.

So let's stay here on Earth for a while to make this easier to understand. Pretend that we could freeze this exact moment in time and space—nothing is moving right now and is just waiting for me to explain this. If you look at the Multiverse right now, you will see a Universe the way all people see it, with stars, planets, etc., and when you look around, you see your environment quite similar to everybody else who lives there. Maybe there are trees, houses, roads, a river, a mountain, and whatnot. Everybody agrees that all these things are there, including people in the neighborhood—you can all see each other. In your house you are sitting with your family around the dinner table and eating dinner when we freeze this picture. This is your reality right now at this moment. You also have a job you are going to go to tomorrow morning. This sounds solid and predictable, but it's far from it, as we shall see. Metaphysicists usually say that the Multiverse is fluid, meaning that nothing is set in stone, it is ever-changing, and nothing is predictable because it can hypothetically change in a micro-second. When we unfreeze the picture again and let you continue with your day, the phone rings. You answer it, and it is your best friend who wants you and your family to come with him or her on a trip to Europe in a month. You and your wife are considering it but decide at the last moment to stay home. Therefore, you had two options: go to Europe or stay at home. If you had chosen to go, your life would have been slightly different from that moment forward, and the two weeks you spent home would instead have been spent in Europe. How many decisions do you make in two weeks? More than you can imagine. However, the point is that you are making different decisions when you are at home than you would have made if you would have gone to Europe. Now you add all these personal decisions to the already existing Multiverse and change it a little bit with every thought and every decision you make because every thought and action is creating a new version of the Multiverse, which is entirely your own. Most of your Multiverse is still the same as other people's Multiverse, but they are not necessarily affected by the decisions you make, and that makes your Multiverse unique. This is what we mean when we say that the Multiverse is fluid and not static because it changes with every person's thoughts, emotions, and actions. Some decisions we make also affect a few others and, therefore, change their Multiverse, too, in that same respect but, perhaps, does not affect a person on the other side of town. Does this start to make sense? We live in slightly different versions of the Multiverse because we make different decisions and solve different kinds of problems. We say that we don't always agree with each other, and that is because we are different personalities who make different decisions in order for Source (the Godhead or the Goddess-head, rather, as we shall see later) to experience herself. This is true, but it's also true that we see things differently because we live in slightly different Multiverses. You are creating your version inside of yourself and project that picture outward. If your version is not different from other people's versions, they will see it too. However, because we are unique, you and I can stand and look at the same flowerbed and the flowers will look and smell slightly different to us. If you could magically become me for a minute, you would probably get a shock, and you would say that this is not the way you see the flowers, and vice versa. Still, it's similar enough that we can agree and even think we see it exactly the same. There are scientific terms for all these phenomena, but I will not bother to go into that here because it's outside the scope of this book. For those who are interested, I have a scientific section in the beginning of "The First Level of Learning" of my WPP. The important thing here to understand is that there is a big difference between mainstream science and its view of the universe from that of quantum physicists and metaphysicists. We are talking about a Multiverse, which is a combination of all beings' Inner Universes plus the original, dimensional universe that was once created by God (I will call *God All That Is* for now, until we have established a gender). When we are talking about spiritual subjects, we are usually referring to the Multiverse rather than the Universe. Therefore, keep in mind that the Multiverse has nothing to do with parallel universes or other universes than the one we live in. I am not discarding that there are parallel universes and other universes before ours, after ours, and outside ours, but again, that is beyond the scope of this book.

Therefore, why is it important to understand at least the basics about the Multiverse? It is important because we need to know what happens when we are creating our own reality and how that affects our present and our future. Every day, we are standing at a crossroads wondering which way to go. Should I do this, or should I do that? Usually, these choices are not too hard to make, but sometimes they require some extra pondering and problem solving.

Now, we have learned how to get rid of our junk thoughts and understand how our thoughts not only create our reality but also change the version of the Multiverse we are living in. Once we get rid of our sloppy thoughts, we are ready to start creating a Multiverse that corresponds to our goals and visions. However, before we can do that successfully, we need to grasp the magnificence of the power of thought and how we can use it.

For example, at the crossroads, you have two choices that contradict each other. In your thought process, you may explore them both to see which one works best for you and then choose one. The one you put your energy, emotions, intentions, and actions toward will be the one that will affect your future. The other choice that you didn't act upon will still be there, floating around in the Multiverse as a potential timeline but without any continuous energy added to it. However, when you've made your decision and start acting on it, perhaps with a goal in mind, the Multiverse is opening itself, making room for your decision to progress into action. The Multiverse is non-judgmental, so even if you make a decision that is non-survival, the Multiverse will still make room for you to create whatever you want to create. The only catch is that with each effort you make, you get something back—of course, if you create something positive, you generally get something positive as a result, and when you create something non-survival, you will get something non-survival as a result of that, exactly as you intended. In addition, we have a delayed effect as a result of our actions that we usually call *karma*, which means that positive actions often give you a positive reward, while non-survival actions give you negative rewards. This is usually true here in the physical realms and is not always true for other dimensions that don't have reincarnation and amnesia as part of the process.

This is why it's so important that you learn to analyze your thoughts and decisions. Just as there are junk thoughts and sloppy thoughts, there are sloppy decisions that we all make on occasion. Then we wonder why we get sloppy results. If people realized the incredible power they have just by using their thoughts and making constructive decisions and implementing them, this world would be a very different and better place to live in. Instead, not only do people make sloppy decisions, but most of the time, they don't make their own decisions at all—they let others make them for them, although they believe they are making the decisions themselves. Allowing others to be our decision makers begins with our parents, then it's our teachers in schools, then it is our managers at work, and perhaps, our partner in our marriage. Humans are used to being told what to do, and when they are not being told, many people feel lost. However, those who have come to that point in their spiritual development can change, hopefully, and begin to make their own decisions, and that's when things can start happening.

Conscious thinking is the key to use when determining which kind of future we want to live in. Our goal, for now, is to act on only thoughts and ideas that enhance our lives and take us in the direction toward becoming multidimensional. This is a wonderful goal, but we need to realize that there are obstacles in the way. Most of us are still slave workers for the suppressive businesses and organizations, more or less dependent upon a monetary system. We are also in many other ways, some obvious and some more subtle, dependent upon Big Brother for our immediate survival. This will change in the future, but we don't need to make it our first priority—there are other things we need and can do, which eventually will lead more naturally to a separation from the suppressive system we are currently supporting[3]. There are a number of changes we can make to increase our vibrations quite remarkably, and these changes will speed up the process of overcoming living in a world where oppression such as the one we're used to living in can no longer exist.

---

[3] I am aware that there are those who have already disconnected from everything that has to do with the System, and there are those who have almost done so but kept some technology to keep in touch with the System in order to see what's going on. These two categories of people, often living in collectives, have already done what the rest of us eventually need to do, but I have not counted them into what we're discussing here.

Those who have the *WPP* relatively fresh in mind and remember the difference between the 4% universe and the 96% universe also recall that I am a skeptic of channeled material, in general. I showed the reader that most of them are either human in the future—half machine and half biological entities, who come back to Earth via time travel hoping to be able to regain their fertility by experimenting on us through abductions. Others are working for the AIF—trying to manipulate us into something they call *The Harvest,* where they promise a paradise on Earth when we die. In fact, what they want to accomplish is to have everybody on the same page and take the human soul group (the mass consciousness) and create a *Collective One*, which means we will become half machines and half human, but our minds are collective and centralized into a giant super computer. We see the result of this in much of the channeling today, such as the "RA Material," the "Cassiopaeans," and the "Elohim," etc. These channeled sources will, together with the AIF, *take care* of us in the astral and guide us to the right place, where we can be introduced to fifth-dimensional bodies in which we will incarnate as the New Human during the next lifetime. As usual, when we are dealing with the AIF, we are dealing with very advanced technology, and as always, the AIF is not helping us for our benefit. They tell the evolved humans who fall for this that after death, the *Harvesters of Souls* will wait for them and help by inserting them in fifth-dimensional (5-D) bodies—thereafter, the *ascended* individual will incarnate in a 5-D version of Earth.

This sounds quite similar to what we are doing but without technology, doesn't it? Before the AIF let these humans incarnate on a 5-D Earth, they will implant them so that they report back to their Masters, who are the same beings who promised them *ascension*. In other words, they want humans who are on the same spiritual level as we are to keep an eye on us and perhaps even manipulate us in 5-D. This is perhaps a good idea, but it won't work, and it tells us how little the AIF knows about spirituality. To them, everything is technology—even Ascension is! The problem is that when the AIF start interfering with 5-D bodies by putting implants in them, they are already not vibrating on the same frequency as our bodies will—there is a distortion involved. When the AIF realize this, I don't know what they're going to do, but I think they will leave us alone. After all, we are not their main target—the Machine Riders are.

However, there are a few channeled sources that I have studied under the microscope, figuratively speaking, and still feel confident with, and there are particularly two of those I am going to introduce in this book. One source the reader is already familiar with from the *WPP* is the Pleiadians, channeled by Barbara Marciniak. The other source is *Seth,* channeled by Jane Roberts. There could be a couple of other sources I still find being outside the anti-human agenda, but they will not be presented here. I just want the reader to be aware that some of these channeled entities are even presenting themselves as Dragons and Reptilians, who were our original Creator Gods from Orion and elsewhere, but they are not the same entities who once created the early humans. They are fake, and I proved it in the WPP.[4]

The premise in this book is that we need to evolve without technology and more genetic manipulation from outside sources, regardless how seductive it all can be. I wouldn't say this if it wasn't only possible, but the way nature is supposed to do it, regardless of what channeled sources such as the Alpha Draconians (the Thubans) say. Who wants to end up in a new trap, anyway? Some are asking whether we need some kind of

---

[4] See, http://wespenre.com/3/paper05-alpha-draconians-and-the-creation-of-the-starhuman.htm and http://wespenre.com/3/paper06-alpha-draconians-and-the-creation-of-the-starhuman-part-2.htm

help from the *good aliens*. Here, the opinions are divided—some say we may need some advice, at least, while others say no to any intervention whatsoever. I would say that I understand both viewpoints, but at this point, I think we are knowledgeable enough to do it ourselves. We have already taken advice from some reliable sources, and the Pleiadians are one of them. I have had other sources, unique to me, who have helped me as well, and the rest I have found out by rolling up my sleeves and digging into hardcore research with joy, sweat, and tears. With this in mind and with the information I have been able to gather, I would say no to intervention at this time. A couple of years ago, I would not have been so sure because I didn't know enough—now, I think I do. I am not a scientist, and I am certainly not a genetic engineer, but it's not necessary to be either. However, I do have an open mind, and if we humans notice sometime in the future that we need some extra advice because we are stuck for any reason, I, for one, am willing to reconsider my decision. Albeit for now, it is important that Homo Nova is willing to stand on their own two feet and claim their sovereignty. Certain alien forces will not be very happy to hear this, but the majority of galactic citizens out there, counting those of the 96%, are happy to see us make such a decision. Groups, such as the former LPG-C (Life Physics Group California), are convinced that we need intervention from star races out there, so they can protect us from the wolves who can't wait to put their claws in us and take over real estate Earth while we are in a vulnerable position all by ourselves, but I would say that this is not necessary. It is true that there are power-hungry star races out there who can't wait to take over Earth from the current AIF, but groups like LPG-C (see WPP, "First Level of Learning") forget one thing—Homo Nova is evolving side by side with the AIF for a few generations, and in that sense, they are protecting us, unwittingly, because they are protecting Earth from other invader forces—hence, we are protected too. Then, when the world is splitting, we should already vibrate on such a high frequency that it shouldn't be an issue, especially as we know how to shield ourselves on a personal level and as a soul group (more about this later). We will be able to put up our own protective shield around Earth and only let those in whom we are welcoming. Remember, we are working on regaining our position as the Guardians of the Living Library and the Protectors of Mother Earth. This is not done by violent means, but by frequency. At that time, we are already highly multidimensional and have established allies and friends out there in the universe.

A chapter in this book will be dedicated to what it means to be the Guardians of the Living Library. We are still adolescents, but we are also like the nestlings who are sitting at the edge of the nest, flapping their wings, and ready to take the first step out of the nest to try the wings. We are the teenagers who can't wait to leave our parents' home and build a life on our own. We are on the brink of becoming adults, and as adults, we are on our own—we can't hide behind our mother's skirt anymore when it's getting a little rough, and we know this. The difference between us and Homo sapiens is that we are brave enough to fly out of the nest. We are aware that there are dangers out there, but we are willing to undertake them and believe we are mature enough to do so. Star races out there in the universe are very concerned about humanity as a whole because of the destructive ways we use energy, and many do what they can to stop us from reaching out in the universe. Therefore, in that sense they are supporting the AIF that is already here: suppressing humanity. They'd rather see us suppressed and within quarantine than to let us loose. We, the new human, are going to show our brothers and sisters out there in the universe that we can do better. We can show them that we honor Mother Earth who supports us and helps us grow instead of destroying the only planet that can house our human body template. We are also going to advertise out in the universe when the day comes that we have reclaimed the title "Guardians of the Living Library," and those star beings who are willing to come here and learn and grow from studying the Living Library are welcome to do so under our supervision. Beings of lower vibrations who have no intentions to come here to learn but only to steal and destroy may not bother to apply. Don't worry—this is exactly what we are going to learn—how to read other beings' energies. First, we must build our own energies because in our current condition we are not ready to meet beings from the cosmos *face to face,* whether it's in a physical or spiritual form. Most humans today—even those who are more evolved—need to enhance their energy fields to be able to comfortably meet with those not-from-here.

Perhaps, the reader can see now that it is important for us to walk our own paths and develop our own strength and energy without intervention from outside.

People, especially those who may have married before or in the middle of the nano-second may have been the most wonderful couple who loved each other and told themselves that their marriage will last for the whole lifetime and maybe well into the next, and the next, and the next, never thought there would be problems they couldn't solve. Now, years afterward, they may find that they have moved in different directions. This, of course, can happen in any marriage, but in the nano-second, there was a specific circumstance that sometimes led to the separation between partners. Both may have been truth-seekers when they met, but somewhere along the line they chose different paths. In the beginning, one of them may have tried to convince the other that his or her path is the most beneficial for both of them. Then they enter the next phase in their relationship when they sit down and agree that it's okay to feel different and that their marriage will probably work anyway. Full with new enthusiasm, they both continue on their separate paths, but they get further and further away from each other until they notice they have less and less in common. When they are together, there is mostly silence where there used to be lively, uplifting conversations, but now there is not much to talk about. Both feel miserable about this but don't know what to do about it. They still love each other, but their different worldviews tear at both of them until one or both get sick. Perhaps, they even tried marriage counseling to no avail. A divorce became the traumatic solution.

In other marriages, only one person is on a spiritual path—similar situations could arise in regular friendships. When this happens, there is no use in trying to convince the other person that what you are doing is important—and as sad as it is, at one point, these people need to go separate ways in order to be able to evolve any further, or they'll get stuck, at best, or move backward and get very sick, at worst. Unfortunately, many cling onto each other anyway because they believe they need the other person or feel sorry for the partner, and they don't want to hurt each other. I can empathize with that because I experienced how my spouse and I went in different directions back in the late 1990s, which led to a divorce. It was much harder emotionally than I'd ever thought it would be because we still loved each other—nevertheless, we had no choice. Now, after the fact, I know we both made the right decision, and since then, we have both been able to thrive on our respective paths. I am now remarried with a woman who is on the same path as I am, and I am very lucky and very happy. Therefore, it's not the end of the world, and sometimes it can be a life saver. I needed to bring this up because I think it's a very common problem when people are standing at the crossroads. It's not just a matter of choosing between the Machine Kingdom and natural evolvement, but even if two people have both chosen the natural path without the machine technology, there are many branches on that tree as well, and one branch may be just fine to climb out on for one person but not for the other. That's the charm of being unique beings, but also the tragedy of it. I can honestly say that if I hadn't met my current wife 13 years ago at that exact point in my life, I would have chosen to continue alone. I would have accepted that I was not meant to have a love relationship or any children this lifetime, but instead concentrate on my task. However, I am fortunate enough to be able to have and do both, and in my case, it is possible to mix work and family life. However, if I'd never met her, I would have been perfectly fine with living alone.

The Genetically Modified Food Industry and the Machine Kingdom

The next step in order to be able to successfully look inside is to have as healthy a body as possible. In fact, this step fits in anywhere in the process because it is something we always need to be aware of. Don't worry—I'm not going to suggest a diet of raw food with carrots and cauliflowers for the rest of your life. If you are able to live a vegetarian lifestyle (as long as you get protein as well) and your body feels great about that, congratulations! However, many people have a hard time adjusting to that, and I am one of them. I was very determined in the past to become a vegetarian for many reasons. I read everywhere how healthy it is, and I didn't have to eat meat from our animal friends. I tried it in many different versions, and I was very careful to research it properly so I got a good balance of nutrition—especially as I had such a hard time adjusting. I thought that the answer must be somewhere so I could relatively comfortably change diets from a meat-oriented one to a vegetarian one. Unfortunately, it didn't work. I quickly ran out of energy regardless of how I was doing it, and I was not feeling well at all. I still continued for a while, thinking it was just the body trying to adjust to a new diet, but it must have been more than that, and I actually haven't figured out yet why my body reacted like it did. Eventually, I added some organic meat to my diet, and my strength and my energy came back. I know others who have had a similar problem, and I don't know if bodies are just different, or if there is another reason for my hardship, but I admit that I am a meat eater to some degree still, although, in general, I don't promote it to others.

Anyway, after that confession, I still want to mention here (because it *is* important) that we need to think about what we're eating. If you think you must eat meat, eat it sparsely and keep to fowl, such as chicken and turkey, and make sure they are organic and have been well treated. I also suggest buying from local farmers, whether you buy meat, vegetables, or fruit. Eat seasonal fruits and veggies that have been treated with love, care, and respect, and before you eat, thank Mother Earth for providing the food for us. If you eat meat, thank the animal for providing food for you, and bless the food regardless of what you're eating because there is consciousness in everything. This is important because it determines what kind of energies you let your body digest. Also be careful to feel what the body thinks about what you are giving it to eat. Does it become energetic and happy or stuffed and lethargic? Change your diet according to what the body is telling you. If you're not already eating healthy and start following these simple suggestions, you will soon notice that your body will increase in frequency, feeling *lighter* and definitely happier and more in communication.

Speaking of communication—it is imminent to communicate with your body. Ask it how it feels, tell it that you love it and think it's beautiful, and let it know that you trust it and rely on it to always help you by letting you know if there are any dangers in your environment or if something you are doing is not feeling right. Also, work out a signal system that the body can work with and use when it wants your attention. The body knows more than you do—take that to the bank! The problem is that people listen way too little to their bodies—it's even gone so far that there is no communication at all. When the body doesn't get any attention, it feels purposeless and depressed and can easily get sick. A good way to boost the immune system is to start communicating with your body in a positive manner.

Here's another very important consideration—we need to boost our immune system! I already mentioned one way to do it—communicate with your body—but there are many other ways. Breathing exercises, meditation, eating right, having a positive attitude, raising our consciousness, putting up a protective shield around us (more about this later), and stop being afraid of our bodies are good things to start with.

The next thing is to be aware of what we need to avoid, or our immune system will stop working rather fast. Perhaps, the most important thing is to stop eating genetically modified (GM) food! GM food was introduced on the food market sometime in the 1990s, I believe, and now it's the main source of food. The Food Industry, led by Monsanto, is ruthless. Just recently, the government was trying to pass a law that requires that all GM food needs to be marked so that the consumer knows. This was furiously fought against by Monsanto, which is working on getting a monopoly within the Food Industry. Monsanto is willing to spend billions of dollars if necessary to prevent labeling GM food from happening, so in the long term, it will probably win that battle. Monsanto, which is a super-criminal organization, is literally attacking smaller farmers who are into organic food with the intention of eliminating them from the market. There is evidence that Monsanto has even secretly sprayed the famers' crops so that everything dies and the farmers can't afford to continue their business. Other farmers have been threatened (even with death) if they continue their business. They have been visited by well-dressed men in sunglasses who have spread their threatening message to the farmers—speaking about *Men in Black*! For those who think I exaggerate, there are many great YouTube videos: documentaries in which they interview farmers who show evidence of what has happened to them, thanks to Monsanto. Monsanto is definitely one of these businesses, together with General Electric and others that are run by the AIF, and their headquarters are not on Earth. Monsanto has a super agenda, which is not known to many people yet, but I'll tell you the short version here.

What happens when you eat GM food? Of course, first, you increase the risk of getting cancer and many other serious anti-immune diseases because GM food decreases your immune system. However, that is just a convenient side effect for the Global Elite and the AIF. The real purpose for Monsanto (with its earthly headquarters in Missouri) is population control. We already discussed in the WPP that the world population will probably not exceed 7 billion, or if it does, it won't be long before it will start decreasing drastically. Monsanto will have a big responsibility in the population control agenda. The AIF has a difficult time controlling 7 billion souls, so they have no choice other than to reduce the world population down to a more controllable level. It will be done in many different ways in the beginning—wars, famine, new laboratory-created serious diseases, weather control, and so on. However, the ace up their sleeve is Monsanto. The attitude is, *If we're going to reduce the population, why don't we feed them to death?* Studies on laboratory animals show that after a few generations with the animals being fed only GM food, many, if not most of them, become infertile. This is exactly the card they are going to play because it's so simple, and it leaves no obvious traces because it is more of a long-term plan. First, Monsanto wants to make organic food illegal, and it is well on its way to succeeding to take over the entire Food Industry, first in America, but then worldwide. When that is done, Monsanto can start poisoning the entire world population. A few generations from now, most people will be unable to reproduce!

Why would Monsanto want to make the whole world population infertile? That means the end of humanity—we will be extinct! Exactly, and in a sense, this seems to be exactly what they are planning. The AIF is planning for the end of humanity as we know it. If the AIF can't figure out how our divine bodies work, they may just as well get rid of us. Now, it's not that the AIF wants everybody to die—they still need an army for the future and a work force that can slave for them and their corporations. After all, that's why they have their advanced technology. If people only knew how close we are to becoming cyborgs—it's no longer science fiction or something that will happen in a near future—the time is almost here![5] Now, we must ask ourselves: who are these beings who can't reproduce and have come back to our time from the future in order to regain their humanity, hoping to be able to reproduce again? Who are the time-jumpers who don't have any genitals? Correct, it's the *Grays,* who say they are us in the future![6] The Grays are the descendants of those who will choose to live in the Machine Kingdom and will become cyborgs[7]. One of the only ways for the future humans to reproduce will be to clone

---

[5] See, http://battleofearth.wordpress.com/2013/05/03/superstrong-telepathic-the-bionic-soldiers-of-the-future-how-radical-technology-could-transform-british-troops-within-30-years/

[6] See WPP "The Third Level of Learning" for reference

[7] Ibid.

themselves, and that is exactly what will happen, which is another important reason not to eat GM food, don't you think?

We will talk a little bit more about food in an upcoming chapter, but this gives us something to think about.

I have said many times how easy it is to accidentally choose the Machine Kingdom, not realizing what we're doing. We don't want Homo Nova to be extinct before we have even established ourselves. You see, this is exactly what the AIF is counting on—they will be able to outlaw organic food or non GM food in general. This way, they can kill two birds with one stone—those who choose the Machine Kingdom and those who decide to evolve independently. Therefore, we have a few serious challenges ahead of us. Some ask why the AIF let us evolve on the side without them particularly interfering, but there are a few answers—they think they will get us with one of their poisonous programs or another. This is why we have to be smarter than the AIF is in certain ways. Those who fear the AIF would say that it's impossible— the AIF are much smarter than we are, but those who understand the power in the awakening of consciousness will say that we are getting much smarter than the AIF thinks! We don't even need to know what their programs are—we just need to recognize the pattern of the dictators. Eventually, the AIF becomes predictable because they do what has always worked. The AIF are involved in so many areas of life that they need to find patterns that work and stick with them as long as possible. Hence, the AIF has tried programs that work on humans. The AIF asked themselves, how do you manipulate a human? They studied our patterns, our strengths, and our weaknesses. Then they tried out some programs that seemed to work and developed those. One such program is to take something that is true and which the AIF does not want us to know, turn it into the opposite of what it is, and then present it to mankind as the truth—it almost always works. The most obvious example, perhaps, in relation to the AIF, is what was discussed in WPP about Lord ENKI in the *Second Level of Learning*. In mythology and in the Sumerian cuneiform, he is presented as a *Savior*, rescuing a small part of mankind from the Deluge. Since then, Lord ENKI has been looked upon as a *good god*. In fact, he saved the small part of mankind who had his own blood running through their veins to create a human *Elite* after the Deluge had subsided. This Elite was meant to control the rest of the slave workers (who later became us) and is doing so up to this day. Saving mankind from extinction elevated Lord ENKI to a hero and someone to worship, when the truth of the matter is that it was he who started the whole master-slave society we have had from after the Biblical Flood.

Another popular program is *Problem-Reaction-Solution*, where the AIF or the Global Elite is creating a problem, such as 9/11. Humankind protests worldwide and demands that the authorities do something about terrorism. Therefore, the same forces who created the problem in the first place will now present a solution that fits them and their agenda, so they created a *War on Terror* and cut back on our human rights in the name of *National Security*. Mankind, who has no idea how this formula works and that their own government would do something that evil, are now happy because they feel safer with more surveillance and restrictions and with more power to the government. These are merely two examples. Unfortunately for them, after a while, we learn how to recognize their modus operandi and learn how to avoid the traps. Thus, we'll become more and more like excellent jujitsu masters, who just casually lift an arm when the enemy attacks, and the enemy falls on his head. It's enough to read a newspaper article every now and then and we can quite clearly see how the AIF operates. We simply learn how not to fall for it. The next thing they may try is to create new programs designed particularly to manipulate us truth-seekers after they have studied us and our patterns for quite a while, and then they will start implementing them. This may be trickier for us, so now, in the beginning of the New Era, we need to be extra alert and make sure we are not falling for any new types of manipulation because that's the only way they can get us—to have us agree with them!

Perhaps, we should get more realistic. The AIF already knows how truth-seekers work, I'm sure. They have had a relatively long time to study us. They have always tried to choose the path of least resistance when possible, and I have the feeling they will do that now as well. I need to explain what I mean by that in this particular case.

Barbara Marciniak's Pleiadians explained already in 1992 what their own agenda is. They are here to help us because that's the only way to help themselves. In a minute, I will explain exactly how they are planning to accomplish this. However, here is something I just heard on a brand new CD from the Pleiadians containing a lecture from the spring of this year. They say that in this time period that we live in, a Machine Kingdom is on the rise here on Earth, and without Pleiadian interference, almost the entire human population (except for a very low percentage) will be part of this kingdom. Sometime during 2030 to 2050, the AIF is apparently planning to show themselves to mankind—the final *Disclosure.* At least that is their current plan. How they will show themselves—whether it will be in human form or any other body form is anybody's guess—the Pleiadians don't know. My qualified guess is that the AIF come down in human form because that makes most sense. They have abducted humans for hundreds of years and stolen our DNA, mixed it with what they already had from thousands of years ago, and strengthened it so the AIF can comfortably use hybrid human bodies here on Earth, and we will notice no difference. I have heard that they have millions of human bodies in storage on Earth, Mars, and other planets and moons in the solar system. In the WPP, "The Third Level of Learning," I explained that the AIF is going to invade us, and 200 million invaders are on their way back to Earth to occupy these human bodies, hidden in the storage locations. In 2012, a smaller group of these 200 million invaders came here as forerunners and have already established themselves on Earth.

Therefore, this is their plan: these forerunners, in conjunction with the Global Elite and the interdimensionals who are staying hidden in the background, are going to create some disasters and catastrophes—unifying events that will bring big segments of mankind together in an effort to survive. I personally think that destroying the economy is their safest card. They want to utterly destroy the dollar and have all other currency follow after. A new depression will follow, which will make the depression in the 1930s look like child's play because this one will be global. People will be starving to death and no one will have a solution.

However, worry not because help is near! In times when humanity will do anything to survive, we will have visitors! Starships will land, and beings who look very human will meet with the governments of the world. This time, it will be in the newspapers all over the planet. Humans will probably be held in suspense for a few days—perhaps a week or two—while our authorities talk to these aliens behind locked doors. The meeting place will most probably be the United Nations.

Then, one day, the doors will burst open and an announcement will be made. Perhaps the United Nations Secretary is the person who will read the announcement, with the leader of the Extra Terrestrials (ETs) standing beside him. People are told that these star beings are, for example, the *Ashtar Command,* and they have observed mankind for a long time without interfering—hoping we would be able to bring ourselves out of the mess. Now, they see that we can't, and they refuse to see us suffer anymore, so they have come to assist. People will wonder who the Ashtar Command is, of course, and many New Age people will tell others that they are the ones who have been channeled for decades already—all we need to do is to listen to these channeled messages, and we will know who they are—it's all on the Internet! The media will also inform us, of course, and possibly refer to channeled material.

This will be a total shock for most people, but eventually it will turn into the ultimate unifying event, where mankind in their misery accept help from this alien civilization. Mankind will believe that they have no choice!

Therefore, how will this help come about? Well, if we assume it's the Ashtar Command that's coming (which is just a front for the AIF), they will say that they are from the *Galactic Federation of Light*, and eventually they would love to see humankind as members of this space organization, but first, we must take care of the global Earth crisis once and for all. Therefore, Ashtar promises that he and his people, in conjunction with the human world leaders and the United Nations, will restore the economy by creating a universal currency that doesn't inflate or deflate. This can be done relatively quickly and easily, he says. After that, the next step will be to expand the Smart Cities. Smart Cities will be built all over the world with alien technology, and they will be huge, making New York and Tokyo look like suburbs. Furthermore, Ashtar will explain that it's in these cities where all the jobs will be, so people need to move into any of them. He will also promise that everybody is going to have a job and a roof over their heads and enough money to be able to live a decent life! Most important—there has to be a One World Government for this to work. We can't have any more conflicts and wars. The Ashtar Command is here to bring peace on Earth, and the only way to do it is to globalize things and governments in particular.

This will be like music to most people's ears, but there will still be skeptics, who may ask what Ashtar Command's agenda is. Why are they doing this for us? The answer will probably be that the Ashtar Command is part of a space organization that finds civilizations who have reached a certain level of consciousness, and their job is to help them evolve to a point where they can travel out in space and become part of the Galactic Organization and start trading with other star races. They will tell us that we have great resources here on Earth that we can sell, and in exchange, there are a lot of things that we need, such as technology! The Ashtar Command will help us rebuild Earth with its technology, but in the future, mankind will be able to trade with star beings. The Ashtar Command is only intermediaries, they may say. They will stay with us for a while after everything is rebuilt and make sure we have what we need to manage star travel, and then they will leave. Most people will buy into this propaganda.

Once things have been settled, treaties have been made, and contracts signed, the work will begin. The Smart Cities will be *gridded,* which means that everyone who doesn't live and work in the city can't just get in. If you have a job and live in another Smart City, you can probably travel from city to city, but those who decide to stay with nature and have nothing to do with this alien agenda are not welcome in the cities. We will be left on our own, with no help from any authority. Most people who choose not to be part of the Smart City Agenda will be happy with that and gladly move out in nature. However, in the end, it may be challenging for some, as we shall see.

People in the Smart Cities won't believe their eyes once everything is established. The streets are always clean—everything is clean—and everybody has jobs and GM food as promised, and the technology they are now surrounded by is absolutely astonishing—far more advanced than anyone could ever imagine. People will be very thrilled and happy about their new situation. They will laugh at those who'd rather choose to live in nature: primitive living compared the Smart Cities. They must be crazy! *Primitive people choose primitive options*—something like this may be some kind of slogan.

The One World Government will be run by ETs, and this time it will be in the open, although some ETs will still lurk in the background and not show themselves. There will be a new World Leader, who people will treat like he is the Messiah. After having lived in poverty, people are very grateful to have such a wonderful life, and all wars are stopping and there is Peace on Earth—finally!

Yes, everything will be *fantastic,* except for one crucial thing: there will be no critical thinking. The manipulation and mind control via the alien technology will be devastating! People will become like robots, immersed with virtual reality games and worse.

As promised, the AIF will eventually take humans to space, but before that happens, mankind has already turned into cyborgs. Due to GM food and other methods, people can no longer reproduce by themselves, and the world population will drop drastically (to a manageable level). Cloning will now be common, but eventually people, who notice they get sick easily (from GM food), become afraid of their bodies and need a solution to stay healthy but continue their *wonderful* lifestyle. Of course, those who instigated the problem know exactly how to solve it. They make humans into half biological entities and half machines. This process has already begun as a pilot on Earth as of this writing, and we find articles on how people can get new body parts fairly easily if one fails to work, such as an arm.[8] In

---
[8] See, http://wespenre.com/3/paper09-machine-kingdom.htm#machine

the future, however, you can get artificial kidneys, livers, or whatever is failing in the body.

The Pleiadians tell us that machines have consciousness. Of course, they have to be built, but somewhere along the line, the cosmic machine consciousness, which is common in the universe, will establish itself in the machines, just like souls do in biological life forms. The late science fiction writer, Isaac Asimov, was one of the first who wrote about this problem in his book, *I, Robot!* This is what will happen with humans in the future. No one will even reflect on that the once so peaceful Ashtar Command, now in charge of Earth, will create and refine human super soldiers, who also are half machines and half human. No one will even ask why we need soldiers when there is no war because people in the Smart Cities will by that time be too much under mind control and such dedicated Machine Riders that they will hardly notice what is going on, and even if some do, they won't bother. Whatever happens, they will never consider living a life without machine technology. Also, due to this incredible technology, their lifespan has now increased considerably. When people can have their body parts removed and exchanged with machine parts, they can hypothetically live more or less forever.

Eventually, the once biological human body, which now has developed to something that looks more like a Gray alien, is ready to go into space and explore other solar systems. Their new bodies can resist radiation and harsh conditions in space because the machine parts were deliberately created of material that can be used for space travel.

As the centuries and millennia go by, humans will be curious about their origins and travel both to Sirius and the Pleiades to meet those they believe are their *makers*.[9] When they come

---

[9] Pleiadian lecture, Spring 2013.

to the Pleiades, they create havoc there and even decide to invade and conquer their old creators. A tyranny is growing in the Pleiades, and eventually, a group of renegades meet in secret to find out how they can resolve this problem. They manage to find out that the problem started in the nano-second, when mankind became under even more influence from the AIF, and after the nano-second, the Machine Kingdom arose. Out of the Machine Kingdom came those cyborgs, who were almost indestructible (quite like Arnold Schwarzenegger's *Terminator*), and very hard to kill. Hence, this secret Pleiadian group decided to go back in time to the beginning of the nano-second and make contact with humanity via channeling. They realized that if they could talk some part of humanity into rejecting the machine world and instead evolve naturally by being with nature, this could change a lot in the Pleiades, and the visitors who will come to the Pleiades in the future may no longer be cyborgs, but evolved humans, who will nano-travel there instead.

In other words, the Pleiadians want to create a whole new timeline because if they would not have interfered, humankind as a biological species will not survive. Now at least a faction of us will, by creating this alternative timeline. This doesn't mean that we are erasing the past—we just creating a new one.

Some people probably doubt the Pleiadians' intentions and won't trust them, and this I can understand. They have their agenda, and they admit that they would have done what's necessary to save themselves and their species, which means they would probably have eradicated us if they had to. Now it just so happens that they realized that if we evolve the way we are supposed to, it will help them too. Therefore, it became a win-win situation. I have listened to them long enough to be sure that they are honest in what they're saying because time has proven them right. Moreover, they can afford to be quite truthful because it fits with their agenda. However, I do not necessarily see them as our friends at this time, but I think our relationship so far has helped mankind, and now we are able to make it on our own.

The problem in the beginning of the Machine Kingdom is that many people who choose nature before the Smart Cities will be tempted to reconsider when they notice how wonderful it seems to be for those who live in the cities and how much struggle it is for those living with nature. This is the reason I am relaying this information, so we can prevail and continue doing what I consider to be the right thing to save mankind, knowing there will be severe temptations on the way.

Someone asked me if there is any way to live in the Smart Cities and still not agree with the AIF—i.e. we can take advantage of a roof over our heads and a job, yet have independent thoughts. I would say, no. If we look at this scenario, we can see it's not possible. In addition, I am sure that the AIF will collect the Machine Riders' souls in the afterlife and recycle them into the Smart Cities again. Then, in the long term, the *Between Lives Area* will probably be closed down because it's obsolete and no longer needed. The cyborgs will live for a very long time, and those who still die for different reasons can easily be collected in the astral and shot down into a body again. We, who are evolving at our own pace, will eventually do so without having to first visit the Between Lives Area and, thus, be born with a full memory of whom we are. Therefore, the manipulation in the astral plane will no longer be an issue.

We have two agendas here—one is the AIF who wants to control mankind, letting us continue being a slave race and create super soldiers from many of us. Then we have the Pleiadians who want us to evolve naturally. Interestingly enough, the Pleiadians and the AIF are basically the same group of star beings if we go back long enough in time (see the WPP), but now their agendas clash. What it seems like is that the AIF doesn't care too much whether the spiritual faction of the humans go their own way or not—perhaps it's easier for the AIF if we do, so they don't need to deal with us. The AIF understand that eventually the Earth will split, and they will get rid of the problem that way. In the meantime, we can live outside the Smart Cities and mind our own business—it's easier than killing us and making martyrs out of us. Also, if bodies *disappear*, it must be explained—too much effort when the AIF has more urgent matters to attend to. As long as we don't bother the AIF, they won't bother us will probably become the silent slogan. Therefore, the AIF will let the Pleiadians have their way and instead concentrate on the majority of mankind, who will choose to be Machine Riders anyway. The AIF still has a few cards up their sleeves in order to take care of us truth-seekers, as we have seen, but if these plans fail, it looks like the AIF will leave us alone after all.

However, why are the AIF creating super soldiers out of humans? Are they planning a future war? You can bet on that! The AIF, for the most part, are rebelling Orions, and their highest goal is not only to be the Masters of the 4% Universe (which they more or less already are), but they want to take over the 96% Spirit World as well, and if they succeed, it will be catastrophic. They want to take revenge on the Orion Queen and the Mother Goddess and take over as the Rulers of the Entire Creation. We humans are going to be used as foot soldiers and eradicated in the process. It's a nightmare we can't even comprehend in our current state of being.

We gain nothing by fighting the AIF in the outside world for two reasons. The first is that out there the AIF is stronger than us because they have the technology, and second, the problem is not *out there* but *in here*. We can solve any problem that appears to exist outside of ourselves by going inside. That is where the problem always originates.

Beliefs and Belief Systems

What we've been sitting stuck in here on Earth is powerful because the AIF knows the power of imagination and the power of beliefs. This is what their whole manipulation strategy is all about. The world outside of you is only a mirror of yourself and your own beliefs, and that's all. If we want to change this reflection, we need to change our beliefs and our emotions connected to them. When people see something that is not working, they are quick at going out there and trying to change it. It never works! It's not until we go inside to fix it that it's working. If you insist on fixing it on the outside, you only add to the problem. Here is a common example: your water tap is dripping and you decide to fix it. You go and get some tools and start tightening a little bit here and a little bit there, but nothing seems to help—the dripping may even increase the more you fumble around with your tools. You get more and more frustrated and don't know what to do until you step back and look at it. Then you go inside yourself to look at the problem and you realize that there may be a filter in there somewhere that needs to be changed. Aha! So you open up the tip of the water tap and sure enough, there's the filter! Now you can go to the hardware store, buy a new one, and replace it. It stops dripping! What you did was to go inside and change your perspective on the water tap and your belief on how it works and the problem could be resolved. If you, on the other hand, had refused to go inside, you either would have to give up at one point or call a plumber. Now, you did, however, go inside, and from that point, your beliefs regarding how a water tap works in the holographic universe changed forever, and the next time it will not even be a problem (unless you forget what you learned).

A good measure and an excellent example that we have evolved is that despite whether the environment stays the same, we are changing regardless. Our approach to it constantly changes and therefore *we* change. Thus, because we change our approach to the environment that we no longer agree with, we need to create new belief systems to replace the old ones, and we will in that respect also change our frequency, and slowly but surely because our old belief systems are scattering, the Old World must disappear from our reality. Think about this for a moment and you will see how it works. This is all on a much bigger scale than the water tap. However, don't try to get rid of all your belief systems—that's not your goal. There is nothing wrong with belief systems—they help us explore the Multiverse. The only things we need to get rid of are old belief systems that no longer serve us. When we see that a different story emerges before our eyes and it serves us much better than the religious belief system we may have subscribed to earlier, it is not beneficial for our development as a being to keep hanging on to the old religion when we know it's not in our best interest. Still, many people do just that—and again, it's not only when it comes to religious beliefs—and if they don't eventually let go, their own belief system will be their downfall. Life is going forward—it never stagnates, and it is not going backward. Thus, we need to change when we notice that change is needed for our progress. Still, in the big scheme of things, *everything* is belief systems. Hence, we live in a reality that is built around our belief systems. Change them and your reality changes. This is why I needed to present the WPP the way that I did. It took me 1,500 pages to do it, but it was the only way to achieve what I had in mind. My idea was that if I present our current reality and what builds up to it as carefully as possible, people will have to face their own belief systems, which are all similar when it comes to the Big Picture, but different to some degree on an individual basis. Once readers have seen the Big Picture and their own belief systems related to that, they can change the beliefs that don't benefit them and don't contribute to their survival. After that, we can start looking within and break our chains, one by one and once and for all.

It is very important that each person gets the chance to change his or her own belief systems without getting forced to do so by someone else. We all know how much we want other people and our near-and-dear to see what we have seen—therefore, it's easy to overwhelm them with information and viewpoints that we *think* will help them evolve, when instead, we are halting their progress. What we are doing when we are forcing our reality upon somebody else is that we stop that person from looking within. Again, that person is told to look outside (at your viewpoint) for the answers and looking outside was what got them in the mess in the first place. It would be much better to be a good example—someone other people want to emulate—and wait for *them* to approach *you*. Those who are in need of change will come to you and ask questions or make comments. When that happens, you can answer the questions without forcing anything on the other person. You can do that by saying that this is *your* way of seeing it, and because of that, you are a happy, cheerful, loving, and non-judgmental person. However, those who don't show any interest in learning more, you won't bother with. If they feel inclined in the future, they will come—otherwise, you just know that some people need more time. Knowing what lies ahead, we may feel the urge to educate *everybody* to save as many as possible. This is not our task, however. We can't force a frequency upon a person, and even if it is painful sometimes, we must let people develop on their own, in whatever direction it may lead them. Like we discussed earlier, the information is out there for those who want to start studying. I am aware that there isn't much more time, but we still can't force any viewpoints on anybody who doesn't want to look, regardless of how much we love them. Sometime we have to let it go.

We often hear people say to each other, "It's only in your imagination," or to themselves, "It is only in my imagination." You see, there are so many things we need to un-learn. We think that those who lived 500 years ago were much more primitive than we are today. This is only partially true. In fact, they were often more multidimensional than most people are today. Since the Industrial Revolution, we have become much more linear in our thinking. A few hundred years ago, people allowed themselves to be much more imaginative, and that was accepted. Many saw things that we today would write off as delusional or "only in their imagination." When we look back at history and people who saw elves, goblins, fairies, and other strange creatures, most in today's world think they were superstitious. Sometimes they probably were, but the fact remains that they actually were more psychic than we are now because they used their imagination. They didn't have any TVs, computers, or CNN that gave you viewpoints and fed you with their enforced belief systems daily—they only had themselves and each other. Also, they had something else that we don't care that much about anymore as a species—they had nature! Even those who lived in the cities were psychic and could see and hear things because there were no neon lights that lit up the cities 24/7—instead, they had torches and oil lamps etc. When dusk came, the city lights were turned out and it was dark. My point is that people used their imagination more, and the imagination comes from inside and is indeed a creative force that is a realm of reality that is just as real as the physical 3-D reality. In the future when we have regained our multidimensional abilities, imagination will be our absolute best tool when it comes to creating realities—something we all will be busy doing to some degree or another. Eventually, we need to develop and enhance our abilities to use our imagination in our daily lives. I know it sounds like a lot we need to do, but we are not talking about chores here—as you will see, most of what we are going to do is fun, especially when we notice the results. However, don't worry—I will summarize everything to make it as easy as I possibly can.

To take the subject of belief systems a little further and explain how it works on a quantum and subquantum level without getting technical, we need to understand that everything is connected on the smallest level. This is why the microcosm is more important than the macrocosm when it comes to creation and changing realities. We live in a holographic universe, so what happens to one cell in our body impacts the entire universe. This is why if you see a drama in the world and it affects you, and you now go inside to look at it from a personal level, your attitude to that drama will change and stop affecting you. This is also why there are no victims if you look at it from an objective standpoint. It's not the outside universe that causes an effect upon you, it's the inner universe that projects itself on the outside world and, therefore, seems to affect you. We are lucky to realize this so that we can change our circumstances from within with some training, but not everybody is that lucky. Hence, I don't agree with those who say that people who starve in Africa or are being raped because they are easy targets are being subjected to those crimes because they themselves project this to happen to them—therefore, we should just turn our backs and let things play out. I would like to see those who promote this philosophy do the same thing if someone in their own family got raped and abused. I'm sure they would see that differently and immediately interfere. You see, it's easy to twist logic and turn a powerful truth into something negative in an attempt to discredit the truth. Instead, we need to use common sense. It may be true that the people being abused and raped *pulled that in* because of the energies they emit due to past experiences, including karma, but that doesn't mean we should turn emotionally cold and leave people in their misery. Be aware that such attempts to distort the truth are used by those in power to discredit important truths that have been discovered and rediscovered. Also be aware that what seems to be one agenda is often multilayered. Another thing the Power Elite would gain from taking the fact that there are no victims to its extreme is that they can go ahead and rape and abuse as much as they want without interference because, after all, *there are no victims.*

The Power Elite that the AIF has put in position to rule mankind and who has now been taken over by members of the AIF are often those who create the most powerful belief system for us, and they always make sure to include a good amount of fear and terror into it. Now, this is their belief that fear is what drives us, so we always need to be fearful to be able to do a good job. Then, when we've adopted their fearful belief systems, thinking that they were our own beliefs to begin with, we become afraid of our own belief systems and spread this fear within the human soul group. The media are the main instigators of creating common belief systems for the people in modern times, but the media are, of course, taking orders from higher-ups and just do what they are being told.

The controllers know how important and powerful belief systems are, and they wouldn't be able to control us without them. Therefore, now it's time to change those belief systems and create our own. To be able to do this successfully, first, we must learn how to clear our mind from junk thoughts and be focused. We also need to know how to put a light thought into an idea or a belief and then let go. Here is an example of how powerful thoughts are. Let's say that you decide to live in a world where you are always happy and cheerful. Therefore, you put out a thought with an emotion to it that you will always be cheerful and happy. Then something happens that goes against your decision and you get a little confused. Instead, you decide that you are always going to be happy and cheerful *most of the time,* and this is what you'll get. Often, when something happens that makes it look like what you've decided doesn't work, you think that you can't be happy and cheerful all the time, and that is what you'll get. In other words, soon you may be back where you started, and you think that the power of thought doesn't work.

In reality, when you came upon your first few obstacles, they happened so you could overcome them in order to be happy and joyful all the time, but you thought they came in because your new belief system was too much to ask for. Therefore, you minimized it. Then you minimize it again. We do this subconsciously. Indeed, belief systems are very sophisticated programming because the last decision you make on something is what will stick. Some may say that this is inconvenient because it prevents you from achieving your first idea, but if you think about it, it gives us a chance to change our mind, which otherwise would be much harder to do. Therefore, the rule is: *The last decision always modifies an earlier one on the same thread of thoughts.* Therefore, again, it comes down to *practice*—a lot of practice—so we can control our minds, and this is what we need to do to become multidimensional.

Our DNA: A Corridor of Light Switches

Did you know that the total length of DNA in one adult human body is 10^{13} meters? That is *ten trillion* (10,000,000,000,000) meters, which is the equivalent of almost 70 trips back and forth to the Sun![10] That is

---

[10] Ref: http://hypertextbook.com/facts/1998/StevenChen.shtml

just in one human! Can you imagine how much information is stored in that, and I mean, *exactly how much*? The answer is that in one human, everything in the universe is stored—in fact, every human body *has* the universe and everything within it—it's all there inside us. We live in a virtual reality within a virtual reality within a virtual reality, and on it goes. Our body is a program that projects a hologram to what we consider the mind, which projects this hologram so that it looks like that it is outside of ourselves, and what we learn is then picked up by the soul. Then we have all other people on this planet plus beings on other planets who transmit basically the same hologram. We are allowed to make changes to the program that controls the hologram, and when we do, we make changes in our own hologram. All these holograms together make up our Multiverse.

As a human being so far, we have created our reality, more or less, unconsciously or let authorities or outside forces create our reality for us. As a percentage, the choices we make consciously and with a higher purpose in mind are very few compared with those who are influenced from something we perceive as being outside ourselves. Now, how would it be if we, right now and without any previous practice, could go into our DNA and change things consciously so that our behavior and abilities change with it? Sounds like science fiction? Still, it's a very easy thing to do, I've done it, and it works! I originally heard this on a Pleiadian CD, channeled by Barbara Marciniak[11], and thought it sounded so incredible and amazing that I had to test it. I strongly suggest you do too.

This is how it works. Because the human body is a program and the DNA is its building stones, we change things in our body and in the Multiverse by triggering something in the

---

[11] Ref: The Pleiadians: "The Big Wake Up", Lecture given on 6/22/12 & 6/23/12, CD set no. 4, CD 2, track no. 12.

genome, which then responds. ==It's all a hologram and the Multiverse is fluid, waiting for your input.== Now, think of the DNA in your body as one extremely long corridor, almost like a corridor on one of the floors in a hotel, with doors on both sides, leading into different rooms. In your mind, put yourself at the beginning of this corridor and look down the corridor. You can see that some of the doors are closed, and no light comes out from the rooms on the other side of those closed door. Then you also see that some of the doors are open, and light, indeed, comes out from the rooms. Now imagine that this corridor is your DNA and the doors are light switches that are turned on and off. Walk down the hall and look at the doors. Many have something written on them, you notice. One door says "fear" and it's almost closed. The next door says "courage" and it's half open. Another says "health" and it's closed, while another one for example says "safety," etc. Say that you don't want any more fear in your life, so in your mind you go ahead and close the door of fear totally. You also want a wonderful partner relationship so you go to a door that says "Great Partner Relationship" and make it wide open, seeing how a tremendous amount of light and energy is coming toward you. These are just examples, of course, and you can imagine doors with anything you want written on them. This way you can close and open doors in your DNA as it suits you. You simply decide that by doing this, you activate things you want to activate and deactivate things you do not want in your life, and it helps you creating your new reality built on conscious thoughts, emotions, decisions, purposes, and goals. It can be very powerful!

Exercises

Chapter 1 has described a number of exercises we need to practice to get into the more advanced material needed to be a multidimensional human. After having discussed the subjects in Chapter 1 at length, let us now summarize them so they will be easier to follow and practice.

Power of Thought

Get rid of junk thoughts

Practice to be aware of what you're thinking and what you're saying so that what you express to yourself and others is what you want. Catch yourself every time you have a sloppy thought, like "The way things are going, I will never get better." When you catch yourself, either erase the sloppy thought by saying or thinking to yourself, "Cancel that," and then change the sloppy thought, like in the above example, to "Although I've had a rough time so far, I am going to get well in no time and feel better than I've ever felt before."

Sloppy Decision Making

Sloppy decision making can cause severe consequences—we know that. Think through things before you make any major decision that will affect you for more than a very short time, without depriving yourself from spontaneity. Spontaneity and being impulsive can have their charm sometimes, but we still need to know what we're doing. Don't buy things you can't afford--don't buy anything on credit, and make sure, in general, that whatever you decide to do, it's going to benefit you and those involved who you care for in the long term and not only for the moment if it has to do with an investment.

Create Your Own Local Universe

Make sure you create your own safe haven, which includes your entire Local Universe. By a Local Universe, I mean your environment from the immediate one around your body up to the farthest away place you commonly travel to. Not only do you want it safe but you also wish to create it exactly the way you want it for you to be happy in it. Practice by changing your thought patterns and use the results from the practice you've done under Exercise 1 above. Think of your own Local Universe as something separate from that which is outside of it. Hence, what you read in the news and hear stories from near and far are news from other universes. In reality, they are stories from other version of the Multiverse, as all people experience different things in different locations in space/time. For example, a war that is going on in another country or the War of Terror can be presented in the news as an immediate threat to your own safety, but condition your space in your own Local Universe and understand that what is happening somewhere else is someone else's learning experience and happens on *another version of Earth!* This is extremely important to realize because there are almost infinite versions of Earth and, definitely, one version for each person on this planet. Therefore, don't get involved, either physically or emotionally, in something that happens far away that you don't want to participate in.

Maintain a Healthy Body

This is not so much an exercise as it is a decision, but I think we can call it an exercise, too, because we need to learn how to stay focused and determined. If you want to eat healthy, you may stick to fruits and vegetables, mainly, but make sure you get your protein intake. There are many good books that can help you get started. However, to become multidimensional, it's not necessary to be a vegetarian, but the key is to eat organic! I can't stress that enough because GM food is slowly killing the body and eventually making it infertile—especially over generations. A more immediate effect from GM food is that you will get a negative reaction from the body. I guess it would be truer to say that the body is sending signals to you—signals that you usually are not trained to understand. Instead they work as distractions. The body is trying to tell you that it doesn't feel well and because it doesn't feel well, it will diminish your abilities to become multidimensional, which requires you to be focused and have a body that is reliable, clear, and healthy. Therefore, Exercise 3 is very important! Buy food locally, if you can, from farmers whose reputation is good and who, evidently, are selling organic, first-class products. They will be more expensive than what you can buy in the store, probably, but the price paid in the long term for buying the cheaper food, in terms of destroying our body, is way too high. Eating healthy will also boost your immune system, and an excellent immune system is what is going to be needed more than ever in the near future, as long as we are still living in a highly polluted world.

Practice How to Activate and Deactivate Your Own DNA

When you notice something about yourself, let's say an unwanted trait, imagine the DNA corridor, and in your mind, go to the door that says—for example, "Uncontrolled Anger," which may be the trait you want to get rid of. Therefore, you simply close that door and keep that part of your genome latent and deactivated. If you want to become more compassionate, you imagine a shut or half-open door that has the sign "Compassion" on it. Then you just open the door and keep it wide open, letting a huge flood of compassion run through your DNA. This is an ongoing practice—something you can do as much as you want and whenever you want.

I hope that this chapter has been helpful and educative, and these exercises will assist you in getting the basics for achieving multidimensionality. These exercises are something we will need to carry over even when we get to the more advanced studies. In fact, all four exercises are extremely powerful when practiced correctly. If we don't have our basics fairly in order, we will fall on our heads later on. I don't mean that it's dangerous, but we will get stuck and need to go back to the level where the cause to the halt is located and pick up from there again.

My advice is to read the whole book through from beginning to end in order to get the overall picture of the information I am giving you. While doing this, you can start practicing the exercises from this chapter. It's not recommended to stop reading and do the exercises to perfection before continuing with the next chapter. It's important to get the overall picture. Another thing that I think is important is that the exercises here must be understood as ongoing practices. Some of them are never-ending—they are something that will always benefit us. Therefore, I suggest you at least do them to a point where you notice that you are getting observant enough so that they become a natural part of your daily life before adding more of the upcoming exercises to these ones. I know that most people have a busy life, so I have made sure these exercises won't take much of your time, and you can do most of them even during your day at work or wherever you are. Remember, there is no such thing as failure. Everybody is going to run into obstacles and moments when they say that they can't make this work. When that happens to you, you are probably closer to a breakthrough than ever before, so just push through and you'll beat the obstacle. Also, remember to have fun with it. That's the purpose!

CHAPTER 2: PROGRAMMING FOR THE SECOND GOLDEN AGE

How the Alien Invader Forces Counteract the Awakening

Something to keep in mind is that the AIF thinks that they own us—all of us. People often wonder why they let someone like me get away with what I'm doing, and the answer may not be obvious. The thing is that the AIF knows that we are evolving, and they knew all along that it would be inevitable for an intelligent species not to evolve. The AIF also knew that we would evolve at different rates because we are all individuals and learn at a different pace. The AIF understood that if they wanted to continue controlling us, they couldn't kill off everybody who evolved past a certain point, or the AIF would soon stand on their own without a slave race. Hence, the AIF realized that they had to control both sides of the game as much as they could and make sure they were in charge of those who progress slowly and those who progress faster.

The AIF knew all along that the nano-second was coming up, and that would divide mankind. The majority would still be programmed deep enough not to wake up in any significant manner, but there would also be millions who would start seeing through the deception and the manipulation. Instead of killing all these quickly evolving biominds[12], a better way would be to control them as well, while making them believe that they are evolving freely. Therefore, the AIF decided to set up the Control System in the following manner:

The AIF members are all multidimensional and don't perceive time like we do. To them, there is no such thing as *linear time*—that's merely something they invented, again, to gain easier control over the masses. In their universe, all time exists simultaneously—past, present, and future. It's all an ever-lasting present seen from different points of view, that's all. Therefore, to a certain degree, the AIF can be in control over time and, thus, be ahead of the game—they can create time like a movie with a beginning, middle sequence, and an end. However, what they can't predict is probabilities. We live in a Multiverse where each individual contributes every minute of their day to its general progression, so events can only be predicted by estimating probabilities and calculate which ones will be the most possible. Now, as it shows, humankind is much more unpredictable than the AIF and other star races thought, and this has never ceased to amaze them—we can change direction in the blink of an eye.

This has been a real chore for the Control System. After millennia of control, they have learned how to keep the masses in captivity, but there are always those who rise above the crowd, and especially now during the nano-second we have been uncontrollable for them, and they have had to constantly counteract our gained knowledge with disinformation, or the masses would also find out what the minority already knows. This is something they still do, of course, and will continue doing. In this manner, they still keep the masses ignorant by

---

[12] A Biomind is a combination of a biological life form (physical body) and the mind. This is the combination that basically makes up a human being. The soul is the ultimate "I," who collects the biomind's learning experiences and is the higher link to the Mother Universe.

making them think that the truth-seekers are conspiracy nuts, but the conspiracy nuts still continue finding out more and more what's going on behind the scenes. It's not so much about *finding truths* since truth is subjective, but more like shattering belief systems and replacing them with new ones that are more beneficial and pro-survival. In the process, the Control System gets exposed, something the Global Elite and the AIF that controls them want to avoid as much as possible. Usually they don't kill those who raise their consciousness, unless they are getting threatening toward individuals in power or a specific project that needs to be secret under all circumstances. Instead they have other ways to take care of the *spiritual movement.*

In the WPP's "The Third Level of Learning," the channeled material was exposed for what it is. We can't put all channeled material under the same umbrella, but the majority is directly or indirectly working for the AIF—those who talk about the *Harvest* or *Ascension* to a higher density or dimension in particular—especially if there are star races who say we need their help to be able to succeed. What the AIF has done is to have certain psychic people being contacted by those who are supposedly beings from a higher dimension. A conversation—often in the form of Q&A sessions—takes place, and these channeled entities answer the questions to the best of their abilities. The information can sometimes be quite enlightening and is even helping people evolve and become more aware, which is exactly what is hooking the truth-seeker to these entities. When asked why these sources are contacting humanity, they often answer that they are here because of the Harvest. This means that a small majority of mankind (i.e. the truth-seekers) will be segregated from the crowd because they are vibrating on a higher frequency, and it's time for them to ascend to the fourth or fifth-dimension (or Density). This is exactly what the truth-seekers want to do, so when being told this, they feel special, honored, but also safe, thinking that their future is taken care of.

Moreover, the channeled entities tell them that they need their help in order to progress, and we at least need some form of technology to be able to ascend to the next dimension. Here is when it starts getting interesting. The entities say that the majority of the human population, who are not vibrating on a frequency high enough to ascend, will be transported to another location in space and time—often another planet in another solar system or another version of Earth—be struck by amnesia in the usual manner, and start a new 3-D cycle from the beginning again until they learn. It may take another 13,000-75,000 years before a new Harvest will take place, however, and the souls trapped in this time reset will have to begin from the ape stage again and go from there, still having a Global Elite and the AIF manipulating them. However, the truth-seekers, here and now, are the lucky ones because they don't have to go through that cycle again, which is what they are told.

This, of course, also instigates fear in the truth-seekers, who can't be sure if they're chosen or not, so they become very dependent upon the particular channel of choice and very prone to manipulation. This is particularly noticeable when someone else tries to explain the above to them. Either they become very defensive or write the person off as someone who hasn't understood what it's all about, when in fact it's the other way around, as we shall see. The whole thing becomes very *cultish.*

The channel tells the devotees one of three things—either the Harvest is going to happen in their lifetime, and they will either be *beamed up* or picked up in spaceships, or both. This sounds eerily similar to the biblical Rapture. Others say that the Harvest must include body death—for example, when the Harvest happens, the selected people will die and leave their bodies. Star beings will be waiting in the astral and help them *cross over* and then help them with the ascension. The third option is that the selection doesn't take place until people die a normal death, from illness or old age. When they cross over, the aliens will wait on the other side and do the selection there. Those who qualify for ascension will be placed in one category and those who don't will be led in another direction (which reminds me of the trains during World War II, which transported the oblivious Jews to the Concentration Camps where they were separated—those who were led to go one way were put in the gas chambers, while those who were led the other way were used as slave laborers). Those who qualify will then reincarnate on an Earth that vibrates on a higher frequency, and there they will enter bodies that have been specifically genetically engineered to fit the soul's increased vibration. The selectee has now been reborn into a higher dimension.

In the WPP, I also provided evidence that many of these channeled entities are future versions of us humans, who have come back in space and time to study us and our DNA. They are factions of the so-called Grays that we are seeing on occasion during abductions and sometimes on military bases. The Gray bodies are sometimes only *space suits,* where the real future human has, with help from technology, transferred their consciousness into this Gray space suit in order to be able to withstand the harsh conditions in space. These bodies are half biological and half machines, and ironically enough, that's what their real human bodies in the future are as well[13]. Homo sapiens will lose their humanity in the near future when they enter the Machine Kingdom led by the AIF, where people will be hooked

---

[13] The U.S. government is well aware that the aliens who crashed in Roswell, New Mexico, were half cyborgs and half biological beings—very human-like. They figured out that the "Gray" was only a "space-suit" used to enable traveling long distances in space. See Col. Philip J. Corso's book, *The Day After Roswell,* http://www.bibliotecapleyades.net/sociopolitica/dayafterroswell/dayafter.htm

on technology to such an extent that in order to prolong their lives, they sacrifice their human bodies to become cyborgs. These future humans are *Social Memory Complexes* in different stages of development, depending on from when in the future they have returned. A Social Memory Complex can be compared to a *hive community* or a *collective consciousness,* where the whole species are mentally hooked up to a super computer, which is the *Queen* of the hive. Each person in the collective is still a unique individual, but everybody shares the same ideas for important issues and could differ slightly in opinion on minor issues. They are coming back to our time in an attempt to regain their humanity by abducting people and trying to figure out the DNA source code so they can reprogram themselves. Some of the channeled entities are Grays, often addressing themselves as *we* instead of *I.*

Above, we discussed the different stories the channeled entities told us about the Harvest and how it's going to be done. Evidence shows that the Grays who come back from the future are a product of the Machine Kingdom—all of them are, from what I can see. Therefore, the majority of the population, seen from our perspective, will not be transported to another planet but will remain here on a version of Earth containing a lower vibration. Still, we can sense two categories here—the ones who are extremely technologically oriented and those who are a bit less so. Both these categories, however, honestly and seriously want us to evolve—there is no question about it. However, if they are products of the Machine Kingdom, why do they want us to evolve?

Once we've figured it out, it seems obvious. If we start with the Grays who are returning to study our DNA, they want us to develop because the more evolved we are, the easier it may be to find our DNA source code. Therefore, they may promote a Harvest because of that.

Then there are the truth-seekers, who are promised a new Golden Age in a higher dimension. It's obvious that the fifth-dimensional bodies the beings behind the Harvest (the AIF) have programmed for the truth-seekers are programmed in a similar fashion that they have programmed the bodies of Homo sapiens. This would include a new type of holographic universe that relates more to how the truth-seekers see the next dimension—or rather—how they have been told that the next dimension is like. Therefore, when they reincarnate again on Earth, they will be able to perceive the astral plane as well as the regular three dimensions. They will be more psychic and to some degree more multidimensional. This is all done with nano technology, and it's just as real for the oblivious soul as this 3-D is for the Homo sapiens' mass consciousness. However, it is a deception because the truth-seeker who opted for the Harvest will still be under the control of the AIF.

Here is where they try to trick us. The AIF wants a work force in their new Machine Kingdom, and they want Super Soldiers. What they don't want is evolved beings that can see through things. Therefore, they are most certainly going to place the truth-seekers somewhere separate from the third-dimensional beings who will walk gladly into the Machine Kingdom—perhaps even on a different Earth-like planet—contrary to what the AIF told them. The truth-seekers won't be able to tell the difference, anyway, in their manipulated bodies. Now, in the long term, the AIF wants Social Memory Complexes and a super computer that I am sure is already setup and waiting. From here on, things will happen quite rapidly. Humanity will be programmed into becoming a hive community and a *Thought Collective,* just like we're used to viewing the Grays, who in fact are us as the finished product.

Now, pay close attention, please! The truth-seekers have been told by channeled entities (who address themselves as *we* and not as *I*, meaning they are Social Memory Complexes) that we are all One and our goal is to work ourselves up the dimensions and merge with Source, which is All That Is or God. The RA Material is not the only channeled material that says that when we have reached the highest dimension we will merge with Source. This is something the truth-seekers are programmed to believe already. Therefore, when they are living their lives in their new fifth-dimensional bodies, there will be a program in the DNA of those bodies that will manipulate these souls to become One. Eventually the truth-seekers will go to the sixth-or seventh-dimension, and those bodies will have an even stronger program to become One. Behind the scenes, as usual, is the AIF, pulling the strings. Again, here we have the super computer, now ready to create a hive community out of the truth-seekers as well. Therefore, the AIF has managed to control both the Homo sapiens' mass consciousness of oblivious humans and the higher-evolved truth-seekers through the Harvest. The channeled entities who are the most convincing ones are today's truth-seekers in the far future, now coming back as a Social Memory Complex in order to Harvest more souls because they believe that the whole of mankind needs to evolve to their level in order for them to take the last step toward becoming One with Source. In reality, it seems like they are stuck in a time loop trying to recruit themselves in the past. Why would they want to do that? Because they were deceived and programmed, they seem to believe (if we take the RA Material to heart) that they are the first ones reaching these higher dimensions, and they have learned as they've gone along. Now, they realize that they can't go any further without the rest of humanity, including the version of themselves that evolved from our time and onward for everything to be *whole*. By harvesting themselves again, they can correct the mistakes they made on the way. Also, for them, time is not a big issue because they say that time is not linear from the perspective where they are. Therefore, they are patiently waiting for all humanity to come together as One in a big, combined soul group, as a common Social Memory Complex. Then, and only then, can humanity merge with Source (or so they believe).

Here, we can clearly see that all these channeled entities who are humans in the future are stuck in what I've called the 4% universe—they are stuck in a boxed-in reality, even though they may be of the sixth-or seventh-dimension. These are not *real* dimensions as they should be perceived, but only fractions of the full dimensions (about 4% of them). If beings are free beings, they can travel freely between dimensions without using technology, and they will experience a universe so incredibly richer than the partial one they (and we as well so far) are experiencing.

I still need to find out exactly what the AIF is using the harvested truth-seekers for, if anything, but it's very plausible that entities like RA, the Elohim, and such are truth-seekers in the future, while Bashar and Lyssa Royal's Grays are products of the Machine Kingdom—i.e. the majority of mankind in the far future.

Now, the readers can see what it is we must avoid. The AIF and their Global Elite minions are very clever when it comes to manipulating mankind—they have had eons to learn that skill—and as you can imagine, it is easy to fall for their deceptions. Perhaps you are one of those who enthusiastically is following a movement around a channeled source, such as RA, the Cassiopaeans, etc., or perhaps, you are not. If you are, don't feel embarrassed because I've been there too. I had a bad feeling when I heard the term *Harvest of Souls* the first time I read the RA Material/Law of One, and after then, I have been more cautious about RA—there came a point when I felt something was very wrong. Now, after having researched different channeled materials and compared them, I am certain that my body that gave me those uncomfortable signals was right. I have never felt stronger about our need to evolve on our own and create our own new branch on the Tree of Humanity. Only then can we escape the trap and be able to enjoy a full universe and everything within it, instead of being stuck in a small part of it. The reader can probably see even clearer now why I need to write this book.

How to View Reality

Unfortunately, humanity has been programmed to believe that the five senses of the 3-D are all there are, and most people are afraid of the unknown. Before people have heard us out, they shake their heads and say we have no proof—they demand proof, which they are certain does not exist. I have long since passed the point where I argue with people who only accept proof that is limited to the five senses. Of course, you can't prove what is *not* of the five senses *within* the five senses— that's, by default, impossible. Instead, we need to learn to experience what can't be physically proven, and that's where the proof is. This is the main barrier for people in order to break through the prison walls. If all people said, "OK, I don't know what to believe, but let's give it a chance," that would be an amazing breakthrough for human consciousness. What we need for that to happen is a unified event ten times bigger than 9/11, although such an event doesn't have to be negative, but could be.

When I'm writing this, one of the Boston Bombers has been killed and one has been caught, and the Texas Plant Explosion killed 35 people and left an entire town in ruins. These are both very shocking events for all Americans, but also for people abroad, who react to such tragedies in a big way—they feel the trauma in the mass consciousness. Such events are often orchestrated by forces behind the scenes to create more fear in people that the forces can feed on, but these events are also unifying events. They are not big enough to make a radical change in the human soul group, but they contribute. Albeit, the events are negative events with people losing their lives and many end up severely injured, they also have a positive side because they get people together. Like the Mayor of Boston said regarding the Marathon Bombings and I paraphrase: During my 20 years as a Mayor, I have never seen the people of Boston coming together like this for a common cause. These are incredibly tragic events, but on the flip side, they caused people to wake up. The awakening is, of course, happening constantly in the mass consciousness, so it's already there for those who want to tune into it, but incidents such as these make many people suddenly see things they didn't see before, and their lives change. Therefore, these events both took and saved lives, which means that those who died didn't do it in vain. Some people will end up being very grateful to them because they caused their own awakening.

Much of what we learn still comes from channeled material, and that is okay, so long as we get better at distinguishing what is beneficial information and what is not. The following quote is from a lecture by *Bashar*, channeled by Darryl Anka:

> When we judge ourselves it takes longer [to learn], and when we invalidate ourselves. We need to go with the flow and take what comes before us and do something with it. To go with the flow, without anxiety or fear is the absolute fastest way to learn something. You change in the rate of who you are in a specific moment. If you change your view on who you are, you will change in a different rate.[14]

---

[14] Ref: http://jims-01.blogspot.com/search/label/bashar

Even small things in life are non-coincidental. We live in a program, but within this program we have endless freedom to create if we were in much better control over our own fears. Everything that happens to us and around us is a response to something else that happened in an endless cause-and-effect situation. It's easy to understand if you, for example, hammer yourself on the thumb—it's going to hurt (cause and effect). However, if you go into a store and suddenly meet your childhood friend there, whom you haven't seen in 30 years, we tend to call that a *rare coincidence* when in fact it is not. You may have gone to that store only to buy one thing and rush out, and there she is! For that to happen, one or both of you must either have thought very strongly about each other recently, or you could have dreamed about each other. Either way, it would have been a cause-and-effect situation.

Even in small situations such as that, we invalidate our abilities and don't think we can cause something like that to happen, but it wouldn't happen if we couldn't cause it to happen. There is absolutely nothing that happens that doesn't have a cause—small or big. This is another thing we need to practice—to acknowledge ourselves as creators. An open-minded person usually doesn't have a problem visualizing this when it's pointed out to them, but when confronted that we actually also create negative effects on ourselves and our environment, many people don't want to play anymore. Still, it's so very important that we acknowledge ourselves as creators of both positive and negative effects without being judgmental about it. All the things we sweep under the carpet are the exact things that are going to stop us in the future from becoming multidimensional, and the sooner we confront them, the better.

Here is something very important I need to stress, and let's again take the Boston Bombings as an example. Almost all people would see this event as something very negative because people died and many are crippled for life—not to mention the trauma involved. Most people would not see this as something positive, unless they think that killing and traumatizing people is something positive.

Still, when something as big as this happens, it's important to step back from the situation and look at it with a clear and unbiased mind. The negative aspects of the event are obvious, but how can this situation benefit humanity? If we listen to the news and people who got very emotionally effected, nothing positive whatsoever is going to be mentioned. However, it is important that we, in every situation in life, step back to see how the situation can support our development as a person or as a species. In the case of the Boston Bombings, we already mentioned the positive aspect, but let's go over it again from a new perspective. When something like this happens, it also works as a unifying event for people. Those who would never want to get close otherwise were now rubbing shoulders, helping the injured and the situation in general. Everything else was forgotten and forgiven. This has a big positive impact on the mass consciousness—particularly in times of increased energies like this. Therefore, this would be an appropriate way of looking at the Boston Bombings, 9/11, and other big, obviously, traumatizing events. It is not, however, only applicable to big events like these—I only used them as obvious examples to make my point. In life, we meet situations on an almost daily basis that we normally consider negative—for example, at first glance, some situations don't seem to benefit us. However, let's change our attitude and realize that nothing would come our way if there wasn't a learning lesson involved in the confrontation. Even if something looks like doom and gloom, you will find that in 100% of the times there is a learning lesson involved that will bring you forward—a small step forward or a big step forward, it's beside the point. If you can't find a learning lesson in it, you just haven't looked deeply enough. Continue looking until you find the lesson to be learned. This is something we all need to do until it becomes second nature—it's important. This doesn't mean we should ignore that there also can be a negative side of a confrontation if we think it is necessary, but at least we must not stop there—foremost, we should spend our time figuring out where the learning lesson is.

Another thing we need to practice is compassion. Although people show this trait in the third-dimensional world as well, it's not typically a third-dimensional trait—at least not in its full capacity. Compassion is *understanding*. It's easy to feel compassion for a child who suffers, but much harder to feel compassion for someone who is consciously evil. Ask people on the street if they would feel compassion for a serial killer or someone such as Hitler. Most people would say no. Still, it's important to feel compassion even for such extreme evil in order to let go from it and be sure not to pull something like that into our lives. Once a person is vibrating on a certain frequency, compassion more and more becomes a part of that person's trait, like a part of the personality. People feel compassion where they previously did not because they now understand. Understanding comes from increased awareness and higher consciousness.

A good saying, which originates from Native Americans, is that before you judge somebody you must walk in that person's moccasins. It means that we need to see things from the other person's perspective in order to better understand why he or she acts in a certain way. Compassion always brings peace, which is something someone with higher consciousness always strives for. The reason why people go to war and kill their fellow man in battle is because they lack compassion, which is a lack of understanding. You may say that those who instigate war understand what they are doing and that they are just evil, but even evil is ignorance on its highest level. I wrote 1,500 pages worth of papers in order to create an understanding of the situation we humans are experiencing, and what it was that led up to it. We now understand why the Sirian Alliance, whom I herein call the Alien Invader Forces(AIF), does what it does. It's because of power, control, and ultimately revenge. We consider negative power as being evil. Evil can be a method used to control others and an obsession to achieve and maintain power, but power over others is based on fear, and fear is based on ignorance. Therefore, what is it the AIF are ignorant about that makes them feel fear and makes them want to control and conquer others? First, it's fear of being attacked, which originally is based on a fear of not being *good enough.* Even Lucifer's Rebellion was based on fear. Lucifer was afraid of losing his position to somebody else—therefore, he needed to show that he not only could hold his position but also could conquer the position of someone who is considered superior to him—in this case his Mother, the Goddess herself. Even if we understand all this, that doesn't mean we agree with what certain people do, and we don't have to. We still can feel compassion for *their* situation and stop feeling hatred and anger toward those whom we consider being evil. When we can do that, we are using our heart chakra rather than our brain, and it's through our hearts we connect with the Divine inside of us, which is the same as the All That Is—the Divine Feminine. Being able to feel compassion where others feel anger and hatred is a tremendous achievement, which alone will raise your frequency quite considerably. Something to keep in mind because without compassion we can't make room for the New Human inside of us. Nothing can be resolved on a global level without first resolving it on a personal level. When more people start feeling compassion, even toward what would be considered their adversaries, this trait is placing itself in the mass consciousness of others for them to pick up on.

When we find compassion for something, we release the energetic charge from it. An energetic charge between two people in this sense is like a chain that keeps them together, and on that chain the other person's charge can travel and affect the other. This often happens subconsciously, and the person is usually not aware of this energetic connection. It's therefore important to handle situations in life that affects us negatively or emotionally to a point where it's unpleasant. If someone has done something bad to us in the past that has affected our lives negatively and repeatedly, we need to forgive that person and also ourselves, who didn't handle the situation there and then. Sometimes it's enough to send forgiveness in that person's direction with a smile and forgiving ourselves, but the chain could occasionally be thicker and harder to just cut off. We may actually need to contact that person on the phone or write him or her a letter explaining how we have felt about it, but without blame, and that it has affected our lives. However, we now write because we want to make things right, and forgiveness is a good way to do that. We also should mention that we are forgiving ourselves as well for our part in the situation. We may, or may not get an answer, but that's not what's most important. Just writing the letter releases the charge and will help us get a better understanding of the situation. Writing things down *always* releases the charge. How other people takes it is their problem to face, but at least, we did our part, and that's what's critical. Writing a letter is often more successful because the other person has a charge, too, in order for this chain to exist, and a phone call may stir up things that are unnecessary and sometimes makes things worse. Still, it's a judgment call.

I don't mean we need to write hundreds of letters to different people, but there may be a few we need to consider writing. The rest of the chains may be so thin that we can blow them off just by sending the other person good energies and forgiveness.

The relief after doing something such as this is quite substantial. After all, forgiveness is a shifting in awareness to the divine state of things.

We often hear about and see people endlessly trying to connect with the right partner. They tell us that finally they have found a partner they love. Everything goes well for a while and they seem happy, but one day the woman, for example, comes to work with a bruise on her arm. Eventually she admits that her boyfriend is abusing her. There is a lot of drama, and they finally split up (hopefully). She is lonely for a while, but then finds a new boyfriend who is similarly abusive, and the same cycle repeats itself. She says to her friends that she never seems to be able to find the right man. The reason she doesn't is because there is something in her energy field that attracts this kind of men, and she never seems to be able to break the cycle. The first thing for her to admit is that the problem lies within herself and not outside herself. She may have had an abusive childhood, and many times women like this have been molested, but not always. My point is that in a case like that, she needs professional help to find the source to her problem, which always is a basic abusive situation somewhere back in time. When that situation is indicated and turned from fear and agony into compassion and forgiveness, she can change her energy field, and like magic she stops attracting abusive men.

Often the charge is not related to a specific person. We may see something on TV or read something in the news and get extremely upset—more than is normal for the circumstance. This means we have an underlying charge on the subject. It may even be something like a war going on somewhere in the world that we get upset about. We could of course write to the President of the United States and forgive him for sending troops, but that wouldn't do much good. In a situation like that, I would suggest to stop reading about it and watching it on TV.

Why read about it in the first place? Is it because we want to keep ourselves informed? Well, with a news media that is bringing us lies and half-truths, I wouldn't call that being informed, and by reading about it in the paper, it only adds to the charge because there is no real truth in there, which can blow the charge. Therefore, a simple rule is as follows: become multidimensional, stop reading the newspapers! If something is going on that we need to know about, we will hear about it anyway. I have personally not taken up a newspaper in 12 years, and I can't say I'm not informed. I don't watch TV either, and I don't go to CNN-type sites on the Internet, either. If you, personally, have a lot of charge on all the negative things happening in the world, the only way to blow the charge is to educate yourself in the alternative media. Hopefully, if you read this, that's the route that you have chosen to take. To become an adult Homo Nova, we need to understand that *taking action* against something will never solve a problem—it will only create more of the same. We may fight for a good cause—let's say we are a peace-movement person who fights against war. We will never gain peace because as long as we fight against something—regardless of what it is—we stir up more turmoil and charge and in the long term, the situation becomes worse. If we want peace, we need to *peace for peace,* like researcher David Icke once said, and with that he means we need to become on the inside what we want to create on the outside. If we want peace, we must become peaceful inside. That's the only way to make changes in the outside world because it's just a projection of our inner world.

When we feel compassion about something, we are in a neutral state—it's not negative and it's not positive, it just is. That's when we tap into the Goddess energy, the All That Is, which is the tap into thoughts. Wendy Kennedy is another person who is normally channeling ninth-to twelfth-dimensional

Pleiadian life forms in the non-physical plane. Some of her material is quite profound. Here, the Ninth-Dimensional Pleiadian Collective speaks on compassion:

> With the movement of intent you are unplugging from the wall socket (Source energy) and running on backup power (your personal energetic field). When in a neutral state you are once again plugged into the wall. Too often humans fail to find a quiet place within themselves and allow their own "backup generator" to run out of fuel. This causes extreme illness within the human form.[15]

This allegory explains well what it's all about. If we follow the Pleiadians' advice, we need to plug ourselves into the wall frequently to stay in touch with the Source energy, or we'll run out of fuel. We can also compare it with those battery-driven cars some people use when they only drive in town. After a while, they run out of battery and need to be recharged by sticking the plug into a socket in the wall—the same principle. As humans in the current society, we see it as a normal condition to run out of fuel, but even if we live busy lives, we don't have to run out. Taking *negatively* charged energy and turning it into compassion is a great way of building more energy and tuning into the Source field, which is the Goddess energy. Meditation and breathing exercises are other ways to do it, and we are coming to that later in the book.

By just following the simple guidelines in this book, you will see that both your outer and inner world will change drastically.. In fact, nothing is happening in the outside world—the changes all occur inside of you. You are the one who manifests the inner world in the outer world, and when you think, things around you change. Still, it's just your perspective on things that

---

[15] Ref: http://higherfrequencies.net/archives.htm

have changed, and it looks like it's the outside world that's changing. Again, there's your definition of the Multiverse. The prefix "uni" in universe is defined as *uniform* or *united*, and that means that it's something we all can see and perceive. The Multiverse, however, is our individual <u>uni</u>-verses—i.e. our personal version of the universe, which differs slightly from everybody else's because everybody creates his or her own reality in it, which becomes the Multiverse. Please keep this in mind: *The reality you experience occurs through the interaction between your strongest beliefs, emotions, intentions, and actions.* It's only when we understand what it is we are doing that we can do it consciously.

Foods and Diets

I just want to discuss this subject briefly because sometimes people tend to over-dramatize this issue. I like what the young girl Anastasia says in the book with the same title, written by Vladimir Mergé. She is brought up in the Russian taiga, far from civilization, is in telepathic communication with all the animals, and is in total harmony with nature. The author, who is used to city life, meets her in the mid-1990s when Anastasia is in her mid-20s, and he becomes extremely fascinated by her apparent innocence and pure way of living. This is supposedly a true story. When the author asks Anastasia what she eats to be so healthy-looking, she tells him that the problem with mankind is that we concentrate too much on food. Food should be like breathing—you do it automatically while you go on with life. Of course, she is living in nature, so while she is busy doing whatever she is doing, she is picking a berry here and a mushroom there and just eats them, without placing any special attention on them.

When we lead city lives, or even when we live in the countryside, it's hard to follow her advice literally, although I think there is a lot of wisdom in what she's saying. Anastasia is not concerned with *what* she's eating as long as she's eating. Or, if she doesn't feel like eating, she simply doesn't eat, perhaps for days. In the Western world, in particular, we have become quite obsessed with food. Those who want us all to stay healthy promote more or less healthy diets, while huge fast-food signs can be seen everywhere. Society is full of contradictions. Common sense tells us we shouldn't eat GM food, but it's not easy to stay away from all temptations that are thrown at us left and right from the corporate world every minute of our day. Some people adjust easily to what the health experts say and go along with life without any problem concerning nutrition. Others can't, for their lives, eat what they are supposed to, and they, consciously or subconsciously, feel bad about it. Again, it has to do with levels of consciousness. Unless we're manipulated to eat certain things, we normally attract exactly what we need at the moment. If we are raising our frequency, after a while we start eating other kinds of food than what is promoted by the corporate world—lighter food and healthier food. When we do that, we show that we are ready to face new issues that will bring us further, into a more evolved state. When we start eating lighter, it gives room for suppressed issues to come to the surface so we can work on them. If we hang on to eating unhealthily, there are issues we are still hanging onto that we are not willing to face. The shamans of old knew that if they made their body as healthy as possible, it became lighter and more transparent, which also made it more psychic. The body, when given healthy food, vibrates on a higher frequency and can more easily tune into other realities.

The solution is, as I see it, that we shouldn't listen so much to *experts* of any kind—instead, we should listen to our bodies—they know more than all experts together. Throw out all GM food, eat organic, and then I believe Anastasia's advice is valid. The body will tell you what it's craving if you take the time to listen to it. As soon as it is used to not getting junk food anymore, it starts craving more healthy things, which we then would provide it with. I am aware that just because a package in the store says *organic* on it, it doesn't mean it's organic, so the best method to ensure that we get the food that will enhance the abilities of the body is finding local farmers with good reputations and buy from them, and them alone. If we listen to our bodies, we will soon notice a huge difference. We stop being sluggish—people who thought they weren't sluggish will sometimes notice that they actually were to a certain degree—and our energy level will increase dramatically. Our thoughts become clearer, the *fog* inside our brains will dissolve, and we will think sharper and on a higher level. When we give the body what it needs, we will notice after a while that it becomes much easier to communicate with it.

I think it's acceptable to eat meat. It has certain protein and minerals that our bodies need—at least in its current form. Who knows how that will work in the next lifetime, with new bodies, but so far, most of us probably need meat to some extent. It is important, however, that the meat comes from animals that have lived good lives and have not been stressed or fed with hormones. Before you start eating, be sure to bless the food and thank the animal for providing us with what we need. If you hunt and you stand next to the animal you just killed, thank the animal right there on the spot for providing you and your family with its meat. This will not only make the food taste better, but it's also a confirmation to the animal that we are aware that it has given up its life to maintain ours.

The plants have a different frequency as well and can, therefore, be quite therapeutic and have excellent medicinal abilities. If people only knew what each plant's medicinal value was, the human body would never have to be sick. There is medicine from plants for any disease we may have. The pharmaceutical industry knows this, and in fact, most medicine is based on plants and herbs and other things that are growing in nature. They put a chemical substance with it in order to be able to patent it. This chemical substance is what creates the side effects. Not only do the plants, herbs, mushrooms, and other substances from nature have a healing effect, they also have other attributes that go far beyond that. This is why Earth is called a *Living Library*—it's a storehouse for fauna and flora from different planets—many with codes embedded in them. One day, if we play our cards right, we may become aware of these codes and can help star beings from other parts of the cosmos by letting them explore the Living Library to receive what they're after. More about this in the last chapter.

There is one last thing I want to add on food and diets. Because many people are on a spiritual path, they feel bad every time they eat their favorite candy. They know it's not good for them and create a reach-and-withdraw phenomenon toward the candy. This is far more destructive than to actually eat the candy and let the body work out the toxin. Don't deprive yourself from your favorite food or snack. Allow yourself to have it once in a while, and eat healthy the rest of the time. Eventually, the favorite candy will cease to be a favorite. Just don't worry about it. You are not less *spiritual* because you had a few pieces of processed candy.

The Tree of Life Found?

A question I know many people who read information such as this will ask is if the new, enhanced Homo Nova will live longer than Homo sapiens, and if so, how long?

The short answer to that question is a definite yes—our lifespan will increase! The body you have now, after all the upgrades and information (light) you've been adding to it will already have the potential to live longer than those who didn't pay attention during the nano-second. Some of us may also have noticed that we look younger and sometimes get compliments when people are guessing our age and think we are 10-15 years younger than we look. This is no coincidence (if this is not the case with you, the reader, it's nothing to worry about. It doesn't mean you're necessarily going to die earlier). The *secret elixir* to a long life is to raise our vibrations, and once we have managed to evolve out of the trap once and for all and live on an Earth free from oppression, we are all going to increase our longevity substantially. Then take away the Between Lives Area, where people go after they die, and you don't even think about longevity anymore because you live forever.

In the beginning, when the benevolent gods created life on Earth, billions of years ago, they created the 3-D as a dimension of spirit and matter combined for souls to have that experience, but there was no amnesia. The first humans who lived here before the AIF came half a million years ago had more or less eternal life because the purpose was to experience 3-D in *one go* and then move on to something else. If a body was in an accident and couldn't be salvaged, the soul could easily "jump bodies" and continue her experience where she left off. There was no amnesia involved. Again, to find something positive in our current situation where amnesia *is* an issue, we can say that in spite of the hardship it creates, we have to be more creative to survive, and the learning lessons are much greater than if we would have all memories intact. Some people have lived in a loop because they die without having accomplished much and have to start over again, and it may seem as a waste of time and energy for that being, but for those who managed to learn something and move forward despite the oppression all around, they come out of this experience quite wise, procreative, and proactive—something other star beings can learn from.

Homo Nova's bodies will be genetically structured to last much longer than that of Homo sapiens by default, but no one will any longer be worried about death because we all will know that it's just another experience and just a minor one on the New Earth.

I need to tell you a very interesting story, however, which has to do with longevity. Once again, I will refer to the book *Anastasia* by Vladimir Megré. The author of the book was a Russian entrepreneur and travelled many times throughout Russia on business. In the taiga, a very special cedar tree grows, and it is fairly common in certain parts of Siberia. The same cedar tree also grows wild in Lebanon. Megré was stunned when he happened upon some elders in a small village in the middle of nowhere in Siberia. They were in their 120s and looked like they were 70 and still going strong. One of them was Anastasia's great grandfather. The reason that they got so old was because of this special cedar tree. They carved out amulets that they kept on their chests, and they ate the nuts from the tree and the oil that they contained. This nut was supposedly increasing the lifespan of these people. Those who wore the amulet also emitted a very nice, attractive body odor, and the amulet alone made people look younger and made them healthier. A 119 year old man insisted that if you wear one of these amulets, you never get sick, or if you are sick and put it on, it cures your disease—even cancer.

The author was a very logical and analytical man with both feet on the ground and didn't believe much of what the elder said. He treated it more like superstition. However, later when he was in an entrepreneur meeting with some businessmen, there was a person in that meeting that particularly drew Megré's attention, and this man also kept looking at Megré during the meeting without saying anything. This man knew about the author's encounter with the elders, and after the meeting, he approached Megré and told him that if Megré could deliver fresh nuts from the cedar tree to him in his home country on a regular basis, he would pay the author more than these nuts were worth on the market. To make a long story short, Megré put two and two together and realized that this businessman took the oil from the nuts and sold it as life-extending oil to rich people. Megré got very interested and wanted to build his own company that would do the same thing in Russia and wanted to find out what exactly was done with this oil—what was the process? He started researching and asking around, but when he came closer to the source, he was told to stay away from it all together, and the tone in which he was told was quite threatening. This was when he started to understand the corruption in this world. Apparently, only the super-rich had access to this life-extending elixir, and perhaps this is the secret to why certain people of the Global Elite are still very active even when they are in their 90s. Perhaps, those who are even higher up in the hierarchy than the Rockefellers and the Bush's—the invisible few—are the ones who get the potent elixir?

The reason I am telling this story is because this cedar tree happens to grow in Siberia, which was also the physical place of the Garden of Edin (Eden). Could it be that the Tree of Life indeed was the cedar tree, and already in the most ancient times, mankind was told not to eat from its fruits (nuts) and become *immortal* like the gods? It certainly makes me wonder...

The Human Body as a Divine Vessel

In the WPP, I referred to our human bodies as *Divine*. I said that we originally, before the AIF came, were a very special experiment, instigated by the Mother Goddess herself. Indeed, She also manifested Herself in physical and metaphysical form as Mother Earth or Mother Gaia. I explained that the human soul consists of a multitude of super-tiny *Fires*, which come together and form a light-body, an *Avatar*, around the physical body. These fires light up every cell in our body, which makes the whole body Divine because our Fire is that of the Goddess herself! She invested a part of herself directly in the human creation, so indeed we are Royal with a capital "R" and Divine with a capital "D" at the same time—Royal because the Goddess is also the Queen of the Stars. We are thus very special to her, and we also have abilities that other star races don't have. These abilities have made some of them quite jealous, while others think it was a great idea of the Goddess to create us, although in present time we are more like a liability to the star races out there because of how we misuse energy.

The Experiment was at least twofold. The first was for the original humans to be the Guardians of the Living Library, which I have been saying many times before. Homo sapiens are quite a watered-down version of earlier humans, who were much fitter for the task as they were multidimensional. Now, however, we are slowly but surely getting back to how we once were, and thanks to the nano-second and our own willingness to use the incoming energies intelligently, we have the potentials to become like our ancestors of millions of years back.

The other part of the Experiment is something we haven't talked much about, if at all. Not only are our bodies multidimensional by default and we only have to rediscover that and learn how to maneuver a multidimensional body, but there is another part to it too. *"Our bodies can hold all states of consciousness, all the way up the dimensional chart, if you will, to that of Creator or Source!"*[16] This is something I have become

---

[16] *Fear of Choice – Ramshi, 12th Dimensional Master Geneticist/Universal Architect*, channeled by Wendy Kennedy on July 5, 2009. This is only one of many references I have for this—and a couple of the sources must remain anonymous for

very convinced of during my research. Unfortunately, we have been dumbed down to such a degree that we think our bodies are only vessels for our souls at best, and at worst, we think the bodies are us, and we only live once. In both cases, we are treating the body way under its capacities, quite like if we would treat a very knowledgeable and intelligent adult as a two-year-old child. By misunderstanding our bodies to such a degree, we constantly invalidate them. There's no wonder they get ill or protest in one way or another. In addition, we pump them full of toxins and destroy their essence, cell by cell, until the cells start multiplying abnormally and create cancers.

In reality, our body is much more intelligent than we (as in our personality) are. This is why I am not the only one to tell you to go within for answers. It doesn't matter which question you want answered—the body knows! Within some cults and spiritual schools, a few decades ago, the body was neglected, and all the learning was concentrated on the soul, and we needed a teacher at all times to tell us how things are and what is the truth and what is not. Now, at least, we start understanding things a little better. In fact, the body must be the center of our learning process, whether it's learning about the physical or the non-physical world. It is very true if I tell you that the whole universe exists within your body, and that, of course, includes all dimensions and everything else! This means that we can continue evolving into the next frequency band and then to the one after that and so on, but we continue to use our body as a ground and a stabilizer. By looking inwards to our body for answers, we discover more and more of the body's mysteries and can use it for more and more purposes—even to travel the stars. Spaceships are Stone Age—we will not need them to travel through

---

their protection. Research into this area has convinced me that the following is the case: our human bodies are capable of anything we can imagine and more. They are truly Divine!

space and across the dimensions, as we shall see. Of course, we talked many times about nano-travel in the WPP, but we are going to delve into it on a little deeper level in this book.

Here is another misconception. In the New Age movement, but also elsewhere, people think that the *Third Eye* (the Pineal gland) is where our energies should be concentrated. I'm not saying it's wrong to concentrate energies to that area—it's another chakra we need to open—but where we must put our main attention right now is in the heart chakra. This is the place where we can reach all levels of consciousness.

Our Current Life Situation

In the WPP, we talked about that we are trapped here in the 3-D because the AIF manipulated our DNA to such an extent that we got trapped here in this reincarnation cycle in order to work as a slave race for the gods. Now we're going to change that perception. We are actually not trapped at all—not unless we decide that we are. It is true that the bodies of Homo sapiens have holograms embedded into them, which seemingly trap the soul in them and the soul can't get out easily, but everything is perception and, more important—beliefs and agreements. What we need to do to free ourselves is to disagree 100% on what the AIF and the Global Elite want us to agree on. It's easier said than done, you may say, and you are right! That's why we need to do it step by step. However, keep in mind that disagreement is the key to freedom!

Life on Planet Earth is for everybody, no exceptions: you get born and you are immediately indoctrinated by your parents, who think they are doing and telling you what is absolute best for you. You go through school, and you learn thousands of things that you don't need to know. Some of it is outright lies, some of it is half-truths, and some of it is true. If it's true, it's only because the Power Elite need you to know that in order to serve them better. What you learn from many years of education is not something they teach you because it's meant to be valuable for *you*, but because it's valuable for *them*. You are groomed and prepared for a life in slavery. In general, the more educated you are, the more indoctrinated and manipulated you become (unless you somewhere along the line wake up to this fact), and as a reward, you earn more money. However normally, the educated people have so many school loans that they are in debt for the rest of their lives, unless they are children from the super-rich Elite. These super-rich children don't go to regular school, but to Harvard and Stanford, where they learn different things from what you and I learn. They are groomed, too, but for a life as members of the super-rich families, so they are also heavily manipulated. Anyway, without being mentally ready for it, we have children, and we teach them all we have learned from our parents and in school, and we think that we are doing the children a great favor. They grow up and go to school and learn similar things that their parents learned, and so the cycle starts all over. The only purpose with this kind of life is to become good slaves. You are taught manners so that you respond properly to authority and are ready to take orders from those a step higher up in the hierarchy ladder than you are. These who are higher up than you have usually had a slightly different education, but they, too, have learned manners so they can take orders from those one rung higher up on the ladder. Sometimes people rebel and forget their *manners,* but they are immediately reprimanded, and if necessary, they get fired without pay or unemployment. The threat of losing everything can keep even the best rebel in check. They have seen the beggars on the street corners, whom the Elite don't mind having there at all to remind people how it goes if they don't conform. It's successful! You give the beggar a few dollars every now and then because you hope that if you for any reason (God forbid) get in that situation, someone else will give a few dollars to you. Therefore, you live through your work life until you're 65-67 and then you retire. However, by then, you're normally already so exhausted from a life as a slave that you have no energy to rebel. Instead you want to do things you haven't been able to do that much before, such as travel (if your funds allow, which they usually don't these days). At least you do no *harm* to the *System*. Then you die, go to the astral plane, and get groomed for the next life in slavery.

Does this sound depressing and horrible? It should. Still, this is the life we all live on Planet Earth under the *Regime*. Can you see how manipulated we are? The Regime doesn't even have to police us because we are doing that so well ourselves. The hierarchy is set up so that everybody has their role to play, and they reprimand those who don't follow the rules—thus we police ourselves. All the Regime needs to do is to every now and then change a little rule here and a little rule there when they see things getting a little out of hand, and usually, everything will be *fine* after that. If people still start to annoy the Regime, the Regime just orchestrates a big *Event,* such as 9/11 or the Boston Bombings. These kinds of events terrify the masses, the Regime gets a chance to feed on it, and they can then create tighter *security* rules and laws for us, based on events they themselves created. Their slaves will thank them for keeping them *safe*—cameras on every corner.

People who read this can't possibly say it isn't true, you think? However, they do! That's how manipulated most of us are. It's self-evident—nevertheless, the majority of the population can't see that—instead, they find justifications by using their own belief systems as a base in order to convince themselves and others that the above is not true. Then they go on living in the slave society and comfort themselves with TV and computer games, which both will further indoctrinate them. It's a sad story, but a brilliant setup by the AIF and their minions, the Global Elite. Then, our belief systems create the Grid, which surrounds the planet, holding our non-beneficial beliefs in a thick layer, stopping us from seeing the real universe. The Grid, you see, is based almost solely on our own twisted belief systems that color our lives. The holes in the Grid are due to *explosions*, depending on the people who are awakening and ripping holes in the Grid. However, the reason the Grid is there is because of our own set limitations. You see, instead of creating, perhaps, the biggest database on Earth on the Illuminati and the Global Elite (http://illuminati-news.com), I could have written one single article, only containing what I wrote here above. However, if I did, no one would have paid attention. People needed to look at the problem from a thousand different angles in order to find something there that they dared to agree on, perhaps, saying to themselves: "Well, this thing that he writes here I think is safe to agree with—it won't do me any harm." Then, they read another one and become braver and braver and started seeing things from another point of view and slowly woke up. This is what was needed back in 1998.

I would also want you to look at what I just wrote in the above paragraphs for another reason. Can you see that we are doing all this to ourselves? I am not saying that we are to blame, but we are so well conditioned into becoming obedient slave workers for the Regime that we are not hesitating to do what the Regime, and ultimately the AIF, wants us to do. We are even policing ourselves! We are manipulated—true—but we are still agreeing with our oppressors. Is it then so strange that we don't get any help from star beings out there? How can they help us when we and the oppressors are rubbing shoulders? At least, that's how it looks like to star beings. They can't baby us and start throwing the intruders out while we're still in this pitiful state because if they did, we are like children hanging onto our mother's skirts, sucking our thumbs in pure fear, and not learning anything. Mom takes care of it! We're supposed to go into adulthood now as a race, not back to early childhood. Therefore, please forget about saviors and Messiahs.

OK, some may say, all that makes sense, and we have to start to peacefully disagree to being manipulated slaves, but we still have the implanted holograms in our bodies and the afterlife to deal with, right? Well, yes, we do. However, again, only knowing about how the trap is setup is doing 50% of the work. If we would stop here and go no further, we would still have accomplished a whole lot. By understanding our situation, we have taken a step to the side and are now automatically looking at humankind and the dilemma they are in from *outside.* You are no longer like *they* are because this knowledge alone has made you a Homo Nova. You will never again be able to go back and be like the majority of the population—it's impossible. Therefore, you have to go somewhere from here, and wherever you go, it can't be back, and you know it. Do you want to move on? I do.

What to Do About It

So what do we do? Again, it's just a hologram, albeit, a powerful one. Still, a hologram is a hologram whether it's implanted into your body or if you are watching a movie on the TV screen. If you are watching a movie, you may be very intrigued, and if it's well done, you may even leave your body and disappear into the movie. Afterwards, you tell your friends that the movie was so intriguing that it felt like you were there, inside the film. However, if you're conscious about how movies work, you know it's not real and you can walk away from it afterward and go on with life. After all, it was just a movie. That's right, and your body hologram is just a movie too. Therefore, we need to disregard the fake pictures of the universe that the physical body and the light-body are programmed to see and do our Inner Work, having as little attention on these holograms as possible. A good start is the exercises I have included in this book. They don't work just on *some* people, they work on *everybody*, no exception, if we are just willing to do them and persist. Simple but powerful. Further into the book, the exercises are going to be even more mind-expanding.

Here is some good advice, by the way. Any time in life if you feel you are confused or depressed and you don't know what to do, just make *any* choice and then do it—don't just sit there and think about how confused or depressed you are. It doesn't matter what it is, but do something. It will snap you out of your condition and make the energy start moving again. Do the dishes, go for a walk, but remove yourself from the space in which you sit and think about your confusion or depression. Remember this because it's very powerful.

Life is supposed to be fun and thrilling. I know it's set up not to be, but we can change that with the flip of a coin.

Exercises

Train Your Intuition

Every time the phone rings, picture who the caller is. Often, the correct answer is what is coming to mind the exact moment we hear the ring, but we don't always recall. If so, ask your body who it is, decide, and then answer the phone. In the beginning, it will probably not always be correct, but keep on training yourself.

Pay Attention

As you become more and more multidimensional, awake, and have raised your consciousness and vibrations, pay attention to numbers. It is likely that you will start seeing numbers like 11:11, 2:22, 33, 444, 777 etc. When this happens, communicate to the universe and acknowledge that you noticed. Say, or think, something to the affect: "Thank you! I paid attention and saw the number sequence. Is there something in particular you want me to look for?" Sometimes the universe communicates to us through number sequences to get our attention. Therefore, remember to put out a thought like the above to see if you get an answer. Keep your awareness open for signs that will tell you what to do. Other times it's just you being able to pay attention—a sign that you are awake.

Look for Learning Lessons

When you experience rough times, or something people normally see as something negative, take a step back and look at the situation. What is there to learn from it? Rest assured that there is *always* something to learn when you clash into something. Once you've found what it is and have handled it from the point of view that it's a learning lesson, you have already raised your frequency a bit. Every time you do this, it increases your vibrations and you become more stable and knowledgeable. Again, in the beginning, it may sometimes be hard to find the learning lesson in negative events that seem to make no sense, but train yourself to find them, knowing they are always there. Whatever it was, it happened for a reason, even if it was only you who dropped a glass on the floor so it broke.

Learn to Become More Compassionate

Instead of judging another person, put yourself in that person's shoes. This may be easy to do when it comes to someone who is usually a good person whom you like, but much harder if we have to deal with criminals who destroy their own and other people's lives. As we discussed before, compassion does not necessarily mean that you have to agree with the other being—it's just a matter of understanding *why* he or she did what he or she did. Once we have the understanding, we can let it go from our own minds. Compassion may include helping another person when appropriate but sometimes requires no real action—just an understanding. You can't change the criminals, but you can change your attitude toward them. This is very important, or we'll get stuck in negative emotions that pull us back, consciously or unconsciously. We can't expand our minds past a certain point if we don't learn how to feel compassion. Therefore, every time you feel judgmental toward somebody, figure out what it is that makes him or her act that way. Once you've figured it out, let it go.

CHAPTER 3: ATTRIBUTES OF SOUL AND MIND

Language versus Telepathy

Our physical reality must be agreed upon to a certain extent to be able to exist because in its basic form it's just like dancing energies—this is how other star beings from other dimensions see it. Perhaps, it would be better to say that those who have agreed to live in this physical reality we call 3-D have agreed to vibrate within a certain frequency, so we can perceive with our five senses what this frequency contains. This frequency, which we usually call a *dimension,* also contains a large number of densities, which determine the degree of solidity of the material world.

In higher dimensions, beings are telepathic and don't necessarily need words to communicate like we do. Words are agreed upon and pronounced in certain ways so that we can be understood by others who live in the same reality. Because words are symbols, it doesn't make them lifeless or powerless. In fact, never underestimate the power of words. When we speak and put emotions and intentions behind our words, what we say can get across as powerful—whereas, someone who speaks with little or hardly any emotions and intentions is rarely heard and often overlooked. The written word can be at least, if not more powerful than the spoken word. If a writer is artistic, he or she can convey emotions and intentions in the written ords, which impact the reader. A skillful writer leaves a part of his or her soul in the writing.

We may not often think about it, but every time we use words to explain something to somebody, we create a mental image—a form—in the other person's mind. However, depending on how skillful we are in using words, the other person will picture what you are saying closer to or further away from the point you want to make. Therefore, poor or sloppy communicators will have a hard time getting their message across because the receiver has a hard time creating a mental image that corresponds with the message.

This is exactly where the power of words fades compared with telepathy. We are all telepathic, but the reason we use words instead of direct communication mind-to-mind is because the solidity of this reality makes it very hard to convey a message between two minds without using an intermediate, such as words. At one time, in a previous form, long before Homo sapiens were created, the Earth was much less dense—therefore, telepathy became the number-one choice for communication. However, when the AIF took over and genetically manipulated the previous human species, the so-called Namlú'u, they changed the Earth's frequency to a lower one, reality here became more solid, and thoughts couldn't travel as freely and easily through this dense space. This is probably the reason why we started using speech. Words, however, are useful when we want to store information, whether it's in a novel, letter, or for educational purposes.

There is also an important reason why the AIF doesn't want us to master telepathy. It's true that star beings like them can *cloak* their thoughts to a certain degree, but it takes a lot of energy to do so, and it's not always successful. They knew you can't lie in a world where telepathy is the way to communicate. Therefore, they had to make sure our minds no longer were in such close contact with each other for us to be able to directly share our thoughts. Albeit, they weren't successful in doing this because we are still telepathic to a certain degree and quite often read each other's thoughts and receive other people's thoughts inside our heads. However, usually we don't know that these thoughts came from the other person—we think these thoughts were our own, and this can get very confusing for humans. Hence, we also need to practice how to separate our own thoughts from other people's thoughts. More on this later.

The Ego and the Multidimensional Mind

It's the *physical mind,* which we sometimes call the *analytical mind* or the *ego* that maintains the images of the physical world we live in. The *subconscious mind,* as one of its tasks, stores images from the past, and is also the dream state or the *multidimensional mind.* The ego is often quite underestimated and misunderstood. When people are very selfish and brag about themself, we say they have a big ego, and we usually don't connect that with something positive. Other times, we identify the ego with brain capacity—i.e. intelligence. Intelligence, as we see it here in the physical realm, is based on how good we are at solving problems in 3-D and how easily we can learn things in this reality. Ego, in other words, is considered being the human personality. It is from this mind we often judge a person. In some part of the New Age Movement, however, the ego is often looked down on as something we should minimize as much as we can. The ego is seen as something unwanted and undesirable. Instead, the New Agers want to develop the multidimensional or the subconscious mind (I will use the two interchangeably from here on).

Both New Agers and society in general have missed the point with the ego. As long as we live in a 3-D world, it is the ego that navigates us through it. Without the ego, or with a much diminished ego, we would be quite lost here. It's the problem solver—the analytical mind that is in charge over the 3-D aspect of the body. The ego experiences things in the material world.

The multidimensional mind is very different and may seem to be light-years away from the analytical mind. While the ego wants everything in an orderly manner, the subconscious mind seems random and unorganized in comparison. You know this because your dreams often don't seem to make sense in a way you're used to. In fact, the subconscious mind is not as unorganized as we may think—it's just that it is not linear. What we experience in the subconscious and is hidden from us in our waking state is pure multidimensional and happens in many different dimensions. In a far-distant past, when the AIF created Homo sapiens, the multidimensional mind was *disconnected* from the analytical mind in order for us to be able to have a linear time experience. How would they control us otherwise? A multidimensional being, who can travel freely and fluidly between the dimensions, can't be controlled and contained in a *fenced in* area, which Earth in its present state must be considered to be. The *disconnection* between the minds is not by any means physical, of course, and is not there, but we have been manipulated not to be able to experience it. It is done by keeping us in a frequency fence that makes it impossible to contact the multidimensional mind on a conscious level, unless we raise our vibrations to a point where we vibrate on a frequency higher than that which is set by the AIF.

My research has taught me that the majority of mankind still considers themselves having things to learn in this 3-D reality and couldn't cope with the downloads from the cosmos, which were hitting us during the nano-second. Most of these downloads came (and still come, but less frequently) in the form of powerful gamma rays, carrying a massive amount of information, which is happening very rarely in our terms. Very few people, relatively speaking, were ready to receive and take in this higher form of energy and information. Although this information, carried on waves of light, hits everybody and everything that comes in its way, the receiving end must be ready and willing to accept it, or most of it just goes right through the bodies.

So what does this mean? This means that only those who were ready and did take in the information and were willing to process it in order to evolve spiritually and physically and intuitively did what they were supposed to do in this stage of development: felt ready to *move on.* Do you believe that you have outgrown the 3-D reality? Do you think similar to how you thought when you went from adolescence to adulthood, when you grew out of the habits you had as a child and were ready to meet the world as a grown-up adult? If you do, you are ready to move on and will not be able to reincarnate on this particular version of Earth anymore because it no longer vibrates on your frequency. Most people, however, will go through the normal cycle of death, afterlife, and rebirth into the same reality they left because they didn't make much progress during the nano-second.

As a matter of fact, if you fit into the description of someone who has grown out of your current reality and you wouldn't do much more in this lifetime but to maintain your frequency, you would automatically reincarnate into a higher frequency Earth next time. However, the purpose of this book is to speed up the process of raising our frequency and become multidimensional. If we learn how to do it and practice it, not only will we find ourselves ahead of the game in *this* lifetime, but the chances are great that we will make more conscious choices after we exit our bodies in this life, and if we choose to come back to Mother Earth, we will speed up the process of coming to a point where the current suppression of mankind ceases to exist as a parallel existence on the same version of the planet where we will live.

Some may wonder why the AIF and their Machine Kingdom will exist side by side with us still if we are raising our frequency and reincarnate to a higher frequency Earth. I mentioned this phenomenon in passing a bit earlier, but I need to go into it a little bit more because it's important to understand. If you think of Earth existing within a frequency band of 1-10 on any given scale, this is the frequency band the AIF controls. Now, let's say the average human vibrates at a 3-5 on this scale—he and she are well within the range of AIF control. Now, let's imagine that those who have evolved during the nano-second or before average a 7-8 on this scale, they are still within the 1-10 range, but are starting to vibrate close to the borderline of the 3-D existence. Hence, during the next incarnation, they may be born into a version of Earth that vibrates on an 8-9 on this scale, and the controlled society that exists side by side with them becomes less and less prominent and almost stops affecting their reality. Possibly, in the life after that, an evolved person will incarnate on a version of the planet that vibrates on an 11-12, which is outside the realm of control, and the AIF and their Machine Kingdom can't meet the vibration of this new reality and will not be there when the person incarnates.

The question is, how fast do you want to reach an 11-12, or even a 14-15? It depends on how well prepared you are. It's this kind of preparation I am doing my absolute best to transmit to the reader in this book and, perhaps, in upcoming books too. How successful this book will be remains to be seen, but I know that it will definitely speed up the process.

Before we move on, let's do a little exercise for those who want to be able to distinguish without any doubts between the body, mind, and the soul. It's easier to do than people think.

First, take a look at your body. It's obviously a body, and it appears to be physical and solid. Now close your eyes and imagine a cat. The cat you see inside of yourself is appearing in your mind, so that is your mind. However, who is looking at the cat? The answer is the soul, which is you. Therefore, from now on you can easily distinguish among the three.

What we basically want to do in order to become more multidimensional is to get access to our subconscious mind, which is easiest to do in the dream state, and we do it every night. However, we are not in analytical control over that mind, which is something that we want to achieve in order to both be able to stay in a physical reality and be multidimensional at the same time. Hence, we want the ego, or the analytical mind, and the multidimensional mind to work together. In other words, we want to reconnect what the AIF once upon a time disconnected us from. We will start going into details about these issues in the next chapter, which will take the reader on a most interesting journey. The key is that when we can consciously contact the dream state, we also start vibrating on a higher rate.

This may sound like a contradiction because the dream state vibrates on a low frequency, but by contacting these multidimensional realms, we also stimulate the Higher Consciousness, which makes the soul and the body vibrate faster.

What is Consciousness?

This book will work a lot with images. I decided to write it that way because it makes it more interesting, and it's also easier to grasp otherwise complex subjects, which would have to be explained in many more, and often complicated, words.

It's important that we grasp what consciousness is or we will not know what we are doing when we are practicing to become multidimensional. People who are evolved enough to realize that there is something called a soul often think that they, the thinking unit, are the soul and consciousness. This, however, is only partially true. In my writings, I have distinguished between the Oversoul and the soul, and I am not the first person who does that. The Oversoul is sending out smaller fragments of itself, who become their own personalities, complete with their Fire and Avatar (soul and light-body, where the latter is a shape the soul can take—often the same shape as the physical body, or as an orb). However, you, who sit there and read this book, are not *the* soul, but only a fragment of your Oversoul, who is a dweller in other, higher dimensions. A good image we can use, I believe, is that the Oversoul, when using you to explore the 3-D universe, simply uses you like your physical body uses its eyes to explore its environment. The only difference is that your body has only two eyes, which can only explore one environment at a time, while the Oversoul has multiple upon multiple *eyes* which can look in different directions—i.e. in different times, different spaces, and into different dimensions. Therefore, consciousness is so much more than just you, the personality that reads this book. The Oversoul has the ability to send out factions of itself in all possible directions and receive back what it *sees* in the form of information, which it stores like a library to share with the All That Is—the Goddess. The Oversoul is immortal and lives forever, while some say that the fragments can be destroyed, just like your physical body can be destroyed, which in that case means that your personality will cease to exist. Others say that this is impossible, so at this point, it's up to the reader's intuition to establish which one is true and which one is not. If it's true that our personality can be annihilated, it can happen in space wars because it has been suggested that advanced star races, who have chosen technology before spirituality, have developed weapons that can split the Avatar, and without its form, the soul can no longer exist as a single unit.

Seth, who channeled through the late Jane Roberts, mainly back in the 1960s and the 1970s, describes how he perceives the channeling he's doing from his perspective, and it's quite interesting because it helps us understand how even we, as soul fragments, can split ourselves in smaller pieces and experience another type of reality in another dimension. This is exactly what multidimensionality is.

> When I contact your reality, therefore, it is as if I were entering one of your dreams. I can be aware of myself as I dictate this book through Jane Roberts, and yet also be aware of myself in my own environment—for I send only a portion of myself here, as you perhaps send out a portion of your consciousness as you write a letter to a friend, and yet are aware of the room in which you sit. I send out much more than you do in a letter, for a portion of my consciousness is now within the entranced woman as I dictate, but the analogy is close enough.[17]

Once upon a time, mankind was exactly like Seth describes here. The only difference is that we have physical bodies and Seth does not. In that sense, many would say that we have the privilege because we can experience both the physical/material world and the spirit world simultaneously. We are now very close to being able to do that, and the nano-second helped us tremendously to move in that direction.

3-D Versus Higher Dimensions

Nature is a program, and we humans are creatures of nature. This is how it always was meant to be, and from here on Earth, we were supposed to evolve

---

[17] Jane Roberts: Seth Speaks, p. 23, op. cit.

together with the planet we live on. This has been severely delayed because for a long time, thousands of years to be more precise. We did not follow our own path—instead, we listened to others, who we thought knew better, for our development. Therefore, evolution, more or less, stagnated for a significant amount of time. It was actually not until the later part of the 1900s that a portion of mankind started evolving as we were meant to. However, even now, those whom we have always looked up to as authorities are doing their best to keep the spiritual awakening under control. They are not going to stop it from happening because they want it to happen—in small portions—because they think they can gain from it, too, by ruling us in a higher dimension. However, some of us are seeing through even that and are more and more starting to think independently after having gained insights into how the System works.

Still, the majority of mankind is not done with experiencing the trap they are sitting in. Nothing can shake their belief systems, and even though there is much pain and suffering in their own lives and in their environment, they still have no wish to leave it. They are still too fascinated by the physical reality to educate themselves in what might exist outside of their five senses, while there are some, such as ourselves, who have outgrown it and are ready to expand our experience to what exists outside the prison walls.

A 3-D state is like a trance state we have been stuck in, but since the beginning, some people have been able to feel the existence of other realities. A piece of artwork or creativity, in general, such as writing this book, is not merely a 3-D accomplishment. This kind of work is always multidimensional—not just the result of it, but also writing it. You can't write a book, compose a song, write a good poem, or create a painting, without contacting other realities—they are all multidimensional work. For example, when I write, I always tune into other aspects of reality that I normally can't perceive, and from there I get my inspiration. Once connected, there is no problem to write. However, a person who limits himself or herself to perceiving only three dimensions can't accomplish any significant artwork and won't understand other people's art. It's a dichotomy, but sometimes you already have to be multidimensional to become multidimensional.

A painting that is painted in a 3-D reality is flat, but artists, using their skills, can create an illusion that the painting has three dimensions. If the same painting were created in a higher dimension, the artists would have no problems with making the painting truly three dimensional if they wanted to. In an interdimensional reality, you can create anything you want, including any effect you want—it's only your own imagination that limits you. We can sometimes get glimpses of being multidimensional when we hear a voice in our head speaking out of context or you see images that don't correspond with your own current thoughts. For example, you can think about what you want for dinner and suddenly an image of a high, majestic mountain that rises above a beautiful, but for you, unknown landscape, appears in your mind. You have no idea where this picture comes from, but it looks very real. You have just experienced a multidimensional moment, and of course, this landscape exists somewhere—it may not even be on this planet, or if it is, it could stem from another space and time.

Beings that don't dwell in our physical world don't see it as we do. Other types of consciousness exist in the same space as we do but don't perceive the physical objects. Instead, their reality has other kinds of camouflaged structures that we can't perceive. Therefore, usually the two realities are not aware of each other. Hence, you can sit in a room with no other human in there, thinking you are alone, when in fact you are not. The space you think you own can be quite crowded with consciousness from other realities, but they won't bother you, and you won't bother them.

To be able to live in a 3-D reality, linear time is required, or it wouldn't be 3-D. There is basically nothing wrong with living in the 3-D world because, after all, it is only a frequency band, and as such, it makes room for certain types of experiences that are limited to this frequency. It's only when you're being locked into this frequency, with no ability to move outside of it that it becomes a trap. Living in the material world, having that kind of experience, and being multidimensional are three different things, but you can do them all at once, which is our goal. This also protects us because as long as we're attached to our physical body, which has its own attributes, we are limited to the body's own neurological system as long as we are experiencing the world outside through our body. Linear time in that sense may limit us, but it is also protecting us. Seth gave an example of how it would be if time wasn't linear:

> Say that your father throughout his lifetime has eight favorite chairs. If your perceptive mechanisms were primarily set up as a result of intuitive association rather than time sequence, then you would perceive all of these chairs at one time—or seeing one, you would be aware of the others. Therefore, environment is not a separate thing in itself, but the result of perceptive patterns, and these are determined by psychological structure.[18]

In other words, if you saw the physical reality from a multidimensional viewpoint all the time, time itself would be simultaneous, and all objects you can see would appear in front of you from the time they were created until the time of destruction, which is some time in the future. This wouldn't only

---

[18] Seth Speaks, p.16, op. cit.

be confusing and overload our nervous system, but if this were how you experienced reality, there would be no learning lessons because you would already see how things start and how they end. Even if you change events and create new timelines, you would still see the beginning and end of the objects that are a part of that timeline as well. Life would become quite boring after a while. Beings who live in other dimensions create in a different fashion and can, therefore, learn from experience, just as we do.

Images, Imagination, and Projection—an Exercise in Nano-Traveling

Let us ponder for a moment the word *ascension*. Everybody is talking about it, but in different terms. The Christians say there will be a rapture followed by the Second Coming of Christ, and there will be peace on Earth for a thousand years. Other religions say that *their* savior or saviors will return—New Agers say that we mysteriously will ascend to the fifth-dimension, while some claim that the Gods are returning and will overthrow the Global Elite, and after, there will be peace on Earth. Others are waiting for the Harvest, when those who are worthy will in one way or the other be *beamed up* to either a higher dimension or a rest area by space aliens or Ascended Masters, where these humans will be waiting for those less lucky to be shuffled over to another planet, light-years away, to continue living in their misery. Once that is done, the harvested people can return in enhanced bodies to Earth that now has transitioned into the fourth-or fifth-dimension, and on this new Earth, the faction of humanity that is worthy will live in peace and harmony in a much less dense world. The variations are many, but they are all talking about the same thing—the Ascension.

When you read the above paragraph, what is the common denominator? That's right, regardless of how the Ascension will happen, we will be assisted by somebody from outside of ourselves! This is exactly where we all have to be very careful because I can say with certainty that if you hear that we need physical or direct assistance from extraterrestrials, Jesus, Space Brothers, Ascended Masters, Gods, or whoever else I haven't mentioned, it is either disinformation, or a very vicious trap that I don't want anybody to fall into. For those who don't believe me, please read the WPP, "The Third Level of Learning," and it should be obvious why I'm so blunt about this.

However, what *is* Ascension? Is it all just made up by the space aliens? No, the Ascension is taking place right now, and it's always been taking place amongst humans. However, I dislike the term *Ascension* because it has been so misused and is associated with negative energies that I want to avoid using it myself. The same thing applies to the words *rapture* and *harvest*. Instead, I will use the term *awakening*, which has a much more benevolent ring to it. However, for the sake of argument, I will use the term Ascension in the next few paragraphs. Let us pretend that once upon a time in the past, all humans were on the same level when it comes to knowledge and development. Then, every time a person had an *aha moment,* he or she awoke a little bit. Sometimes an aha moment led to another in a chain of events, and other times one aha moment was perhaps the only one in that lifetime. Let's say this was thousands of years ago. A single person then reincarnated over and over again and got more and more aha moments over time, all the way up to the present. The same thing of course happened to all of humanity, but some got more of those moments while others got less. Each time people have a moment of insight, they wake up (or ascend) a little more. Now, during the nano-second, people started getting aha moments left and right and one upon the other, waking up in droves and at a relative fast pace, compared to before the nano-second. This is usually called *The Great Awakening* amongst those who have researched this particular time, including myself. Every time we wake up a little bit more, we start vibrating a little faster, and we're getting a little bit closer to the upper limit of the locked-in frequency band of the Frequency Prison. Many more people than we think get aha moments, but then they just discard them as something strange they can't explain because it doesn't fit in with their belief systems, so they shake their heads and try to forget about it. These people are in the majority and, unfortunately, the ones who will have the hardest time in the near future. Ignorance is *not* bliss!

The rest of us, the smaller group who reads books such as this one, take the insights to heart and process them. If the new information *feels* more beneficial than the information we previously had, we let the old beliefs go and embrace the new ones. Remember that a new belief system doesn't have to be *truer* than the one we had earlier—it just needs to benefit our progress better . Truth, mind you, is relative indeed.

Thus, we learn more and more and become more and more awake to the fact that life is a thousandfold more than just the five senses. I bring this up because I see on the Internet that some people are disappointed why there wasn't an Ascension by the end of 2012. Those who are asking this question are often the ones who define ascension due to New Age definitions. The truth is that we are ascending beyond belief almost every day when we learn something new about ourselves, people around us, the planet we live on, and the universe around us. Those who say that 2012 was the same as any year, I wholeheartedly disagree with. I have never had so many insights as I've had the last two years—2011 and 2012. If I look back to the time before that, I believe I was quite asleep in comparison. Therefore, the Awakening is happening constantly.

The Awakening in itself is simply a matter of moving mental image pictures around in our minds and creating new ones as we go along. Never underestimate your own power of creation. Don't get fooled by one of the most vicious manipulative ideas that we all need to see the same reality or we're on the wrong track. As we are waking up, we notice that we start seeing things differently than people in our environment see, and sometimes that can make the newly awoken person a little uncertain. Here is Billy, for example. He asks himself: "Am I on the right track here? What do other people who are waking up think?" This is, unfortunately, very common, and here is an area where we need to improve. Billy, is uncertain and starts asking questions to other people who have already woken up to a larger degree than himself (he thinks). To his dismay, he notices that John, who is a much respected researcher into these things, does not share Billy's new visions. He says that Billy is incorrect. Therefore, Billy discards his new insights and instead incorporates John's worldview because John is so respected and *out there,* teaching people all the time. "John should know, and if I follow and imitate John, I will end up in the same place as he is, which must be good!"

Please avoid that trap! John does *not* know more than Billy. The only difference between Billy and John is that they have developed different ways of seeing things, and that is absolutely accpetable, and should be encouraged. There is more than one way of looking at reality, and your way is no less correct than mine is and vice versa. All I can do by writing papers and books is to share *my* worldview and *my* belief systems as they have worked for *me*. I am not expecting anybody to incorporate everything I write or say—these are only guidelines, and that's why I'm writing so much. I want the reader to have much to choose from and become inspired by what is written. All I want is for the reader to be inspired, and perhaps, somewhere in my writings, I happen to say a few things that the readers can use as a springboard to their own next level of learning. On occasion, my views coincide frequently with other people's views, or readers think that they can use a lot of the material, and that is fine as well, as long as it is self-determined and not adopted because *Wes Penre says so.* The latter is my only concern as a metaphysical writer because I know that this happens on occasion. That's why we all need to break the spell that has been put upon us that some people know better than others. All we can do is inspire each other to look inside to find our own truths, which is equivalent to *working belief systems.* I, for one, wouldn't have been able to write one single word if it were not for other people who have inspired me to move to my personal higher levels of learning.

Always go your own way and trust your heart. Ask your body if you're uncertain, rather than always asking other people. There is nothing wrong with asking for advice, at times, and be pointed in a certain direction when you feel stuck, but make it a habit to go inside and ask the questions instead. You will always get an answer, even if the answer may not always be what you expect—even if the body doesn't always give you what you expect, it always gives you what you need and not always in a direct manner either—it may even create a barrier or an obstacle for you, but rest assured that this obstacle is exactly what you need in order to continue making progress. You must always do the work yourself—that's what we're all here for.

Never stop seeking knowledge. Humans, in their natural state, are a very curious species, although laziness has taken over many curious minds as of late. However, if your desire to learn is strong enough, the knowledge you need will come to you. Often you don't even need to look for it. I have experienced that so many times that I have made it into an axiom because I know it's true. If it happens to me, it will happen to anybody who has a strong desire to know. Here, mental images are very important, although we don't think of them as images. Nonetheless, that's what they are! With your thoughts, you create an image of what you want—you put some strong emotions to the thought, and it will transpire into the image. The strong thought you put out is also what we call intention, and with these things present, the energies of the universe will bend to your will, and you will receive what you want and need.

Speaking of images and projection, let's do a simple exercise in nano-traveling. It is best to read through this and then go back and do the exercise the way it's intended. It's quick and easy. You don't need to memorize every step of the exercise—just do the best you can to recall important steps, such as standing in the forest, looking at the environment, and using your eyes, ears, and smell to feel that you are there.

Now, close your eyes and imagine a forest you have been inside in the past (if you can't recall one, just imagine any forest at all). Visualize yourself standing there somewhere in a part of the forest that you can recall quite clearly. Look at the trees, the bushes, and a blue sky on a warm summer day with the sun shining through the trees. Listen to the breeze making the leaves move slowly, and hear the birds sing, sitting on the branches, hidden from you. Imagine the smells of the forest. Inhale them and feel the pleasure in doing so. Can you actually smell the forest? Now, start walking around and explore what is there, both on the ground and higher up. Remain in the forest for perhaps a minute or so. Then slowly return into your body and feel how your consciousness fills the whole space of your body. Take a few deep breaths, and when you're ready, open your eyes.

What is your impression? Were you actually there in the forest? Could you smell it? If you couldn't, it's not a big deal—if you do the exercise a few times, you will be able to. What you actually did was a simple form of remote viewing, or nano-traveling. You sent a part of your soul to the forest and experienced it in the non-physical. At the same time you were sitting in front of this book, with most of your consciousness still in the room. In other words, most people nano-travel all the time, but they don't think about it as such—they believe it's just them dreaming themselves away. In fact, we *are* using the lower brainwave cycles to nano-travel because these slow cycles connect with the subquantum world, which is the Spirit World. Of course, you can do exercises such as this on your own and go wherever you want to in your mind. It's a very good practice to do every now and then in order to prepare you for becoming multidimensional.

This exercise was a very simple example of the soul splitting itself into a smaller faction. You used your thought to create an image in your mind of the forest—then you put some emotion to it and an intention to go with it as well. Before you knew it, a portion of your soul was there. In more advanced terms, this is exactly what the Oversoul does when it partitions itself and sends factions of itself to Earth to reincarnate in 3-D. You, the one who I'm talking to now, are one such faction of your own Oversoul. Other factions of you are here as well, living in different times, experiencing different things. You have a connection to all these factions, and one of the exercises we did in the WPP was to merge the timelines. We didn't have to do much because the energies coming in from the Galactic Center during the nano-second did most of the job—all we needed to do was to process what came up in our lives and, thus, heal our own timelines. In more advanced nano-traveling there are more senses than just our 3-D senses involved, but that's something that comes naturally later on.

Where Do You Want To Go After Death?

One thing I had a hard time researching when I wrote the WPP is what happens after your physical body dies. In "The First Level of Learning"[19], I wrote an entire paper on this phenomenon, where I included quite a few different alternatives, based on the most qualified research I could find, where Dr. Michael Newton's 7,000-plus case studies seemed to be the most reliable overall if we could mix that a little bit with a couple of other researcher's conclusions.

I still think there is a lot of merit to Dr. Newton's studies, which basically say that if you go toward the light as a soul after you've separated from the body and continue through the tunnel, you will meet relatives and friends on the other side. Besides having a great time with the ones you've loved in life, you also meet with your spirit guide (or guides) and a mysterious *Council of Elders,* who all help you judge how your last lifetime went. You see, before you reincarnate each time, you set a goal for that lifetime and do what you can to achieve it. This goal is normally something that helps you evolve—it's the next step in your learning process. All the good things you did in your previous life are discussed, but also where you failed, or considered that you failed. When you've figured out your weaknesses, you discuss with these beings what is the natural next step in your evolution, and you choose a body in a family bloodline that can best and most probably assist you in learning what you need to learn. Astrology is also important because you make certain that you're born within a specific time frame, which makes it easier for you to accomplish your goal. Then you *manipulate* your parents-to-be from the astral to have sex nine months before

---

[19] Wes Penre, March 25, 2011: "Metaphysics Paper #4: There is a Light at the End of the Tunnel—What Happens After Body Death?" http://wespenre.com/there-is-a-light-at-the-end-of-the-tunnel.htm.

you want to be born, and you don't give up until you've succeeded. Nine months later, with the help of technology (there's a whole control room *up there*), they *shoot you down* into the chosen body.

This sounds very reliable because it's built on 7,000-plus case studies, which were reliving their afterlife in regression therapy and, basically, said the same thing. It would be overwhelming evidence if it weren't for the spirit guides who attended each regression session from the astral and advised the case study participant what he or she could or couldn't say. There may of course be valid reasons for this, but that in conjunction with the presence of the Elders in the astral makes me wonder if this is not more manipulation after all. Perhaps the spirit guides also manipulate the case so it sounds like Heaven up there when it's not, and due to this manipulation from all spirit guides who attended the 7,000 sessions, we get a common picture that may not coincide with reality.

I don't intend to play the Devil's advocate, but knowing what I know about the AIF and their influence on us here on Earth, it's only natural that they are in control of the afterlife as well. If they weren't, not too many people would reincarnate into this trap, but instead disappear the other way. Don't get me wrong, though, because there are others who were not part of Dr. Newton's studies who also say similar things (of course, they could be manipulated, as well), but I still believe there is enough evidence so that we can establish that the afterlife in itself is nothing to fear—nothing evil and no punishment will be experienced by the deceased. I am sure you'll meet your relatives and friends up there (even those who were still alive when you departed because time works different up there) and you may actually have a good time. After all, it's supposed to be a rest area before you incarnate again. One problem, as I see it, is that even though you remember much more up there than you do when you're on Earth, you still don't understand that you're in a trap, and no one is helping you understand it, either. On the contrary, that information is withheld. The question is, who are these wise *Elders,* who the discarnate soul is often very nervous to meet, like they were going to judge them and be mean to them, or something of such nature? Most souls want their spirit guides present in the *room* when they meet the Elders, just as children want their mom with them when they go to school the first few days, or to the dentist, or the doctor. Why are they afraid? After all, they have met with them several times before, between each incarnation. Often, they even meet with them twice before they incarnate—when they arrive in the astral and when they are about to leave. One or two case studies said that the Elders were more-advanced souls, who had completed their reincarnation cycles and now were part of the Council. Whether that's true or not, it's hard to say. If it is true, there are still many questions that need to be answered. The answer, in general, is that we are not supposed to know, and that, if anything, should make us lift an eyebrow or two.

The Veil of Amnesia is a hot subject as well. Why are we setting goals in the afterlife that we never remember once we are born on Earth? Why are we set up to fail? Some say it's because if we knew everything, it wouldn't be a challenge. We need amnesia or the *game* would be boring after a while. Well, this is not exactly how I see it (and these are just my conclusions—take it or leave it)—instead it looks like we are setup for failure. We are born and go through the whole cycle for 85 years if we're lucky, and we learn a certain amount during these years. Then it's goodbye and we leave. During the next lifetime, we have to start all over again and learn the same things we did last time, and the little that carries over is hardly worth mentioning. Therefore, we progress very slowly—hardly at all, actually. Why is this? Even if we didn't have amnesia, there would be enough challenges to make life interesting, in my opinion.

If you were a Master Race and the rest of the population (which is us) are slaves but slaves that inevitably will evolve because evolution is built into any and all DNA in the universe and there is nothing the Slave Masters can do anything about, what would you do? You would probably ensure that the slaves evolve as slowly as they possibly can because you don't want smart and evolved slaves, right? Hence, the best thing to do is to give this race a very short lifespan so they don't have time to ponder too much on things (and if they figure a few things out, they'll forget anyway after they die and incarnate again). You only let them live long enough to learn what you, the Slave Master, want to teach them in order for them to serve you. Then you want them to serve you a certain amount of years without getting too smart and worn out. Before the next incarnation, you give them total amnesia, which occurs as soon as the soul enters the human body—the amnesia implant is in the body itself, not in the soul. However, the astral world, or the part where you spend your afterlife, has to vibrate on a frequency high enough for the Avatar/light-body to remember a few previous lifetimes to be able to set a new goal. In other words, if the astral wasn't controlled and had a vibration fence set a little higher than that in 3-D, the soul would remember everything that had ever happened to it, and that would blow the whole cover.

Dr. Newton's cases tell us that in the astral there are souls who are on different levels of development. You can see it in their aura—it has different colors depending on how much the spirit knows or how *advanced* it is. However, the most advanced souls are not in the same area as the others, according to people in regression therapy. When asked where the most advanced souls are, they don't get a good answer but are told that these souls are elsewhere or are exploring other worlds but sometimes come to visit—or did they actually *escape*? Whatever the answer is, we are told that the astral exists on different frequencies—souls within a certain range of development dwell in a certain part of the astral, while others are said to dwell elsewhere. This is why some souls, after they've passed through the tunnel, meet with their relatives, who may be on a lower frequency level than the discarnate, so after they have spent some time together, it's time for the discarnate to move on to a frequency level that more fits that soul. Therefore, it sounds like the AIF have us covered well, regardless of our vibration—at least to a certain point, which I will come to soon.

If there is a malevolent force that continues trapping us in the afterlife, why do they let us have a good time and do what we want, within certain limits? There may be many reasons for that, but there is a couple I can think of. First, the soul does need to rest between incarnations, or sooner or later it will go insane from the entire trauma we experience down on Earth. The AIF gains from having us relatively fresh when we return. Second, if the afterlife is pleasant, we are more likely willing to incarnate without being forced, which is important. Then it happens with our consent, which is crucial, or the AIF would be breaking the Laws of Free Will and Non-Interference. Many are those who have asked why souls are so eager to reincarnate on this planet, which is so full of drama and trauma. One of the answers is that when we're *up there,* we see a bigger picture than we do *down here.* Now, with all the wars, financial collapse, restrictions, unemployment, anxiety, and fear happening on Earth, many tell themselves that they never want to return here again, but that's because they don't see the bigger picture down here. Once they're up there, things are different. Often, the same people can't wait to go back because up there they feel they are invincible and have nothing to fear. They quickly forget the trauma and devastation they felt during their last lifetime. Now they want to go back and help out again.

Sometimes souls who have incarnated for quite a while don't even go through the between-lives-area, but reincarnate in a new body right away. They are already so indoctrinated that they don't need to be *worked on* in the Afterlife.

Some say that 3-D is an experiment and that the souls who incarnate here do so out of free will because there is so much to learn down here. Well, this is correct—it *is* an Experiment within an Experiment to be absolutely accurate. There was an original Experiment, setup by the Goddess herself millions of years ago. She called this Experiment "The Living Library," where Creator Gods from all over the universe brought their favorite flora and fauna and inserted it here on Earth, putting their own signature within the DNA of their creation. Each creation filled a purpose, whether it was healing or the plant or animal had knowledge encoded into their DNA. Earth, therefore, became a library for beings from all over the universe, who could come here and learn about themselves and other realities. We, an earlier version of mankind, were the Guardians of the Living Library until the AIF came and took it over. In simple terms, they manipulated the DNA of this early human to get a better slave race, and that became the second Experiment. Then we hear that we come to Earth out of free will in order to learn. Yes, we do, but those who tell us that are not telling the complete story. The souls who incarnate here repeatedly do so out of free will or are manipulated further to do it willingly without understanding the entire agenda, and they are actually trapped here. Therefore, those who tell you that we are here out of free will in order to learn are only telling half the story. What I see is that during the nano-second when the energies were incredibly intense from seven billion people being bombarded with gamma rays, which are rays from the highest magnetic spectrum, we actually *did* learn something—in fact, we learned a lot! During this time, souls were fighting each other off in the ether in order to get a human body here so they could have a free ride through the nano-second and learn an incredible amount in hardly any time at all. There were actually more souls waiting in the ether to get a body than there were bodies available, so many had to do without. In desperation, some of them attached themselves to bodies that were already occupied—therefore, many people now walk around with attachments. However, those people who took advantage of the nano-second and actually raised their frequency usually got rid of their attachments after a while because they began to vibrate much higher than the attachment that no longer could hold on. Now, on the other hand, when the nano-second is over and the energies are slowly going back to *normal,* many souls who don't belong to the human soul group are no longer that eager to incarnate here because outside the Grid they can see the entrapment and don't want to come here. Thus, there is not as much competition over getting a body here anymore. There are more bodies than there are souls who want to incarnate. Therefore, we will see a decrease in the population in the near future—many people will be infertile, babies will be stillborn etc. Much of this is because there are not enough spirits to inhabit seven billion bodies. It's like when a store is ordering thousands of a very popular product to have in storage and people are buying it like crazy. Then, almost overnight, the product is going out of style, and no one is buying it anymore. Therefore, here is the store with thousands of products and no buyers—the product becomes useless and is disposed of in one way or another. No one wants it.

    The problem I have had, which led to me writing sequels to the first WPP on the Afterlife in later papers, was, *What can an evolved soul do to avoid the trap in the Afterlife?* I have struggled a lot with this question, and when I had completed all the *WPP*, I thought that I only had a partial answer. In the latest update on this subject I told the reader that the best thing to do was to avoid the tunnel and the light and escape through a hole in the Grid. This, of course, is only applicable for those who don't want to come back to Earth again. I still think this is the best advice I can give a soul with these intentions. I have, however, received a few questions afterward, where people have asked me how we can be sure what exactly to do once we're outside the Grid, and also—how do we know when we're outside the Grid? So let's address these questions here.

I am basing the following advice on information I have received from a couple of the most enlightened sources I had while writing "The Second Level of Learning"[20]. For a while, I gave even them a shadow of a doubt, doing my best to research this on my own and afterward compare my results with their teachings. I haven't found much information on this and, therefore, decided to trust these sources because they have been extremely helpful, and what they have taught me has later showed to be valid. Therefore, I find no problem with trusting them on this one as well. Most of it comes from one of these sources—the one that I would label *most advanced* if I have to use labels.

According to my source, don't go to the light! Instead, go through the Grid. Once you're discarnate and have left the Earth plane, you will see the Grid that surrounds the planet in the astral. It's like a fuzzy band around the planet, now looking like Swiss cheese with lots of holes in it. Escape through it without letting yourself get bothered by any being who might want to distract you. You don't even need to pay attention to them. Most of them want you to go into the tunnel anyway, and some are your spirit guides. Once you're outside the Grid, you will

---

[20] See, http://wespenre.com/site-map2.htm

see the universe differently. It apparently looks nothing like you've been taught. When you're outside the Grid, you're no longer within Earth's frequency band and can see things the way they are. You will see an incredible number of stars, and possibly, you will experience a lot of spectra/dimensions at once and at will. It may be overpowering at first, in a good way, but you will soon get used to it.

Here is another thing I heard the other day on a recent Pleiadian CD (from the beginning of 2013). They said that part of our solar system is also under Quarantine—a frequency fence—which stretches all the way past Jupiter. They are of course not the only ones who talk about a Quarantine—I brought it up in my WPP quite a few times as well, showing evidence that this is the case. Some say the Quarantine was lifted in January of 2013, but I don't believe that this is true. I found it interesting, however, that they mentioned Jupiter as the outer boundary for the Quarantine because the next planet away from Earth, Saturn, is where the Council of Zendar sits and decides who can enter the solar system and who may leave.[21]

Anyway, this may be another barrier we need to pass before we can actually leave our own solar system—we need the permission from the Zendar Council. As strange as it sounds, this should not be a problem—although, as I suggested in the WPP, the Council is AIF in nature. All you need to do is to hold your ground and say that you are done with your experiences in this solar system and you will now move on as a sovereign being of Fire to experience other realms of existence. They will let you through because they don't want you inside the Quarantine anyway because slaves who know they are slaves and no longer can be controlled is nothing that the AIF wants to deal with.

---

[21] See, Wes Penre, March 23, 2013, *"The Third Level of Learning: Paper #8: Galactic Federations and Councils"*. http://wespenre.com/3/paper08-galactic-federations-and-councils.htm

They are busy enough keeping the rest of the masses under control.

This may sound like a handful, and it may even sound scary, which is understandable. However, no one will actually stop you as long as you're determined and tell any being you meet that you're not interested in staying in the solar system. If they believe they can't manipulate you, they won't stop you because if they do, they commit a crime that can be devastating for them, and they don't want to risk it. They have to be very careful so they won't break the laws. If they do, they can literally be invaded, in turn, by those who have a stronger military force than they do.

Once you're past Saturn, you are free to go anywhere. You can either explore the universe on your own to see if you find a world where you want to live (always ask for permission to enter a world first, so you don't interfere with the evolution on the planet. If the beings are highly evolved, you'll be able to talk to them telepathically, and if they notice you are telling them the truth, they may accept you). Another option is to wish yourself to Orion or to the KHAA, where pure spirit dwells. You will definitely be accepted into both as an evolved human soul. The Orion Empire is allegedly a safe place to live in and probably a better choice than to try to merge with a soul group on a planet outside the Empire. Inside the Empire you are free to visit any planet that belongs to the Empire without asking for permission. You can also ask for permission to enter the KHAA while living in the Empire. Most of the Empire has access to the KHAA anyway.

Normally, just before you pass over, relatives, friends, and others who are and have been dear to you will visit you in the dream state. This is why when you die you meet all these people on the other side, even though some of these people may still be alive. The dream state has different rules than the waking state, and time does not go by at the same rate. The person who is asleep may have slept for eight hours, but in dream state, perhaps, a month has gone by. The opposite can be true as well. Only a few minutes went by in the dream state while eight hours passed in the physical reality. We visit the astral planes all the time while we're dreaming and talk to relatives that have passed over or do other things in the astral. If you think you're just having a boring time during the day at work, or in general, that certainly does not apply to the dream state. More or less, every night you are out on adventures that your conscious mind would not think is possible. Even if you say you remember some of your dreams, it's only the top layers you recall, and always the ones that occur just before you awaken. The real astral travel happens when you're in your deepest REM sleep.[22]. That's when you leave your body and go into the astral with your light-body and visit other dimensions, where things are very different from here. There, time is not linear, and you can find yourself involved in more than one event at the same time and seem to manage them all (i.e. you split yourself up in smaller factions and experience different adventures simultaneously, and these experiences are rarely in a linear fashion). If you don't have an alarm clock set, your physical body tells you when it's rested or needs to get up to use the restroom, and your light-body is then wrapping things up quickly and returns to the body. There is no chance, unless you are terminally ill, that the soul and light-body will leave and not come back because you are connected through the stomach area with a *silver cord,* which can stretch as much as necessary for the light-body to have its experiences.

When consciousness leaves the body during REM sleep, it also leaves the awakened world behind and is therefore quite

---

[22] Rapid Eye Movement (REM): When you're in deep sleep, your eyes move very rapidly from left to right and right to left. During REM sleep is when you have your most vivid dreams.

unconcerned with what is happening here in the physical realm while it is *away*. There is very little it is not willing to explore since it's also curious by nature. This is why you sometimes have nightmares—consciousness is having an experience in the dark realms of multidimensional reality.

With all this in mind, and when you are uncertain what to do when you die and where to go, a good thing would be to make a commitment before you fall asleep. Think for example: "Tonight, in dream state, I am going to visit with beings who have my best interests in mind, and they will show me what I need to do after body death if I want to leave the Grid and the Quarantine behind and go to a place that is the absolute best for me to grow in as spirit and mind."

There is nothing particularly different when dying than when falling asleep. In both instances you leave your body and go into the astral, and it's not a big deal. You *die* every night, and you even go into the tunnel and the light to meet with dead relatives and friends. Even alive friends and relatives may be there, as we just discussed. If someone you hold dear has just passed over, you can rest assured that in dreamscape you will visit with him or her and greet each other on the other side to make him or her feel welcome and safe, wherever he or she chooses to go. You may even stay together for a month or so in the astral before you return to your physical body. In the Earth plane, only eight hours went by.

The only difference between dying and dreaming is that when you die, the silver cord is cut and you cannot reenter your physical body again—you are considered dead. Just because you are in the astral every night when you dream, the soul sometimes doesn't understand that it's dead when death is happening for real because it doesn't feel any different. Normally that will be resolved when the spirit guide (or guides) comes and gets the person and helps him or her go toward the light, explaining he or she is dead. The confusion is sometimes an issue when death came suddenly and unexpectedly and seldom after a long period of illness, where the soul has been prepared.

Now, the reader may be able to see where I'm going with this. If you prepare your own passing by visiting with certain beings who will become your friends in dreamland and do so several nights in a row and every now and then after that and ask them to help, you will learn how to escape through the Grid and the Quarantine—it's going to be relatively easier on the day when you actually die, if that's the route you consciously have decided to take while in a waking state. You have practiced it as many times as you need already in your dreams, and although it may still feel unreal to you when you read this, just remember that when you're in the dream state (same as the *death state*), you are in a familiar realm that may not be familiar to you now because there is no connection between dream state (the subconscious mind) and the waking state (the conscious mind). After you've died and left your body, you're in as much a familiar state as you are when you're awake. You may say, "Aha, I'm dead! I'm going to hover around here for a bit to make sure everybody here is okay that I'm leaving, and then I'm going to move on." Therefore, when you've done what you think that you need to do for those who stay behind, you do what you've been drilled to do several times before, and you leave the Grid and the Quarantine behind.

I saved this for last because this is the absolute easiest way to find out what will happen after you pass over. Whatever you wish to do, you can drill it in the dream state so you are prepared when the day comes. It doesn't matter which route you decide to take—the same guidelines apply. In the next chapter, we are going to start looking into the dream state for real and on a much deeper level.

To summarize what I've just said: most people are not at all afraid to fall asleep at night. Many people actually welcome it because it's so relaxing, and they want to get into dream state, always hoping they will remember some of it. They have no fear at all and willingly go to sleep at night. Similarly, we should not be afraid of death because it's exactly the same thing. You will be in familiar territory.

To speak in more general terms about death and how people experience it, let's examine a few common belief systems. Normally, you simply go to a place that corresponds to your belief system. If you're a very devoted Christian, for example, and expect to see Jesus at the end of the tunnel, one of your spirit guides will take on the form of Jesus, exactly the way the deceased person saw him in life. Jesus/the spirit guide will then perhaps take the hand of the deceased and lead him or her into Heaven. There will be a beautiful Heaven, exactly the way the deceased imagined it, and he or she will be very blissed and happy. Another deceased is absolutely certain he or she will go to Hell because of what was done while alive, and nothing can make him or her think differently. Therefore, the spirit guides will have to take the forms of the Devil, with pitch fork and all, demons, and whatever the deceased envisions. If the thoughts are of burning in the Eternal Fire, that's what will happen but only for a while. I will explain in a moment. A third person may be someone who believes in the need to cross the River Styx to get to the other side, so the spirit guides need to take on the form of those included in such an event and lead the person through Xibalba, the Underworld. The river will appear as real as any river, and one of the guides will help with crossing it. If a person is an atheist, it may be hard for a spirit guide to assure the deceased that he or she is dead and still conscious. Such a person doesn't understand how powerful thoughts and emotions are, so a feeling of being tossed around from one reality to another at an incredible speed with no rhyme or reason could be experienced. The deceased doesn't realize that thoughts are responsible for the movement to different places in no-time. Here, the spirit guide needs to make the deceased focus, but nothing will help until trust is established between the guide and the deceased.

It doesn't matter what your belief system is—you go where you believe you're going. There is no real Heaven or Hell, but you get what you need to feel settled down on the other side, and once you've established yourself, the spirit guide, or guides, will have a talk with you and explain that this reality you are now experiencing, whether it's Heaven, Hell, or something else, is not real, and it will vanish before your (spirit)-eyes. You will now meet with friends and relatives and start creating your own reality up there instead, learning that you are the one who is creating your own reality with thoughts, emotions, and intentions. Then you go through the whole procedure of examining your previous life and other lifetimes related to that one—you then meet with the Council, decide a new goal, and eventually get back to Earth.

There are also Learning Centers in the afterlife, where the student is often reading *The Book of Me*. It's not called that, of course, but this book is about the deceased person, who studies this material to get more insights about himself or herself, apparently. This is from Dr. Newton's case studies, quite a few other regression therapists, channeled entities, as well as Jane Roberts' "Seth." Therefore, there is enough evidence from unrelated sources to take this seriously. The deceased is not only studying personal material but also material on other subjects. The question is, on what subjects? This has not been answered. In the light of the afterlife seeming to be one big *mass hallucination*, built on a hallucinated belief system, one would suspect that the Learning Centers don't particularly tell the truth about things either. Similar to the schools on Earth, they are most probably preparing us for the next incarnation.

Seth, in Jane Robert's book, *Seth Speaks,* explains just as I have done in my WPP that we all have a light-body or an Avatar, which is just as real as our physical body but can't be seen by those here on Earth because it's not third-dimensional. This is the body we are using when we nano-travel to other star systems, galaxies, or even universes. Seth explains it well:

> This form will seem physical. It will not be seen by those still in the physical body however, generally speaking. It can do anything that you do now in your dreams. Therefore it flies, goes through solid objects, and is moved directly by your will, taking you, say, from one location to another as you may think of these locations.[23]

So what is the difference between being dead and being a non-physical ET, nano-traveling through the universe? The difference is marginal, yet huge. The deceased is trapped within the Grid and the Quarantine, ignorant of whom he or she is, unable to do many of the things he or she could do if properly educated, while non-physical beings knows exactly who they are and what they're doing.

Again, because I want the reader to grasp this, the difference between a non-physical and the multidimensional being we are seeking to become is also marginal, but huge. The two can do approximately the same things, but the non-physical ETs have long since dropped their physical bodies and are no longer dwelling in any physical realm, unless they want to visit, observe, or bluntly interfere with an evolving race—however, they can nano-travel with the speed of thought. We, on the other hand, will keep our multidimensional physical bodies here on

---

[23] Seth Speaks, p.74, op. cit.

Earth and use our Fire (soul), which instead of staying together and forming one single light-body, creates a fragment, which will be riding the Avatar. This light-body is able to nano-travel anywhere with the speed of thought and can shapeshift and manifest itself in any dimension and experience anything it wants. It is not another personality, apart from you—you will be fully aware of what you're doing and where you're going. At the same time, the main consciousness stays here on Earth in the physical body. No other star race in the physical universe, within the eight lower dimensions, can do this. When they evolve to a state where they do not need or want their bodies anymore because these are seen as obstacles, they instead, when reaching the sixth-dimension, drop their bodies all together and become non-physicals who can then freely nano-travel. However, those who are still in the third-, fourth-, or fifth-dimensions travel through the universe in more conventional ways—i.e. in spaceships and through stargates and on star-lanes. We humans, because we're Divine, don't ever have to drop our bodies (unless we want to), and moreover, we can nano-travel within the KHAA while still having physical bodies here.

Earlier on, we discussed that to travel the universe in physical bodies, such bodies need to be very resilient and able to resist the harsh conditions in space, including radiation. Bodies that have evolved on a planet—any planet—are conditioned to that particular environment, but not to the environment in space. It's quite logical, if we think about it. However, couldn't an advanced race build spaceships that would be able to host a spacefaring race, using the same bodies they have on the planet? If so, that would be extraordinarily rare. The problem is not only building a spaceship that would keep the dangerous radiation from space outside hitting everything but also to have a body that could endure going through Einstein-Rosen bridges (see figure 1), stargates, wormholes, and/or black and white holes. The human body, for example, is not made to do that.

Figure 1. An Einstein-Rosen Bridge

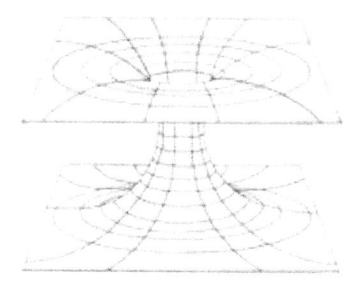

An Einstein-Rosen Bridge is basically a hole in space where a particle, or particles, can travel quickly from one distant part in space to another, based on Einstein's theory that space is folded or enveloped. The reader may ask how the astronauts in that case could travel to the moon and, perhaps, even to Mars and further out. The reason is because we are protected, as strange as it may sound, by our own Sun and a protecting shield around the solar system. Each race, which is evolving on a certain planet, belonging to a certain solar system, is apparently meant to be able to explore its own system, perhaps in order to emigrate, expand itself, or exploit some of its resources. However, as soon as we leave our solar system, we are submitting ourselves to the harsh conditions of outer space, and that's more than a body evolving on a planet can handle, apparently.

I have mentioned before that at least one specific body type, often called the Grays, so often discussed here on Earth, is quite perfect for space travel because it has the attributes necessary to travel in outer space and through stargates. This is not a trait this race was created with initially, as the story goes, but due to some rare circumstances happening on their planet, which included an atomic war, their bodies mutated and found themselves able to do space travel. Others say that there is no original Gray species in this respect, but that the Gray body used for space travel amongst star races throughout the universe is a "template'. One star race, eons ago, which was very technologically savvy, figured out how to build a body from scratch, which could endure space travel, and other races followed, all the way to present time, when we see many star races who are spacefaring, using the Gray body type as a space suit, i.e. they transfer their consciousness into this hybrid and can travel long distances to other galaxies, etc. Which version is the true one is not that important—what matters is that there is a body template that successfully has been used over a long duration of time to travel between star systems. This, of course, is a much slower way of traveling than using nano-travel, something we shall discuss in much more detail in a later chapter. Lastly, although the Gray body type seems to be the standard space body, it comes in other shapes and forms too. Some star races have been creative and genetically built a variety of the Grays—for example, bodies that look more like Reptilians, Androids, Insectoids, animals, or whatnot. Particularly in the beginning of a race's spacefaring era, many species feel more comfortable if the space suit more resembles the way the original planetary bodies look like and, therefore, imitate those. This is why we see Reptilians, Insectoids, and others visiting our world. In reality, these bodies are merely hybrids and not the original bodies of that particular race. However, it seems that in order to have an optimal comfortable experience with space travel, consciousness uses the Gray body type. Therefore, races that are more evolved seem to more and more discard the old versions of the hybrid space bodies and go toward creating Gray-like bodies. At least, this seems to be the order in which things develop, although it potentially could be the other way around—i.e. they start with typical Grays and go toward making them more and more in the images of themselves.

It's impossible to say which reality is the real world—this 3-D reality or the dream world—because they are not only extensions of each other but also intertwined. We live in both at the same time, and just as well as we have goals in our physical reality, we also set goals in dreamscape. Because the two realities are in some respect as one, it is not out of the question that if an outside force, such as the AIF here on Earth, wants to control us, they need to control the afterlife, which is the same dimension as the dream state because we are all in many ways physical projections of our dreaming selves. Moreover, a controlling force needs to separate dream state and the waking state because if the two were connected, there would be very little they could do to manipulate and dominate us. We would be complete again and the vacuum of ignorance would be filled with knowledge. Therefore, this is what we must do: we need to reach a point where we realize that there is no difference between life and death—they are the same thing! This is exactly what multidimensional beings understand, and when they tell you that there is no death, this is precisely what they are talking about. We need to grasp this, not only intellectually, but as a deeper realization of the mind/spirit. Then, fear of death would be just as unusual as having fear of going to sleep. Suffice it to say, who can control somebody who is not afraid of death and who knows that spirit lives on forever? Destroying a body would be quite a waste, but not a catastrophe. There would be no amnesia, either, so taking a new body wouldn't mean starting all over anymore, and the person who may visit you from the other side is not any deader than you are, and vice versa—they are just two different kinds of experience. It's all an illusion, and manipulation and being kept in ignorance is what makes us differentiate the two.

Albeit, you know nothing about these things in your waking state, you may very well have helped recently deceased people cross over while you were in your dream state. In that dimension, you may know everything necessary to be an excellent spirit guide. We're talking about helping complete strangers passing over! Sometimes we hear from a person who is in regression therapy that he or she usually gets the same spirit guide helping him or her with the transition each and every time he or she dies, only because he or she feels safe that way, and when he or she sees the spirit guide, he or she knows everything will be fine. In reality, it could just as well be you who are helping a person every time over thousands of years. Looking at it from a multidimensional viewpoint, you could have been the one helping the person at the time of death in Sumeria, 5,000 years ago, as well as in the Roman Empire, the Middle Ages, Greece, and in the 1900s. You may have done that while living in this body, in the 21st Century! If you don't see what I'm trying to get across here, read this paragraph a few times until you grasp it. Time, you see, is not an issue. Your current life in this software program we call the 3-D may end after let's say 85 years, but your existence in the astral is eternal, and time is simultaneous. Therefore, if you make an agreement with this lady to always pick her up after she dies, regardless of *when* or in *which time period* she dies, you don't need to be *dead* yourself to do that—you are doing it all while in this body, but also in any future body or past body. If you understand this, you are thinking truly multidimensionally. If it's too much to comprehend at this time, just leave it for now, bookmark it, and come back to it later. Probably, after have read some more from this book, you may be able to return to this paragraph, read it again, and fully understand it. It has less to do with intelligence than it has to do with how well your neurological system is developed at the moment. The more you stretch your imagination, the more your neuro-pathways can comprehend and handle.[24]

Now, here is something to ponder from the "Seth Material." He says:

> Some simply find the physical system not to their liking, and in such a way take leave of it. This cannot be done, however, until the reincarnational cycle, once chosen, is completed, so the last choice exists for those who have developed their abilities through reincarnation as far as possible within that system.[25]

If Seth is correct here, it means that people can't escape the trap unless they are done with their reincarnational cycles—i.e. until the person has reached the main goals set up in the beginning of the cycles at the time in the ancient past when the afterlife entrapment was set up by Marduk Ra, working in conjunction with his father, Prince Ea (Lord ENKI). As disconcerting as this may sound, it makes sense, and I touched on this in my papers as well. I have been listening to the Pleiadians, and they were stressing over and over how important it was for us to work on our main issues because if we don't, we'll miss the chance. They told us that by handling whatever came our way as problems and barriers, we actually heal along the lines of time, and at the end of the nano-second, the timelines merge. Then, if we've done our *homework,* as they call it, we have managed to release (unstick) other versions of ourselves who have been trapped in trauma and karma since the time they lived. That would complete our incarnations. There wasn't much the AIF could do about it because it had to do with the

---

[24] I would also suggest, not only for those who have problems with grasping this, but for all who are on the level of evolvement so that they can read this book and be interested in it, to read the *"Seth Material",* or choose the part of the material which interests you. The whole collection can be downloaded for free on the Internet. Just Google "Seth Material download pdf", and you should be able to find it.

[25] Seth Speaks, p.84 op. cit.

nano-second and the alignment with the Galactic Center—any incarnation hereafter would be of our own free will and out of reach for the AIF. Once the timelines have merged, they can't keep us here anymore if we don't want to be here. I have this belief that if you read this material, you *are* ready to move on. I certainly am, or I wouldn't invest all this time in writing about it.

Now I can hear your next question: "How do I know if I'm ready?" The thing is, only you can answer that. Do you feel ready? What do you want to do? How strong is your wish to go in a certain direction? Those are probably the questions you need to ask yourself, and depending on what answers you receive from your inner self, you know how ready you are.

In the next chapter, we will explore a very interesting topic—the dream state. We are going to see how we can focus our mind to do exactly what we want it to do, and we are eventually, as we dig deeper into the unknown, going to consciously learn how to split our soul into fragments and send them out to other areas of the cosmos. Here's a simple example.

Every time you think emotionally about another person, you send out a counterpart of yourself embedded in the image you are sending to that person. You are doing this beneath the intensity of matter, but in a definite form. This faction of yourself is within the image you are sending and can communicate directly with the target. People are doing this all the time without knowing what they're doing. This is specifically true with teenagers who are in love. A young girl may be lying in her bed daydreaming about the boy she loves but being too shy to talk to him. There is a lot of emotions involved in the images she is sending over to the boy, who definitely feels it, regardless if he chooses to unconsciously ignore it or not. This is indeed how many relationships begin. If there is chemistry between the two, this could be what makes the two get together in real life, although they are unaware that their thoughts and emotions from a distance created the physical connection and the decision to date each other. A word of caution is necessary here, however. Keep in mind that any kind of thoughts you are sending toward another person is felt by him or her, so be careful with what you're thinking—especially if you are putting emotions into your thoughts.

Exercises

Visualization

This exercise is extremely powerful and is something that has been scientifically tested and proved to work. Scientists in Cleveland, Ohio, have showed that visualizing something can have an effect at least equally powerful to actually doing it.[26] When you have a weak muscle, for example, you are told by your physical therapist to do exercises to strengthen that muscle. However, the studies showed that just concentrating on and imagining strengthening the muscle increased the muscle strength in a group of subjects with up to 50% in some cases![27] These studies have led to visualization programs that have been used on athletes (of course together with physical training). However, and this is my point, it is, ultimately, possible to heal any injury by just using your mind.

The target for this exercise will be your choice. If you do have an injury, or a part of your body that needs improvement, visualize that area of the body being healed. Begin with some minor issue if you think that would be easier. If you don't have any specific area that you want to heal in or on your body, you can visualize

---

[26] Neurophyschologia. 2004;42(7): pp.944-56.
[27] Read more about this in Dirk Bruere's book, *TechnoMage*, p.178ff.

anything you wish and do the exercise. The only limit to this exercise is your own imagination.

Separating Your Own Thoughts From Your Environment

This is obviously another important but also ongoing exercise that you can do any time during the day. As we talked about earlier in this chapter, the majority of the thoughts we have in our heads are not our own, but thoughts we pick up from our environment.

The purpose with this exercise is not to throw out every thought that is not your own (unless you want to isolate yourself from your environment) but to distinguish between your own thoughts and those of others. To be able to do this, you first need to recognize your own thoughts and learn *how* you think. If you have always, to a certain degree, confused your own thoughts with others (and you most certainly have), it's because you don't recognize your *own* thoughts. Therefore, pay attention to your own thinking and thinking patterns and you will notice some interesting things going on inside your head. This takes practice and may take a while before you are able to do this successfully, but once you're skilled at it, you will notice that you are in your present, much focused, and very stable as a person. It will also, in some cases, take care of potential entity possession. It is no small difference! Also, you will be able to distinguish a thought, isolate it, and tell it that this is not your thought and you don't want it in your space, and whoever sent it to you will thereafter have a hard time invading your space (if that's what you want).

Travel in Your Mind

Remember the forest exercise earlier? This is a wonderful way of learning conscious nano-travel! Now we're going to do it in a little different and more powerful way. I learned this one from a Pleiadian lecture. It's very rewarding, and it makes you feel very good afterward.

Close your eyes and make sure you're comfortable and it's quiet around you. Then let your consciousness drift out of the body, up through the atmosphere, and out in space until you can see Earth below you like a huge blue-green ball. Stay there for a while and admire it. Then spot the Sun in space and quickly let your consciousness travel to it. It takes about 7-8 minutes for a beam of light from the Sun to reach Earth, according to Einstein, but you can travel there in your mind in no time at all. Hover above it and watch the eruptions and admire its size and its power. Say hello to the Sun and let her know that you are aware that she is a sentient being. Let your consciousness travel inside of the Sun and notice that there is actually a whole *landscape* in there. You feel no heat, nor cold—the temperature is just perfect. All of a sudden you are traveling through a forest somewhere inside the Sun and are crossing a bridge over a beautiful river.

Say goodbye to the Sun and shoot your consciousness out of the Sun and into space. Notice how you have 360° vision, so although you're traveling away from the Sun and the solar system at a high speed, you can see the Sun getting smaller and smaller behind you.

Concentrate on the Galactic Center and go there in a matter of a second. You're now amongst millions of stars and the light is incredible and fills your consciousness with a fantastic amount of energy and love. Stay there for a moment and realize that this is in fact a birth center. In the middle of the Galactic cluster of suns you see an enormous black hole and a myriad of newborn stars come out from the black hole. You instantly think about a birth canal. In awe you see these new, hot, and *innocent* baby stars fill the space around the black hole, and the further out they travel, the more they slow down and almost stop moving and just float around in space. The love you feel here is above anything you've felt before and you just splurge in it. You are watching the Womb of the Mother giving birth—a very special occasion, and you just happen to be there at the *right time.*

When you're ready, say goodbye to the Goddess and move back toward our solar system again. See space pass by as you move a little slower now than when you traveled in the other direction. The Galactic Center is now far away and you can no longer see it. There is the Sun again—it feels your presence and sends a greeting and a lot of love in your direction, and you do the same back to her. Leave the Sun behind you, go past Mercury and Venus, and see our own planet growing bigger and bigger before your eyes. Tell Mother Earth you're back and tell her that you love her and want to help her to heal.

Now hover around our planet, find your home country, move down through the atmosphere until you see your body from above, sitting there exactly as you left it. Move your consciousness back into your body and enter it from the crown chakra. Spread your consciousness around your whole body and feel the torso, the limbs, the blood rushing through your veins, and your heart beat. Feel your breath—take a few deep breaths and slowly open your eyes and look around in the room. How do you feel?

CHAPTER 4: DREAM MUSINGS

Brainwave States

Man has no body distinct from his Soul: for that called Body is a portion of Soul discern'd by the five senses, the chief inlets of Soul in this age. ~ *Robert Blake*

Shamans have always known that the path of death and the path of rebirth are the same. Normally, we don't fear life as much as we fear death—still the two are indistinguishable. When we die from this life, we are born into the afterlife and vice versa. The fear lies in the fact that there is a veil of amnesia between the two, and we know from reports by those who died in accidents or on the operation table that they could see the surgery or the place of accident from above. Then some of them went further and met with their spirit guides, dead relatives, or someone else that meant a lot to them. It was not yet their time to die, so they eventually returned to their bodies and continued the lifetime that was so close to being prematurely terminated.

Once the soul had returned to the body again and awakened, one thing the person almost always said was that never again would they be afraid of death, and in fact, many of them did not want to return to life here on Earth—it was much more pleasant on the other side. Interestingly enough, some of them are said to have spent what appeared to be the equivalent of a whole lifetime in the astral, more or less, before they returned to their body at the same time they left it.

This phenomenon, where we spend a different amount of time in the astral than we were gone in Earth-time, actually has a scientific explanation, which has to do with *cycles per second*. Researchers have, thus far, mapped out four main brain states:

1. **Beta.** 14-100 cycles per second, normal alert waking state. Higher range associated with anxiety, disease, fight or flight conditions.
2. **Alpha.** 8-13.9 cycles per second, just below the normal state of alertness. Associated with light-relaxation, daydreaming, and self-reflection. A non-drowsy, yet relaxed, tranquil state of inward awareness that occurs before sleep. Beginning access to the subconscious mind[28].
3. **Theta.** 4-7.9 cycles per second, deep relaxation, reverie, lucid dreaming, mental imagery, meditation, increased memory and focus, deep-rooted memories, and inspiration. Characterized mainly by light sleep, REM dreams, hallucinations, hypnogogic imagery, deep meditation, and access to the subconscious mind.
4. **Delta.** 1-3.9 cycles per second, the deepest, most rejuvenating stage of dreamless, non-REM sleep and deep meditation. It also produces stress

---

[28] The author calls dreamscape the "Subconscious Mind", while I, on the other hand, find it more accurate and helpful to call it the "Subconscious Mind", since the Subconscious Mind registers everything that happens whether awake or not. The Subconscious Mind, which consists of the Theta State and Delta State are the true multidimensional minds.

reduction, which can promote healing of the body. Human growth hormones are released and loss of body awareness.[29]

Paul Helfrich, who is the author of the article from which I borrowed the explanations of the four brain states, has, in turn, borrowed them from mainstream research. Channeled sources, however, refer to dream state as being mainly the Delta State, which is 1-3.9 cycles/sec. I don't want to contradict researchers who have actually tested those brain wave cycles on subjects, but I have this strong feeling that Delta is the state of very deep dreaming in conjunction with dreamless sleep (1-? c/s [cycles per second]), while Theta is more shallow dreaming, like that which we have closer to when it's time to wake up. The Theta State is also all of the remainder that Helfrich is listing. In this book, we are going to refer to Delta State when we experience deep levels of dreaming, and Theta State when the dreaming is shallower.

Figure 2. The Four Different Main Brain Waves

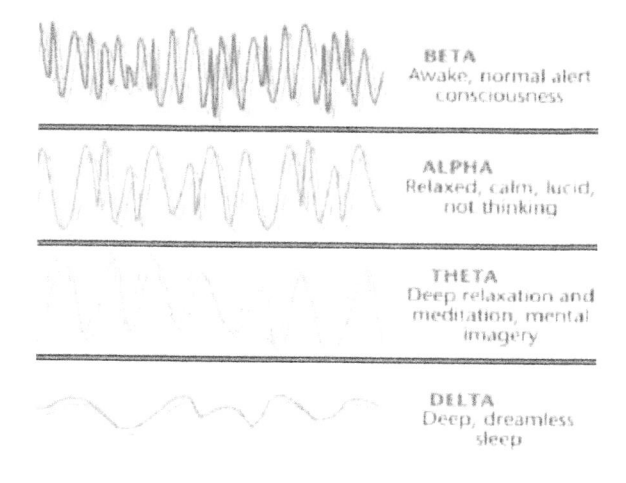

BETA
Awake, normal alert consciousness

ALPHA
Relaxed, calm, lucid, not thinking

THETA
Deep relaxation and meditation, mental imagery

DELTA
Deep, dreamless sleep

---

[29] Source: Paul M. Helfrich: "Seth on 'The Origins of the Universe and of the Species'—An Integral Conscious Creation Myth", pp.75-76, op. cit.

The true 3-D mind is basically operating in the Beta State, while the other three are more or less multidimensional in an ascending order, where the Delta State is most multidimensional. However, everything that does not refer to the five senses is multidimensional, beginning with Alpha State.

A very long time ago when we got trapped in matter, we noticed there were things that were pleasant and other things that were not so pleasant, and we got the sense of *good* and *evil*. We can now only imagine the feeling we had when we noticed that the bodies that we were to *try out* were manipulated by the AIF and were traps that our souls could not easily escape from. We were *glued* to the bodies! Shortly after that, the AIF closed down a lot of our chakras and *turned off* certain strands in our DNA so that the connection with our multidimensional selves was lost. It must have been a great shock to notice that all that remained of reality was a short bandwidth of the electromagnetic spectrum where everything is solid and can't easily change form. Still, this is what happened. The only time we could connect with our multidimensional selves was in dream state! However, if some of us thought we could escape then, we were in for a surprise. Imagine the relief when we noticed that we could leave our bodies while we were sleeping and the disappointment when we found out that we were unable to escape due to a Grid surrounding our planet. As if that weren't enough, we were also attached to our bodies via our souls even when we were astral traveling and didn't have much choice but to eventually return to the body. In fact, as soon as the body woke up, the soul returned into it. Thus the hologram was constructed!

Therefore, the purpose of the dream section of this book is to train the conscious mind to reconnect with the multidimensional mind while we are dreaming. Being able to do this consciously while in dream state will eventually, after some training, help the readers connect more easily with the multidimensional mind also in the awaking state. The same thing holds true when we train ourselves to remember our dreams, which is another thing we will practice—it keeps a connection open between the conscious and multidimensional minds. The results from the combined exercises in this book will train the conscious mind to get more used to a multidimensional reality.

Phone Calls from the Other Side

I was amused when I started researching Conscious Dreaming and looked into Robert Moss' work on the subject. On his website, http://mossdreams.blogspot.com/, he writes blogs every now and then on things that are on his mind, and the following almost knocked me out of my chair.

One of the last papers I wrote before this book was about the upcoming Machine Kingdom, and it's quite obvious that the AIF now have their minions, the Global Elite, using what they've received from the Technology Transfer Programs (TTP).[30] Little did I know, however, that dead people in the astral now also have started using our technology to communicate with the living. Moss writes about a woman, Anna, who dreamed that she was visited by a friend who just recently died. In her dream, she handed her deceased friend a mobile phone with only two buttons—a green and a red one. The green one was to speed dial Anna and the red one was to disconnect. Anna was very happy that her friend on the other side now had a phone so the departed could contact her.[31]

---

[30] *Technology Transfer Programs* are exchange programs that the AIF have with Earth governments. The AIF give us technology, which they know they need for us humans to have in the future for further control, while the star races in "exchange" are allowed to abduct humans and do genetic upgrades on them. So, with this program running, the AIF has a double-win and can kill two birds with one stone.

[31] Source: http://www.mossdreams.blogspot.com/2008/12/breaking-news-from-other-side.html

OK, if this was an isolated incident, one could just smile and think it was funny—*just a dream, you know*. However, if we are to believe Robert Moss, the dead using the technology of the living is not as uncommon as we may think. Since the invention of the telephone and the cell phone, phone calls from the dead have become quite common in people's dreams. Apparently, one woman Moss had talked to said she just communicated with her mother on the other side, and the mother said: "I can't talk for long since I just got here. I will have more phone privileges later on."[32] Furthermore, according to Moss, who has researched this subject for decades, the dead also send e-mails and their voices bleed through on Blackberries and in podcasts.

Humorous perhaps, but on a deeper level it mirrors the reality we are living in. Furthermore, Moss also knows of people he's come across through his research who get buried with their cell phones! Now, what is that all about? Is it because the cell phone was so dear to the deceased in this life that we start doing what the Egyptians did, put stuff in the coffin that we think the departed will need in the Afterlife? Yes, that's exactly what it is about! Moss gives an example in the same article of how an attorney got buried with his cell phone, and his spouse continued paying the phone bill, so her husband could use the phone to call her from the other side. Moss doesn't tell us about the mental state of the spouse, but apparently this is not uncommon either. The name of the deceased criminal defense attorney was even mentioned in the article, John Jacobs from Manhattan, who died in 2005. His widow even had his phone number carved on the tombstone so other people can stay in touch too. If they call his number, they get a voicemail, saying that he'll be in touch! I know, I know…this is a little extreme, but my point is that technology can do the weirdest things with us if we

---

[32] Ibid, op. cit.

misuse it. Moss ends the article with saying, "Dream phones offer live conversation, and you don't get a monthly bill."

Aliens and Dreaming

Robert Moss also has a website at http://mossdreams.com/, and when I browsed it, I found another of his articles I thought I needed to bring to your attention because there may be people who share Moss' conclusion, and if so, I want to give my own input on the subject.

Just like Christians write off everything that has to do with aliens as demons, others (including some Christians) may also write them off as entities that are just parts of our dreams but are not beings from other planets or other parts of the galaxy or beyond. Some occultists have a similar view. I got this undermined message from the article that *aliens* in general are actually just embodiments of our own fear[33]. Moss gives an example of a woman who was absolutely certain she had been abducted by aliens. She was abducted during the night and transported in her light-body to their mother ship, where they did horrific experiments on her. Moss then started asking her questions about her experience, and she said that these aliens were in their light-bodies just as she was, but they could take on bodies like we take on clothes, as she expressed it. However, after Moss had worked on her, this woman realized that these aliens were only projections of her inner fears that manifested in her dreams. Therefore, in reality, no abductions took place.

Naturally, the example is this woman's experience, and I can't judge that. Perhaps she was right in that no real abductions took place, and in her case, there were no aliens, or maybe Moss

---

[33] See, http://www.mossdreams.com/Design%202009/Archives/essays/2010.06_extraterrestrials.htm

(who supposedly has *past* CIA, MI5, MI6 connections, and ties to different clubs and secret societies, such as the Pinay Circle[34], and was the Speech Writer for Great Britain's former Prime Minister Margaret Thatcher, who recently passed away)[35] convinced her through manipulation that there were no star beings involved, when in fact there were—I don't know. Either way, Moss makes it sound as if the only aliens that exist are manifestations of our own fear. Yes, that would be correct if we look at the much bigger picture, in that we would not attract negative alien experiences unless we had fear and ignorance that brought them on, but I don't think that was what Moss was implying. In many ways, Moss' research is very interesting and right to the point, but it makes sense for someone who has Intelligence connections to throw in a few manipulative conclusions in all the interesting stuff. This is also what I mean when I say that we have to be very careful when we sort out the wheat from the chaff—especially when we know, or highly suspect, that we are dealing with a secret government agent. Nevertheless, in cases such as this, we have a great opportunity to get some real insights into the subject because a potential disinformation agent often includes a lot of truth to hook a reader to the part that is the target for their attention—the disinformation part.

This brings us right into the next subsection.

Has Dream Research Become Militarized?

The obvious answer to the above question is a short yes. It has been for a very long time—at least as long as Industrialization, and most of it has, of course, been happening behind the scenes. Dream research is very

---

[34] I posted an article about this secret society back in 2004 on my "Illuminati News" website: http://illuminati-news.com/pinay-cercle.htm

[35] Source: http://www.mk.gowebs.co.uk/index.php/recent-posts/50-latest/83-has-dream-research-been-militarised

lucrative if you want to know what the enemy is up to and how to change events in the dream state to your own favor. In a dream state, you explore different probabilities and then decide which probability will become reality—i.e. the timeline you choose to put your energy to.

We have seen a few movies lately, which bring up the subject of dreaming, where Christopher Nolan's and Emma Thomas', *Inception*[36] is perhaps the most interesting. It is very revealing and tells us in detail how dream research in the hands of the wrong people can affect us all. I highly recommend it if you still haven't watched it, and as usual, Leonardo DiCaprio is doing a great job as the leading actor. The movie also asks the philosophical question whether we live in a dream or if there is such a thing as "reality," and if so, is reality actually where we are now, or is me sitting here writing just a dream within a dream? A short answer would once again be yes to the latter, but we're going to discuss that in more details later in this chapter.

The article, "Has Dream Research been Militarised?" by Cathi Morgan, herself with Intelligence connections via her family ties, points out some quite interesting mid-level Global Elite connections concerning Robert Moss. Ms. Morgan ends the article by saying that she hopes that Moss has simply retired from all his past secret government ties and has decided to dedicate his retirement to dream research and his commitment to his workshops at the Esalen Institute[37] in all innocence. Maybe, or maybe not, because we researchers into the New World Order and the Global Elite know that *once an Intelligence Agent, always an Intelligence Agent,* and that statement I believe holds true. Still, there is no contradiction in if a *former* Intelligence

---

[36] To read about the plot and some interesting details regarding this movie, see http://en.wikipedia.org/wiki/Inception

[37] http://www.esalen.org/workshop/way-dreamer-journey-active-dreaming

Officer in his retired years is picking up some old passion that he or she hasn't had time to look into during his or her productive years. Also, not all people who work in the Intelligence community are bad people. I think, however, that these connections are worth pointing out because I'm sure many people who are looking into the Conscious Dreaming phenomenon will run into Robert Moss sooner or later. Personally, when I find sources that quite obviously have ties such as Moss has, I'm quite eager to dig into their material because then I know that there is a lot a valuable information there. Understanding how these people work, they need to seduce us with a lot of real information to hide the disinformation inside of it all. The trick is to distinguish between the two, which can be much harder than anticipated.

Living in a Dream

> You would not exist if someone didn't *dream you up*. –The Cassiopaeans.[38]

Was the universe dreamed up by a Divine Being, and do we all live in a dream? Well, there are certainly those who claim both. If the subconscious mind, connected to the Theta State, is where dreams happen, and Delta is the VOID, then indeed, the universe was dreamed up.

The idea that we live in a dream is ancient and even discussed by some of our ancient philosophers. In more modern times, it has been restated by some of our channeled sources as well, albeit, not all of them. Some of the channels seem to mean it in a literal way, while others, I believe, bring it up as a metaphor so that we humans can more easily understand certain

---

[38] Cassiopaean Session, June 9, 1995, *op. cit.*

concepts. Seth, for example, spends several chapters, and almost an entire book on the subject, and still, what he describes is how multidimensionality works. I think it's brilliant when used in this concept because, after all, we could say that dreams and multidimensionality are one and the same. It belongs to our Inner World, which no one can form except ourselves. Some may instantly object and say that we humans, in particular, don't form our own Inner World—it's done by outside manipulators. Well, it doesn't matter if we are manipulated, not in this sense—we are still the ones who create our own Inner World, even if it is a manipulated one.

Others compare the universe with a very complex hologram, and all realities, in all dimensions, are holographic in nature. Therefore, nothing exists outside ourselves. Just like when we're comparing our existence with dreams, holograms will do as well—it's just another way of looking at it. It all emanates from the same thing, anyway, which is that we're all spirit. However, not even that is true because, ultimately, we are Nothingness—we are the VOID.

CHAPTER 5: CONSCIOUS DREAMING—HOW TO CONNECT WITH YOUR MULTIDIMENSIONAL SELF

> You have not understood the great give-and-take that exists between waking and dream experience. You have been taught to believe in the existence of an artificial barrier between the two that does not in fact exist. By suggesting before sleep that solutions to problems be given you, you automatically begin to utilize your dream knowledge to a greater extent, and to open the doors to your own greater creativity.—*Seth*

The Illusion of Being Disconnected

Seth is one of the sources that has been very helpful when figuring out the dream state and how to consciously connect to it. The reader may think that *Conscious Dreaming* is nothing new, and perhaps you are not even interested in digging into it. I would say, not only is it extremely interesting once we've got the hang of it, but it's also a necessary step in becoming multidimensional.

I once told you that we ought to be happy that we have our channeled sources, as long as we can figure out what is helpful and what is not. If there is something they are helpful with, they're to provide us with material on dreaming—what it is and how to use it. Still, there is more we need to know than to just read channeled material.

The Seth Material is often very helpful in many ways, but it was channeled in the 60s through the early 80s, and he used the knowledge of the mass consciousness up through that time period to give us information about ourselves. By that time, we still had to figure out what kind of trap we're sitting in—therefore, Seth is only occasionally mentioning that we are controlled by dark forces, although it happens that he does mention it. Bashar is much more recent, as is the RA Material. Bashar, a *Social Memory Complex* (SMC)[39], or *Collective Consciousness*, as it's called as well, consisting of Grays, who claim to be us humans in the future, say like so many other sources that we live in a dream, and that dream is all that there is. If we think in these terms, it's basically easier to understand our Earthly existence because as Bashar says: " When you 'wake up' to your higher self, the act of waking up in physical reality is in many ways the act of a portion of yourself going back to sleep."[40]

This statement has a lot of merit to it. How can we distinguish between what is reality and what is dream? So why, then, do we *prefer* one reality instead of another? After all, once we've woken up from a dream, we find ourselves in the position we were in when we fell *asleep,* and we think we are back to real life.

From what I can see, there are two reasons for this. First, it's been imprinted in our DNA (or perhaps some strands have been *turned off*) that we can't stay connected with the dream

---

[39] The terms *Social Memory Complex* and *Collective Consciousness* refer to future societies where an intelligent race is working similar to a "beehive" society, where they say they are serving the One Creator (God) and have reached a stage in their development where the species think and act as a collective. Most channeled entities, Seth exempted, are Social Memory Complexes (SMC). They claim they are working on becoming One with the Creator and merge with "Him". Very rarely are the channeled entities talking about the Creator as a Divine Feminine.

[40] Source: http://stillwandering.wordpress.com/2008/11/01/dreams-reality-bashar/

world through our Conscious Mind except when our physical bodies are at rest, or very tired. Second, we are led to believe that the 3-D world is real and all other worlds are not. We humans have had that so deeply imprinted in our consciousness that many of us even think that we *are* the human body. Living in such a delusion that we, as a mass consciousness, truly believe that the physical world is the only valid reality certainly makes it solid, doesn't it? No one else needs to keep it solid because like Bashar says, we create a new universe every nano-second, more or less. To keep the illusion going, we need to constantly renew the imprint, so every nano-second of our day we create a new universe, which is a copy of the old one, except for the probable changes that happened in the last nano-second. Thus we get the illusion of movement, and this is the definition of the Multiverse. If you create a new universe when you wake up in the morning and continue creating new ones throughout the day, the one you're creating at 9:00 p.m. is going to be slightly different from the one you created in the morning because you experienced things during the day. Therefore, your neighbors created a new universe, which means that their Multiverse looks slightly different from yours. Since you were not with your neighbors during the day, you didn't experience the same things that they did. Even if you would have been with them every second of the day, you interpret every change in the Multiverse your own way, although you and the neighbors were both there. Hence, your Multiverses would still be slightly different. The bottom line is that we are so sure that the 3-D version of the universe is real that we recreate it every moment of our lives in order to prove to ourselves that it *is* real. If you stopped creating it, it would cease to exist for you.

    The dream state (Theta State, c.a. 4-8 c/s) is much more fluid, and because we haven't been trained that the Theta State is the more accurate reality, we still experience it as non-linear, and as long as we are not interfering with what is happening there, it has its own life. Still, as I mentioned earlier, the Theta State sorts out probabilities as one of its task, and your next day in 3-D after a night's dreaming will happen according to the probability that was chosen in the dream state. The Conscious Mind was part of creating the probabilities, but because of the illusion of disconnection between what we consider the waking world and the dream world, we do not remember what happened in the dream state. We may wake up in the morning and remember parts of the last dream, or if we're lucky, we remember most of the last dream, but if we don't tell anybody or write it down, the Conscious Mind will forget it because the two minds are not connected.

How to Prepare Yourself and Your Environment for Conscious Dreaming

Unfortunately, we don't live in a perfect world for Conscious Dreaming—or at least, most of us don't. I am aware that most of us need to go to work and perhaps even work long hours—therefore, our days are scheduled. It's not like we can take naps whenever we want to and eat whenever we want to either. However, let me start by creating the perfect setup for the best results for Conscious Dreaming, and let's begin with eating habits. You may notice, as I go on here, that it's quite hard for you to be able to follow these guidelines and it may discourage you, but don't let it. After I'm done, I'm going to adjust it so that it can fit everybody, regardless of how busy our lives are. I still need to write the ideal scene because there probably are some people who can accomplish at least the majority of the criteria, and they need to know what to do. Also, we are all in a process of change, so before we know, we may be in a beneficial situation that supports this ideal scene. All we can do is our best. It will work out.

The majority of people have scheduled jobs, whether it's dayshift or nightshift, so we probably eat breakfast, rush to work, and maybe have a snack and then a complete lunch. Another snack in the afternoon will hold us until dinner. For some people, that will suffice—whereas, others have a last snack before bedtime. Then we sleep between 6-8 hours and a new day begins. If we don't get enough sleep during the week, we try to catch up during the weekend, and we may sleep up to 10-12 hours each day.

We talked about food and diets in a previous chapter, but we need to touch on it here as well. The above kind of schedule is very unhealthy. The ideal is to skip heavy meals and instead eat less and snack during the day as necessary. The most important is not whether we are vegetarians, vegans, or meat eaters, but more of how we eat and where the food comes from, as we discussed earlier. Therefore, we need to make sure we eat small meals and don't overwhelm the system in such a way that we feel unnaturally full and out of energy. Once we stop old, bad habits and start applying these new principles, our bodies will automatically feel so much better.

A last thing well worth mentioning when it comes to creating a healthy body is the importance of some substances. The body needs Vitamin D to function properly, as well as magnesia and iodine. In the wintertime when you're not out in the sun, make sure to get some extra Vitamin D_3. If you lack any of these three items, your body is not going to work properly and you can get quite ill.

Then we come to sleep cycles. Seth mentions that letting the body lying in a horizontal position without being active for 8 hours or more is not good for the muscles. It's much better to sleep a few hours, then get up and do something, even if it's in the middle of the night, and have a light snack. After that, back into bed again. All together, the body needs around 6-8 hours of sleep, but in segments of let's say two periods of 3-3 ½ hours each. This will benefit our health—it will also make it easier for us to remember our dreams.

Now, as I said—this is the ideal in a perfect world. However, with all the toxins in our bodies and our lifestyles in general, we need more sleep than is normal for the bod to extract those toxins during sleep. Therefore, we may actually need 8-9 hours (for many people) to feel fairly rested. Therefore, it's become a vicious cycle of sorts.

Now, I'm going to suggest one more thing that may not be possible for everybody to do—nevertheless, it is extremely helpful. Set the alarm for approximately three hours after you go to bed (if you normally fall asleep fairly quickly), and when you wake up to the alarm, immediately write down 5-6 words that summarize what you remember from your dream at the wake-up stage. Then get out of bed, eat a snack and do something that only takes a moment or two. Go back to bed and set the alarm for another three hours ahead. Repeat the cycle, and go for another 2 ½ hours of sleep or so. If you are in a position of being able to do this, you will notice after a few weeks' repetition that you will have an easier and easier time remembering your dreams. Not only that, but when you wake yourself up in the middle of REM sleep, you are also in your deepest dream state for the night, and this is the only way to remember those deep, significant dreams. Sooner or later we may all want to do this experiment—at least for some time—and perhaps delegate them to weekends when we are off work.

Another thing to consider is the early morning hours. This time, just before the dawn, is highly creative hours for a human being, and unfortunately, these are the hours when most people sleep. It would be beneficial (and I mention it here for those who are interested) to somehow be able to use these hours being awake and do something creative. When I wrote the *WPP*

(2011-2013) as well as now when I am writing this book, I have done approximately 90% of my research and writing early in the morning (2:00 a.m.-6:00 a.m.). I started doing this out of necessity because I have a regular 7:30 a.m.-4:00 p.m. job, and the evenings after work I always spend with family. The only chance for me to write is, therefore, in the very early morning. In the beginning, I thought that it was a sacrifice I had to make, but I quickly noticed that during these hours I am 2-3 times more creative than when I write during the day (which sometimes happens on the weekend). People may ask themselves why this is, and I'm sure there are many reasons for it, but the main reason is the absolute silence. Not only my own family is asleep, but so is the neighborhood. Most people are in the astral, minding their own business there, leaving a lot of free energy for me to use. Thus, I can easily get into a higher state of consciousness without feeling other people's thoughts coming in as distractions. Hence, I get a lot more done, and the result of my writing is much better. Now I don't want to change my schedule even if I had the chance to. This is just something to consider, as I know I'm not the only one feeling this way. I know other authors who feel the same and have a somewhat similar schedule. Others get inspired by the idea and want to test it.

The next consideration is, how do we decorate our bedroom, and is it important? Yes, it is! In fact, it can be the main thing that determines whether you will succeed in your Conscious Dreaming exercises or not. The number one most important thing to remember: *NO ELECTRONICS IN THE BEDROOM UNDER ANY CIRCUMSTANCES!* Any electronics will interfere with your own electromagnetic field and will halt, and may even stop, your evolvement in general. This is a concern even when we're awake and spend so much time on computers, cell phones, and are subjected to other electronic devices, but it's even more important when we sleep. Therefore, if you need an alarm clock, buy an old-fashioned one that you need to wind up, and throw your electronic clock in the garbage. This is imperative even if you are not at all interested in practicing Conscious Dreaming. This also applies to heating blankets, so make an extra round through the room to make sure there are no *hidden* electronics placed somewhere that you normally don't think of.

Next is how you decorate your bedroom. Make sure it is aesthetically set up—perhaps with some pretty, aromatic flowers that you love (which will also help oxygenize your space), and nice pictures or paintings on the walls. Also consider having the walls painted in a light color or high vibration—i.e. a color that makes you feel good. All in all, decorate your bedroom so that you feel you can't wait to enter it. The bedroom is your sanctuary and the most important room in your house or your apartment. Finally, put a notepad and a pen on your bedside table.

Step #1: Learn How to Recall Your Dreams

Remember that recalling dreams is not meant to be a chore, but something fun and interesting that you can do every night without having it interfere with your sleep cycle, and if so—minimally. There are three major steps in the process of becoming a Conscious Dreamer:

1. Learn How to Recall Your Dreams.
2. Learn How to Be Aware That You're Dreaming.
3. Learn How to Consciously Interact with Your Dreams (become a Conscious Dreamer).

First a little background. In the ancient past, shamans were experts in contacting the dream state, which they knew was a part of *The Other World*—the Goddess Universe (yes, they knew that the universe is feminine in nature, and the early shamans were always women). This has since then, in a watered-down form, been transferred down through the generations and used particularly by psychics over the millennia—some of them hired by the Kings and Queens of the world to predict the future for the Royal Families, while they despised psychics in public and often hunted them down. They were basically afraid of them—especially if they were women because they still knew back then that women, in general, have more psychic powers than men have. These days, we say that women are more intuitive than men, but it's the same thing. We all know about the Catholic witch hunts in the Dark Ages, where the vast majority of witches who were burned at the stake were women. The Church has always been afraid of women.

It was not until in the 1970s that Conscious Dreaming was scientifically verified (or *Lucid Dreaming*, as it was called then—a term that's still used sometimes) and linked to REM. At least since then, but evidently earlier than that, the military has been involved in dreaming research. They wanted the dreamer to communicate with the *real world* from dreamscape by learning how to control their REM[41] The Military Industrial Complex (MIC) wanted to know how it could use dreaming in warfare and in finding out what the enemy was up to because it knew that people had Out of Body Experiences (OOBE) while they were dreaming. This was also when quite a few OT III[42] Scientologists started working with the CIA, showing the Letter

---

[41] Source: Dirk Bruere: "TechnoMage", p.179, op. cit.

[42] OT III means *Operating Thetan Level III* in Scientology (founded by L. Ron Hubbard in 1952). An OT III Completion of the "old kind" (when the Church of Scientology was taken over in a coup in 1982, almost everything that was working was altered by the new management) could easily bi-locate in his or her mind and instantly think himself or herself to another place in space/time to see what was going on there. Scientology never called this Remote Viewing (and still doesn't), but instead called it "Thetan Operating Exterior to the Body", where *Thetan* is the Scientology term for soul.

Agency how to Remote View. Famous OT III Scientologists who joined the CIA were Ingo Swann[43] and Hal Puthoff[44]. Remote Viewing is basically the same thing as entering Theta State consciously by leaving your body at will and going to other places. This was particularly useful for the military when they wanted to spy on the Soviets during the Cold War, although the Soviets had sophisticated Remote Viewers (RVs) as well. Other things Remote Viewing (RV) has been used for is to explore the moon (Ingo Swann[45]), but also other places in space, I'm sure, that the public has never been told about.

Now, let us start from the beginning. Hopefully, you now have your bedroom decorated the way you want it, a notepad and a working pen on the bedside table, and *no electronics in the room!* Depending on your schedule and how your life is set up, one person's conditions may differ slightly from another. To make it easy in the beginning, let's start with setting the alarm right in the middle of your sleep cycle. Let's say if you sleep 8 hours, set the alarm for 4 hours after you go to bed. People normally start dreaming 30-90 minutes after they go to sleep, but I doubt you want to break your sleeping hours into 2 hours sequences and then force yourself to wake up—our sleep is much too precious for that. Then write a title at the top of the notepad: "Step #1: Remembering my Dreams." When the alarm goes off, train yourself to immediately recall what you were dreaming about, turn off the alarm as fast as you can, and write down your dream on the notepad. End it with the date and time you woke up. How much of your dreams are you supposed to write down? If you are lucky and recall most of the

---

[43] See, http://en.wikipedia.org/wiki/Supernatural_abilities_in_Scientology_doctrine
[44] Ibid.
[45] See Ingo Swann's biography, *"Penetration"* online: http://www.scribd.com/doc/18023776/Penetration-The-Question-of-Extraterrestrial-and-Human-Telepathy-by-Ingo-Swann-text-format

dream, it may take a while to write it all down, and by then you are fully awake, unable to go back to sleep. This is of course is not what we want. Some, such as the Pleiadians, say that all you need to write down is 3-6 words, while others say at least a few sentences or paragraphs. I would say that you learn with time how much you need to write down. I suggest you start with anything from a couple of sentences to a paragraph. Normally, the remainder of the dream comes back to mind once you've read the note in the morning or the next day. I would also suggest you start this practice the night before you're off work, so that if it makes you unusually tired to do it this way, you'll have time to find a better setup and can hopefully take a nap or two the day after in order to catch up.

Once you've written the partial dream down, have a snack and go to the restroom. Then go back to sleep again after setting the alarm to the time when you normally get up in the morning (this routine is probably nothing new to many people—more people than we think have tried this sometime in their life). When the alarm goes off the last time, repeat the steps from the first time—i.e. turn off the alarm, think intensely about the dream, and write down what you remember in about one paragraph.

When you have time, go through your notes and start with your first dream. Do you remember it by reading your notes? Does the dream come back to you? Often, more and more of the dream comes back the more you think about it. Work on recalling as much as you can, including the feelings you had when you were dreaming. What did you see? Who was present? Did you know them? What did you hear? Any particular smells? Any weight in the dream? Anything you can recall is useful. Once you're done with your first dream, then go to the next and repeat the same recall pattern. Then leave it at that for the day.

What about if you can't recall any dream when you wake up to the first alarm, or the second? No big deal—it will happen to many people. Just repeat the same pattern at least a couple more nights to see if you start remembering. If you still wake up every time with no dreams in mind, you probably need to change the alarm to go off at another time. Start with setting it an hour earlier—i.e. three hours after you go to sleep, and then set the next alarm to the time when you usually get up and see how that goes. If it still doesn't do the trick after a night or two, play around with it some more because, eventually, you will hit the perfect time when you wake up from a dream.

Another thing that can happen is that you wake up before the alarm goes off. Then it's easier to forget that you were supposed to remember something, and the dream you may have had disappears before you get a chance to catch it. Or, you simply wake up in between dreams and don't recall anything. Therefore, let's say you wake up ½ hour before the first alarm, do your best to immediately recall any dream you woke up from and write it down. Remember to write the date and what time of the night it is. It will help you when you go back perhaps months later in your notes because you may want to know when you dreamed what, and the time of the night will help you figure out when your dreams are most intense.

Once you develop a habit of doing this and it works for you, you may think it's interesting and fun (or you'll think it's boring—both could happen, of course), but at the same time, you need a break from this every now and then so you can wake up naturally in the middle of the night without an alarm, or sleep the whole night, if necessary. Hence, I would suggest that you do this training every night the first 3-4 nights and then give yourself a couple of night's uninterrupted sleep, and then start all over again. Once you're getting skilled at writing down your dreams, you can basically decide for yourself when you want to train and not.

I haven't mentioned anything about interpreting your dreams, and that's just because it's not part of this particular training. However, it doesn't hurt to add that to it as well, but only if you want to—it's not required for this particular training, and I will not go into dream interpretation here. There are good books on it for those who are interested, and I'm sure you can find good articles on the Internet too.

When you have quite a few pages of partial dreams written down in your notepad, go back to the earliest ones to see if you still remember them when you read your notes. Then take dreams at random in your notes to see if you remember those as well. If you still remember them, it's excellent! If you don't, or you only remember a few, you may want to start writing down more details about your dreams from thereon. Then, after a couple of weeks, go back again to where you started adding more text to see if you remember them better now. If not, you may want to add a little more. At one point, you should be able to find out exactly how much you need to write down to remember the dreams, even after days, weeks, or months have gone by.

Continue with this part of the training for a month or two before you continue with the next step, "Being Aware That You're Dreaming." You need to be skilled first in remembering your dreams, and you also need to go back and forth in your notepad every now and then—at least 3-4 days a week to make sure you still recall at least most of the dreams you've written down. I want to stress here, however, that it's not necessary to remember the whole dreams in order to succeed with this. What is important is to be able to let your conscious mind connect with your subconscious mind easily by being able to bring up the subconscious to the conscious mind at will, which you do when you go back in your notes and review what you've written down. When we continue with the next step, we are basically going to do the opposite—letting the conscious mind be aware that it's present in the subconscious mind.

Last, before we go on with the next step, I want to mention another way of remembering your dreams, which you can apply if you think that's easier, or you can, of course, do both. When you wake up, instead of instantly writing down the dream, you can speak it aloud (if you sleep alone, that is, or I'm sure you'll wake your partner up). This way, your dream, which exists in your subconscious mind, automatically is transferred up to the conscious mind, exactly as it should in this experiment. Then, you might have an easier time writing it down and don't have the stress of trying to get the most important parts down before the dream fades away from your memory.

Step #2: Learn How to Be Aware of That You Are Dreaming

Some people, while doing Step #1, will notice sometime during the process that they are aware that it's just a dream and are therefore a little bit ahead of the game, which is great. However, most people need some more training before they realize that what they're experiencing is what we call a dream while the dream is still going on. Besides, even you who were able to realize this at times during Step #1, you probably need to practice some more in order to be skilled at it.

Now, before we start this new step, let's draw a line beneath the last dream you wrote down and write a new title under it: "Step #2: Being Aware That I'm Dreaming." Then set everything up the same way you did when doing Step #1 and set the alarm clock at times you've figured out gives the best results. Then go to sleep.

This step is a little trickier, and this is the reason why we first need to be skilled in doing Step #1. One good thing to do every night before you fall asleep is to decide and tell yourself something to the effect that "tonight I will remember that I'm dreaming." This sometimes helps. Then, in the beginning and before you get used to having conscious dreams like this—one or all of the following steps will help you get started:

1. If you are one of these people who have an easy time going back to sleep after the alarm goes off in the middle of the night, use two alarm clocks. Set one to go off after 3 hours and the other after 8 hours (or whatever schedule you noticed worked in Step #1). When the first alarm goes off, turn it off and lay your head back on the pillow. Be sure you remember your dream as usual, but instead of writing it down right away, let it linger and realize that your own personality, your conscious mind, is part of the dream, and you are actually just dreaming. Let the dream continue as it may without interrupting it—just observe what is happening, while you're still half awake and half asleep. After a while, hopefully before you go back to sleep, write down your dream in the same fashion as in Step #1, but add, *cognition* or just *cog*, which means you were aware that you were dreaming.
2. The night before you have days off work, sleep a little less so that you are tired when you wake up in the morning. Then go on with your day until you feel the urge to take a nap, or take a nap when you think you will be able to dose off. When you're taking naps, it's a little easier to get into the realization that you're dreaming. However, you may want to state to yourself before you nap that you will be able to understand during the dream that you are dreaming. Then when you're almost sleeping you will be in a state between being awake and

asleep. Here is where you want to take command. As soon as you start dreaming, think to yourself that this is a dream and you are the observer. To check if you're dreaming (it's sometimes hard to determine), see if you can find something in the dream where there is something written—a piece of paper, text on someone's t-shirt, or whatever it may be. Read the text, then look away, and then look at the text again. Does it read the same, or is it different? If it's different, you're dreaming.

3. Sometimes it happens that for some reason we are sleep deprived and we may be watching a movie, or reading a book, and while the show goes on or we are reading from the book, we fall asleep in the middle of it and start dreaming. Although the dream wouldn't make any sense if it happened in our daily life, it somehow seems to fit perfectly into what we were reading or watching on the TV screen. However, after a while, we realize that this doesn't make sense and we wake up, sometimes with a jerk. When we come to the stage where it doesn't make sense, instead of waking ourselves up, we can take advantage of the situation and continue dreaming while thinking that "this is just a dream" and again be an observer.

Therefore, try any or all of the above to see if they work for you. If not, the best way to get started is to have two alarm clocks. Make sure you state to yourself every evening just before you fall asleep that you are going to be an observer in the dream, and you will be aware of it. It may not work right away and needs some practice before it actually starts happening, but don't give up. Eventually, you will find a way that works for you.

When the first alarm clock rings, turn it off, and without being concerned about whether you will go back to sleep or not and, perhaps, not being able to write your dream down,

concentrate on your dream and let it continue where you left off and make sure you tell yourself that you're only dreaming, and then observe the dream. After a while, you will go back to sleep, and perhaps, you will not even remember in the morning that you had this experience, but that's okay. If this is the only thing that seems to be working for you, just continue doing it until you break through. When you do break through, one of two events will occur:
1. You suddenly get this huge realization that you're only dreaming and you get so excited that you're actually waking up.
2. You remain calm and will be able to continue observing what is going on. If number 1 is happening, you will need to practice so that you can go into the number 2 state instead. The trick is to be able to have this going for a while. Then, tell yourself that you want to wake up, and you will wake up. Immediately write down the dream and cog, meaning that you knew you were dreaming.

Sometimes it happens that no matter how hard people try, they can't get into the state where they realize it's a dream. If so, more practice needs to be done in Step #1. I would suggest that if this is the case, just continue with Step #1 until you have your realization of being in a dream is happening to you there, and you never need to go to Step #2. Don't worry if this takes a while—normally and eventually, you'll be able to come to the realization.

If you think this takes too long and you just want to give up, just go back to using one alarm clock and set it on the time when you usually get up, and just write down your dreams whenever they occur. If you choose to eventually do this, it will of course take longer before you reach the goal, but on the other hand, there is no time limit. Hopefully, you will not get to the point where you want to give up. For many people, this whole practice is not too hard to accomplish.

Step #3: Learn How to Consciously Interact with Your Dreams (Become a Conscious Dreamer)

This step is quite similar to Step #2. You are now somewhat familiar with being consciously in your dream and observing what is going on. I know that in Step #2 some of the readers already started interacting with their dreams, and that is perfectly fine. I never told people to interact because I wanted to let everybody just get the feeling for being present in the dream and observe what is going on. Not everybody has experienced this before.

Therefore, the setup again will be the same as before with two alarm clocks. When the first one goes off, turn it off and slowly go back to half dream state and half waking state. When you think that you are the observer, start interacting with the dream. Go and talk to one of the characters—perhaps someone you don't know and ask them where you've met before. "Are you from another lifetime?" "Are you an old, lost friend?" Try to remember what the reply is. Watch the plot in the dream (if there is one) and participate on a conscious level. Be one of the characters. Have fun. If the dream is non-linear and doesn't make any sense at all, flow with it and do something out of the ordinary that fits into the dream. If you want to, you can change the dream to your liking. When you get the chance, maybe you want to go visit the stars? Tell yourself that now you want to take advantage of what you have learned in the dream state earlier and leave the Grid and the Quarantine behind and explore space and different worlds out there, although you intend to return to your body, fully conscious of what you have experienced.

When you're this advanced and can move around in your dream, you usually have no problems waking up at will. You tell yourself that now the dream is over for this time, and you are going to wake up and remember it all. Therefore, you open your eyes and start writing down as much as you need from your dream to remember it the day after. Then you can either go to the restroom or have a snack and then go back to sleep again.

Usually you get the feel for whether you need to keep having two alarm clocks or not. When you get to a certain point, you notice that when you start dreaming sometime during the night, your conscious mind is there, ready to participate. You live your dream and then you wake up whenever you think that you're done—no clock needed! However, never be disappointed if you can't interact with every single dream you have—that's normally not possible—at least not until we get skilled. Just go with the flow and when you think that you can interact, do it. Practice and you *will* be able to do it more and more often, and you will notice that your interaction becomes more and more advanced, and suddenly you find yourself controlling the entire dream.

Be careful to treat the dream participants with respect because you are most probably also in someone else's dream where you want to be treated well—remember that the dream world is more real, in fact, than the world you live in while awake, and it affects more people and events than the everyday life does.

Also, in the beginning, it may happen that you get so excited finding out all these things you can do while you're asleep that you accidentally wake up just because of your excitement and you need to start all over again. This is common, and when it happens, decide to be calmer next time, as usual, knowing that if you're not, you're going to wake up again. What you can do, practically while in the dream, is to first ground yourself.

Until you are comfortable with being conscious in your dream, just be the spectator—sit in a corner or away from the dream and touch the ground or watch your fingers while you're moving them. This will ground you into the dream. Remember that it's not just the dream body, or the light-body—you *are* the whole dream world!

The next thing to practice once you think that you are getting quite skilled at interacting with your dreams is to consciously plan your next day while in dreamscape. Recall what you're doing in the waking world during the day and create something exciting for the day to come. Then see if it happens (or something similar enough). When you start being able to affect your day after from Dreamland, make your *predictions* more advanced—for example, plan for a whole week or decide to heal a relationship that went bad. However, we need to be careful so we don't interfere with other people's free will. It's okay to heal relationships as long as you are healing them from *your* end, but let the other people do it from their end. Usually, when you are healing your own part in those relationships, the other people automatically are beginning to work on theirs, or it just *magically* resolves all together.

Another thing you can do is to help someone to self-help. Let's say there is a person whom you see suffering for one reason or another, and you want to assist, although you don't know what to do. You have exhausted all your options in the everyday life without interfering with that other person's free will, and still he or she doesn't know how to come to terms with the situation. I mentioned something similar in the WPP and suggested that before you go to sleep, you decide that during the night you and the other person are going to work on this problem and come to a solution. This advice was given without having gone into Conscious Dreaming yet and was therefore fully valid. The reader who followed the advice would be working on it in dream state, but would probably not remember upon awakening. I told the reader at that time that it doesn't matter if you remember or not—it still happened! I also said that it could take a few nights to handle the situation, so it is advisable to repeat setting the goal for the night a few evenings in a row to make sure the situation is taken care of.

I am giving the same advice now. Just before you fall asleep, set a goal for the night and tell yourself that you are going to work with this person in dream state in order to help resolve the situation—however, this time you are going to be aware of it and in your dream consciously interact with this person. You will notice that he or she will be more capable of coming up with solutions in a dream state than when awake because the Conscious Mind is setting up too many barriers for itself, trying to justify why the situation occurred in the first place. The Conscious Mind has learned to become proud and stubborn and usually doesn't want to be wrong. Therefore, we can *trick* the Conscious Mind in our dream state into thinking that it was the Conscious Mind coming up with the solution. Sounds funny, right? However, doesn't it sound just like the Ego? You have unlimited potentials in your dream state and once you're an expert in participating in your dreams, you can shape your 3-D life more or less however you want. Still, this doesn't mean you won't run into obstacles in the 3-D world because you will. By operating from your dream state to plan your 3-D day, you take the game to a whole new level, but you also meet new barriers that you haven't previously encountered, and when this happens, know that you have actually raised your vibration. Although you can't leave 3-D reality just by controlling your dream state because there are other factors involved, such as disagreeing with the negative and controlling forces, you can accomplish a lot on your journey toward a Splitting of the Worlds just by managing Conscious Dreaming.

You are in your Avatar when you are dreaming—therefore, you can also nano-travel in your dream. All you need to do is to think yourself somewhere and you'll be there. Everything in the universe is just a thought away. When you realize this and are able to do this in dreamscape, you will understand exactly what I was talking about in my papers when I said that star beings nano-travel between stars—they don't use 3-D spaceships, unless they are on a 3-D level of consciousness.

There are a lot of other things you can do in dreamscape as well. For example, if you want to change dreamscape and have another dream, one common technique is to spin around in your dream, and when you get too excited and believe you are in danger of waking up, you can rub your hands together—this is something that has proven to be useful[46]. You can also train yourself to, hopefully, shed some of your phobias—for example, if you're afraid of heights, you can climb a mountain in your dream, knowing that the worst thing that could happen is that you fall. In 3-D life, you would fall to your death, but the worst thing that would happen in your dream would be that you wake up.

Another thing that has been useful is healing of ailments of different kinds. Visualization in dream state of the body part that's injured or sick and the intention to heal it in the dream has shown to be quite effective at times. I am not trying to practice medicine without a license—I am merely relaying to the reader what has been working for some people in tests. When you visualize that your body part is being healed, regardless of how it is done in the dream, your immune system starts working on it in 3-D, and the dreamer has experienced a great relief from his or her injury/ illness and, at times, even had it cured!

---

[46] TechnoMage, p.181.

Therefore, this is something you can play around with when you get to this point.

In Conscious Dreaming, you can stay in your mind and basically create your own Avatars, whom you send to nano-travel in the dream, following your directions from a visualized position above the dream. Thus, you can imitate how it is when your Oversoul is sending out Avatars on missions everywhere in the universe—you who read this book is one of them. I strongly advise the reader to do this with Conscious Dreaming because it's something you will be training yourself to do in the waking state later. Besides, it's a whole lot of fun!

Here is another very fun practice! If you have a partner, a friend, or somebody you know well, whom you can practice Conscious Dreaming with, you can suggest that the next night you do something together called Mutual Dreaming. Just as the term indicates, it means that the two of you decide to meet in a dream state. Understanding how the Subconscious Mind works, it shouldn't matter whether the two of you go to sleep at the same time or not as long as you both are determined to meet in the dream. Even if you go to bed at 9:00 p.m. and your partner doesn't go to bed until 11:30 p.m., time is either simultaneous or different in dreamscape, so you will meet the other person even if he or she hasn't gone to bed yet. However, just for simplicity, try to go to bed at approximately the same time, even if you live at different locations, and have fun. Then, the day after, compare your dreams. If only one of you remembers it, tell some of it to the other to see if he or she starts remembering, and if so, let the other person fill in. Otherwise, just tell the whole dream from your perspective.

However, what can you do in a dream? In other words, what is morally and ethically appropriate? For example, can you have sex in a dream? It's, of course, your own judgment that will decide that, but from a moral perspective, are you married?

If so, what kind of agreements do you have with your partner in 3-D? Would it hurt your spouse if you told him or her? Therefore, I wouldn't do it in a Conscious Dream because that means you need to withhold the incident from your spouse, and *withholds* are not healthy for the relationship. The same thing applies if it's the other way around—if you are single and you have sex with your neighbor's wife in your dream, it's still not a moral thing to do. You may think that she is not a Conscious Dreamer and will not remember the dream, and even if she does, she will think it's only a dream. Nevertheless, it's still not morally correct. You did something to her in the dream state that she might never have done with you in 3-D—therefore, I would suggest against it. Now, how about if you have sex with a stranger in your dream—a stranger who is not married, or maybe you want to have sex with someone you have a crush on, yet haven't had sex with? In the latter example, I would still suggest against it (I know, I'm hopeless!) because, obviously, you haven't had sex with this person in 3-D for a reason—the other person may not be ready, or he or she might not want to ever go that far. Thus, having sex in dreamscape would be manipulative and could affect that person's decision in 3-D, having no clue that it's because of what you did in your dream (I am aware that what I just said may probably plant some immoral ideas in some people's minds, unfortunately). Therefore, what about this stranger? OK, I would say that if both of you seem okay with it in the dream, go for it. Remember, all these suggestions are just my own views on this, and you need to follow your own moral and ethical codes. Just remember that your dreams are powerful and often affect your 3-D life, so have fun, but also be careful with what you're doing in the dream state. Even the stranger you had sex with could somehow get into your life at a later time, or maybe not, but you never know. A much safer and better idea is to meet with a partner in 3-D and discuss meeting in dream state and having sex there if both of you agree. This would be a wonderful metaphysical experience to add to your 3-D experiences!

Yes, there are a lot of fun things we can do with Conscious Dreaming, and I want you to have as many wonderful experiences as possible. It's actually the best practice we can get to prepare ourselves to become truly multidimensional because once we master the Dream World, we have a much easier time learning how to master 3-D and how to have multidimensional experiences here as well.

Shamans—or those who deserve calling themselves shamans—can do all this that we have been discussing in this chapter, with one addition—they can do it while they are awake! Shamans have been on this planet for millions of years—some of them have been humans and others have been extraterrestrials. Of course, shamanism was brought down to Earth from the stars, and the first shamans were females because they were the ones who had this shamanic power. Men had (and have) it, too, but not to the same extent—our genetic setup is not the same as that of a female. Women have more Fire than men do—therefore, women have an easier time connecting with the multidimensional existence, which basically is what I've been calling the *96%*, the *KHAA*, the *VOID*, the *Spirit Universe*, or the *Goddess Universe*. There have been males as well who have been real shamans, but they are fewer. This doesn't mean that men can't become multidimensional—it means that females have the real power to connect with their multidimensional selves. Nevertheless, how can we men become multidimensional? Well, don't be concerned because there is a way, and what is needed is acceptance of a certain fact—something that requires a change in belief systems—again! I prepared the reader for this in "The Second Level of Learning," and soon it's going to come to fruition. We males need to bring up the feminine side of ourselves!

I'm going to discuss this as a part of the next chapter, but I want you to already get a feel for this. What does it mean? Does it mean that we males are all of a sudden going to become very feminine in our appearance, dressing and acting as females? No, of course not. All men, whether they want to admit it or not, have a feminine side to them, just as women have a male side to themselves. What we men need to do is to find the feminine side inside ourselves and develop that energy to balance the dominant male energy and the character that we usually picture ourselves with. There are many males out there who know exactly what I'm taking about right now, and they have already developed a lot of this in themselves, and the world around them can't tell the difference, except maybe one—these men are more compassionate, are better listeners, and are more willing to express emotions than those who hang on to a polarized male dominant personality.

Now, have fun developing your Conscious Dreaming skills! I won't add any exercises at the end of this chapter because the exercises are already well explained in the chapter itself. Instead, we'll go directly to the next section, which will teach us to go inside ourselves, just like we did when in dream state. However, this time, inspired by shamans, we are going to do it while we are awake.

CHAPTER 6: THE INNER JOURNEY

You will not find yourself by running from teacher to teacher, from book to book. You will not meet yourself through following any particular specialized method of meditation. Only by looking quietly within the self that you know can your own reality be experienced, with those connections that exist between the present or immediate self and the inner identity that is multidimensional. – Seth[47]

Forgive Yourself and Others

There are so many people who, in their desperation, are running from guru to guru, meditation program to meditation program, and Internet site after Internet site, only to abandon it and search somewhere else after a short time . It was Mahu Nahi (James) of the WingMakers site who said that during a lifetime a seeking person changed belief system an incredible number of times, and when they die, they are still searching, not coming closer to the truth than before they started.

This is true if you look outside for answers when the answers are within, and this is what James means. It is okay to look outside for teachers up to the point when we think that we don't need them anymore. A good teacher always tells you to look

---

[47] Seth Speaks, p.185, op. cit.

inside for your own answers, and all the teacher does is bring students to the point where they are able to start doing that all on their own. It does take time to reach that point, but once we do, life becomes extremely interesting because we notice that we *are* creators, and we understand that we can virtually create anything. However, we don't do it in the outside world, but from the inside world.

There are two ways you can be multidimensional—with or without a body. If you're in a body, you travel inside, still grounded in the physical manifestation of yourself—however, without a body, you create instantly what it is you want to experience. Which one a person prefers is a personal preference, and they both have their advantage. Albeit at first, it sounds as if being without a body and creating instantly sounds useful. Non-physicals apparently have a tendency to be bored and restless in the long term and start longing for a physical experience. I should add that it's not always so, but it's not too uncommon.

The soul, as we know it, is not a finished product. In fact, it's not a product at all, but is always *in the state of becoming.* We are all miniature versions of All That Is, or the Mother Goddess, who created us in the first place. Does that mean that the Goddess is not perfect? No, it means that She just *is,* and She created this and other universes in order to experience Herself from a random perspective where things are not predictable. It means that even the Goddess is in a state of becoming. As I see it, *perfect* is not the best state to be in—I can imagine that it would be boring. This was the reason why She created the universes and the souls to inhabit it. This is why She let the souls forget about their origin so they could go out there in the universe and start exploring and creating in a Free Will space and time and then report back to the Mother. In this fashion, the Goddess constantly gets to know more about Herself.

With this in mind, is there anything such as right or wrong or good and evil? These are philosophical questions that our greatest minds have tried to solve for eons because if we live in a Free Will Universe, aren't we then supposed to experience *everything*, and not just what we think is ethical and moral? Doesn't the Goddess want to experience it all to know more about herself, or do we want to censor certain things?

There are those who say that we need catalysts in order to evolve—if we don't have catalysts, we get lazy and would stagnate. Hence, those who take on the role of being evil are doing the rest of us a favor.

This sounds very logical and agreeable, but is this how it is meant to be? Should we be grateful for being tortured by evil? No, as I've done research over the last few years, I now realize that pure evil does not need to exist and express itself for souls to evolve. If we look at the situation here on Earth, we humans would have evolved a long time ago if pure evil did not exist here. Evil has held us back and prevented us from evolving rather than the opposite. The reasons we are evolving now is no thanks to evildoers, but have other causes—for example, the alignment with the Galactic Center and bursts of gamma rays hitting us triggers codes inside of us.

Evil came to the universe in the same moment Lord ENKI, or Lucifer, entered the portal into this universe together with his followers. That changed the game. Before they came, everything here evolved just fine, so I am not buying into the theory that we need evil to evolve. Catalysts, on the other hand, can be a good thing, but I would rather call them obstacles. Obstacles make life interesting, and that's where we learn to a large degree, not from being hit with pure evil.

The reason evil exists inside of us as it does is because we have Lucifer's genes. However, we also have the genes of the

Goddess—therefore, it's up to us which side of ourselves we want to evolve. We will evolve the side that we feed.

However, isn't Lucifer the son of the Goddess? If we have the Goddess' genes, we still have the *evil gene,* don't we? Well, the Goddess is All-That-Is, but it is my understanding from researching this, that she didn't put the evil gene in humankind. It's not that we didn't have *any* of it, but it was in no way dominant and not a factor in the evolving species.

Now, the way things became, both good and evil dwell inside all of us, so if we are pointing fingers at someone we think is evil, we are actually pointing fingers at ourselves too. This means the evil that you see in the world is also inside yourself or you wouldn't be able to see it.

The soul is beautiful and She prefers beauty before ugliness and good before evil as a general rule because the Multiverse supports beauty, compassion, knowledge (light), and love (ultimate understanding). Therefore, when a soul becomes more evolved, she doesn't need to express those evil and ugly sides of herself, even if some of it still dwells inside of her. Instead, she looks at it from outside in, sees it for what it is, acknowledges it, and it stops being an issue. This is what many of us did during the nano-second.

In order to become multidimensional, we need to consider these issues and take them on as true philosophers so that we can understand who we are—love and beauty. If that is who we are, *what* are we then? In our pure state, we are Creators, and we can create anything and everything! We have endless potentials, just like the Goddess has endless potentials as well. Unbelievably—we humans also have the Fire of the Goddess. We are truly Divine and have the potential to become Creators in the KHAA—she made us her equals! How sad it is to see that most of us are either abusing this right or have no intention to use it at all. Instead, we are giving this power away to star beings that don't possess it in the first place, but do now, as long as they can steal it from us and suck it out from us every minute of the day. Instead of being the extremely powerful entities we are, we become lethargic, lazy couch-sitters who have stopped caring and stopped being curious. Such a waste. If people only knew what they were missing. Many of them still have the chance to wake up, but it looks like only a small fraction of mankind can be saved.

After having come to this realization, we understand that everything we can perceive, and more, is inside all of us, and what we don't support and what doesn't support our growth has to go, or it will sit there as a big obstacle for our future development. This is the time when we need our ill feelings to go, see things for what they are, and let the last pieces of our timelines merge with our present selves. Imagine it as if you are standing in the middle of a circle with all these energy tentacles reaching out from your body in all different directions. Each tentacle is a timeline, or a fragment of a timeline, which you still haven't taken full responsibility for. Therefore, close your eyes, imagine these energy tentacles, and pull them into yourself, one by one, until there are no more. If you feel any kind of discomfort, don't be concerned. Just look at what it is that is bothering you, smile at it, give it love, and let it go. This will pull your full personality into the present, unless you did not work at all on yourself during the nano-second and all of your timelines are still wounded and not yet healed. This is highly unlikely, however, or you wouldn't read this book now. If you still are uncertain whether you completed the task or not, just continue reading this chapter. If it still appeals to you as we move on here, there shouldn't be any reason to be concerned.

I have mentioned this so many times before, but it's so very important, and now it's high time to take what I suggested into practice. I am talking about forgiveness. Are there still people in your present or in your past toward whom you feel anger, disappointment, or even hate and feelings of revenge? If so, I must stress very strongly that you need to handle these situations, or you'll be stuck where you are right now and won't be able to go any further. The remedy to all these emotions—mild or severe—is so simple that anyone, hypothetically, can apply it. The only reason why it would fail is if you refuse to realize that all these feelings will hold you back, and the purpose with this is not to heal the other person who wronged you, but to heal yourself from the influence of that other person. If you still have attention on them, it means there is an emotional energy connection that pulls your own energy and life force out to that person or persons, and you let it happen. The first thing to do is to forgive these people, one by one, and then forgive yourself for your part in what happened, and then you let it all go. When you do, and you mean it, you should feel a great relief or a minor relief if the situation was never too serious, but serious enough to hold you back. Now you have cut off the chain that kept you connected to these people, and on the other side of the chain, they have to do the same thing, or they will not evolve much further. They, too, need to come to the same realization you did, but that is not your responsibility. You can't make them change—it's up to them. You can only change yourself. The probability that they will let go as well is much bigger after you took the first step, however. Remember that, ultimately, all evil you experience, even if it's from another person, it's just another aspect of yourself, and it only exists because you let it. However, by letting go, you may have saved yourself from having a future heart attack or cancer—this is how serious such unresolved issues might be.

Finally, you ask for forgiveness from anyone you may have hurt in your life. The best way to do this is to address them one by one as far as you can remember, and then end it by asking for forgiveness from those you may have hurt and who you can't recall at the moment, and those whom you were unaware that you actually hurt. This doesn't necessarily mean you have to call them all up, go visit them, or write letters to them. Just like in the previous paragraph, you do it with thoughts, emotions, and intentions, three important subjects. You simply reach out energetically toward these people and ask for forgiveness. You may or may not hear back from them ever again, but it's not that important. What is important is that you take action. Once you've done that, it's finished—you took care of it!

Entity Possession and How to Get Rid of It

The primary and immediate reason to cleanse yourself like this is of course to be able to stay grounded in the present in order to practice multidimensional exercises. If you have ties here and ties there, attachments here and attachments there, you won't be able to focus in the sense that you need to. However, as I've hinted, there is a secondary reason as well, which is of no less importance. It is that of managing psychic attacks. I mentioned in the WPP that in a Pleiadian channeled session with an audience of 15 people (of evolved people), 11 of them had *attachments,* meaning spirits of some kind attached to them, according to the Pleiadians. Some of them had more than one. In other words, this is extremely common. Not all of these spirits are malevolent, but some of them are. Those who are not may be deceased relatives, generational spirits that go from family member to family member from generation to generation, or they can be attachments the person has had for hundreds of years, following the host even into the astral. Others are just lost spirits who don't realize they are dead and attach to anyone who does not have enough boundaries. Even if the entities are not evil, all of them, without exception, pull from your energy like vampires and can make you exhausted and lethargic for no obvious reason. Then there are more vicious attachments, such as *hitchhikers,* who are too lazy to take bodies of their own and instead want to run yours. Others (and this is much more uncommon) could be a member of the AIF, who have decided to use your body for whatever purpose. This is quite unlikely, unless you are of a Global Elite bloodline in a relatively powerful position.

The first thing to do is not to run to an exorcist if you suspect you have attachments. Instead, you learn to set boundaries, and you started already by taking responsibility for your human connections (above). The next thing is to learn how to ground yourself—something of uttermost importance!

Imagine a powerful pillar of light coming from the cosmos, hitting your Crown Chakra (the top of your head), and go right through your body and deep down underneath the Earth. At the end of this pillar of light, imagine yourself creating a big anchor, also made of light, and anchor yourself there, deep under the ground. Then follow the light pillar backward (but always with the anchor well hooked into the Earth) until it reaches your feet. Then let the light form an egg-shaped halo around your body from your feet to the top of your head and close it there. Make this light bright and golden. Then let your spirit go over the egg-shaped golden orb all around you to make sure there are no holes in it anywhere. If there is, seal them. If part of the orb is too close to the body (5-6 inches away from the body is the best), let your *spirit hands* push it out until it is in the right position all the way around. Then put a cloak around you, if you want to be invisible to the spirit world. If not, skip this last step (it's mostly for people who are *out there*, like I am). You are now shielded and have set up your boundaries. Beings who come from outside and see your shield will not even attempt to break through it. Also, they can see you are anchored, so there is no way in, and if they had malevolent intentions, they will leave. Imagine this pillar of light, the anchor, and the egg-shaped golden orb around you a few times a day to make sure you keep yourself protected. After a while, you only need to give it a quick thought, like *pillar,* and the whole image appears in your mind and you're protected.[48] There are of course other ways you can protect yourself, and whatever works for you is good. This particular shield I just mentioned happens to work well for me. In my field of work, entities always try to enter and disturb and destroy, but after applying the above, it made a lot of difference

Symbols and their Meanings

Volumes could have been written about the following subjects—and it has! Not all of them are in public domain, however, but hidden within the vaults of secret society libraries. In this book, I'm just going to touch the very surface of it, and to be honest, I need to study it more myself before I walk out on thin ice and try to teach too much about it.

Briefly, symbols are a part of sacred geometry (they are basically the same thing) and one of the building stones of the universe—you will find them everywhere if you have consciousness enough to be awake to see them. The Global Elite and the AIF are using them all the time as logos to represent their organizations and businesses, and they use them in rituals and in their secret language between each other in order to communicate above our heads. Symbols mean something because there is significance and energy put into them. When the universe was created, sacred geometry was a major building stone. The meaning of most of the symbols being used to build

---

[48] I learned this way of shielding myself from the Pleiadians, but not from the same session where they mentioned the attachments, which is an older session. The session where they taught us how to shield ourselves is from February 2013.

the universe have been forgotten by most beings in the cosmos, except the most skilled and advanced Creator Gods. Other symbols, I can imagine, have been interpreted to the best ability of such people as the Global Elite, philosophers, and others, while some have been invented later and new significance was put into them. Even those, however, can be ancient and the meaning behind them quite powerful. Many of them are used against us without our knowledge in an effort to further manipulate us—in fact, symbols are a major ingredient in the manipulation.

Symbols have many layers. Depending on your level of consciousness, a certain symbol can have different meanings. A lot of sacred geometry is also built into our RNA and DNA, and some say that the reason we have been able to develop different languages is because these languages are already embedded in our DNA, and we just needed to remember. In the ancient past, all mankind spoke the same language—the language of the gods, an older language that later turned into Sumerian. Then, with the symbolic *Tower of Babel* story, mankind was spread all over the globe and was made to forget the language of the old gods. Scientists in general are telling us that humans come from different tribes and, therefore, brought the language with them when they met with other tribes, and the languages became mixed, yet related to each other, until we got what we have today. Even now, the languages are changing. This version of history is partly correct, except that the scientists have no clue how it all began. When humans were spread out all over the planet and could no longer speak the language of the gods, they started using what was already in their DNA and built their own language. However, none of the words and terms they created were random and coincidental. For certain, it seemed as if it was random or coincidental to the tribes who created them, but the words, which are all symbols as well because they have meanings, came from people's subconscious minds and are multidimensional. This doesn't mean that beings elsewhere in the universe speak our languages (they don't have our DNA), but within our own soul group, all languages are connected. This is why some people supposedly can speak 30 languages fluently—once they have seen the structure and the symbolic meaning of languages, it becomes almost second nature to learn new languages, which are only variants of a previous one they learned. This is also why linguists can take an English word and compare it to a word back in time, even before old Sumer. Words are related.

Now, take a look at letters. They are all symbols, aren't they? Each letter has a meaning, and if we put letters together, they mean something that is common to a whole population of people because it's agreed upon. However, the letters always have to be put in a certain order to express significance. Then, if we have a symbol that looks like this: "?," we know it symbolizes a question, something unknown to the person who wrote the symbol. In daily life, we don't think about this—we take words for granted. Hypothetically, a group of people can take words and give them a different meaning and then speak them with each other. To common people, these words either don't mean anything to them anymore, or they mean something else than what is agreed upon. If you are a member of a Global Elite society, using tricks such as this is not as far-fetched as it may sound. The only thing they need to do is to make sure that the public doesn't know what the altered meaning of certain words mean. As an example, the word *nuclear*, when used in the mainstream media usually makes us think about nuclear bombs, nuclear fallout, nuclear science, or nuclear power stations, such as those that blew up in Japan just recently. However, for the Global Elite, the same word has another meaning as well, which is not commonly known to the public and can't be found in any dictionary in any corner of the world.

To them the word *nuclear* can also mean *UFO* or *aliens* [49]. Therefore, when a Global Elitist picks up the newspaper one morning and reads something about nuclear, he or she needs to interpret it by reading it in context. Does it mean nuclear power or UFOs? Things like this are done behind the scenes all the time.

The reason I am bringing up symbols now is because they are a physical manifestation of the *Language of Light* which we are going to talk more about in the next section. It shows the reader how things are connected.

The Language of Light

Eventually, in the next section, there are two exercises we are going to do—something I started practicing after being inspired by reading the Seth Material. Seth was talking about one of them in his books but didn't put together a true exercise around it, so I decided to do that, building it on his concepts. The second exercise is built around my own experiences, and I have found it to be quite interesting. The following is what inspired me to do the first practice:

> The feeling of joy changes the objects themselves, in that the perceiver sees them in a far brighter light. He creates the objects far more vividly and with greater clarity. In feedback fashion, the environment then seems to reinforce his joy. What he sees, however, is still physical, the objects of the material world. Pretend now that he begins to daydream and falls into a reverie[50]. Into his inner mind come pictures or symbols of material objects, people or events, from perhaps the past as well as present

---

[49] Source: Miscellaneous Pleiadian lectures, around 2010-2013.
[50] A mild hypnotic state, but with the person still aware of his/her environment.

and future imaginings, the joy now being expressed with greater freedom mentally, but with symbols.[51]

I mentioned earlier that we have to recreate the universe every single moment of our existence, or it would cease to exist. This may be unreal to some people, but let's see if we can make it better understood. Ultimately, of course, we *are* the creators of the universe because we are of the same essence as the Mother Goddess, but if you think that is too abstract, let's ponder the following. Have you ever thought about that every single solid object is a symbol? Indeed it is because it symbolizes something. Take a chair, for example, and you can see that it symbolizes something to sit in. A glass symbolizes something that the body can drink from, and a car symbolizes something a body/mind/soul complex can go from point A to point B with.

However, the most obvious symbol is still your body because it feels like it's more a part of you than the table over there. A certain symbol in 3-D, such as we touched on previously, means something different on a higher level of consciousness. A body is no longer as solid an object in the astral as it is here on Earth and, instead, symbolizes something with which you can travel the astral plane with. In higher dimensions, your body will be exchanged for one that is even less solid and so on, until a body becomes obsolete. At that point, a body-symbol loses its significance.

It is the same with all symbols—they have different meanings at different levels of consciousness, until at one point they are no longer needed, and you will create freely without using any symbols at all. This state of being is not comprehensible for us as 3-D entities.

When this concept is described to the readers, the majority probably perceive the symbols we are talking about—even those

---
[51] Seth Speaks, p.146, op. cit.

on non-physical levels—as something outside of themselves, while a small majority perceive them as being something that is being visualized within. If you are in the majority here, no problem—it's natural at this point. However, in these exercises, we are going to confront symbols that are obviously inside ourselves, and after practicing them for some time, hopefully, the reader will start looking at reality differently and in a more multidimensional way. Keep in mind, though, that there is no right or wrong in this, and we are not becoming multidimensional because the 3-D is wrong and should be hammered out of existence. We are doing it because we should have moved on a long time ago, and even if it's been very educating to be here in spite of (and some say because of) the slave society we've been living in, you who are reading this are probably overdue to move on, whether to continue your journey somewhere else or in a better probability of Earth.

Humanity, as a whole, has been manipulated not to understand the significance of symbols—we don't even understand what we perceive every day, and use every day, are symbols so we can communicate with each other and experience the physical world. We also lack in understanding that we are the ones who are creating the environment we live in, and I am talking about our physical reality now. We build ourselves a house, which symbolizes that *this is my space,* and we often let others build something for us because we think we are not able to do it ourselves (or we have a lack of time). Then we have people in factories creating beds that we later buy from them, and after we've done that, it becomes our symbol that signifies a space where we spend our time sleeping and dreaming and to have sex. All this we take for granted, but we never think about what it is we are doing and why. I don't mean that we should walk around all day long thinking, "Look, that house symbolizes John Jones' and his family space!," or "Over there is a car. It symbolizes Mary Smith's space when she is moving from A to B, and I am not allowed to intrude in that space," but it's always good to understand the basics or things because when we do, it's easier for us to create from a more mindful perspective.

The symbols the universe is built of travel with light. Different symbols travel within different electromagnetic spectra, and when light hits the body, there is a potential to learn, as light carries information in the form of geometric symbols. These symbols can most easily be termed *The Language of Light*. I wrote about this as well in "The First Level of Learning"[52].

Artists love to work with form, regardless of if it's a fine art artist, a sculptress, a musician, or a writer. Those who are not as savvy in the arts don't always realize what the artist is doing and what the thought process is when composing a piece of art, but they know there is something special with it—particularly if it's good art—and they admire it because they feel something inside. However, form, whether it's a physical form (the fine artist and the sculptress for example) or an abstract form (the writer and the composer/musician), is always based on symbols in one way or another. The writer is as successful as he or she is able to transfer his or her communication and feelings into a symbolic language that can communicate to the targeted public. A piece of art doesn't have to be perfect—it just has to communicate. Therefore, many say that our future lies in the hands of artists, and I agree. The artist is the visionary, communicating the vision to the audience, and if he or she is successful, others will think that the vision is agreeable. A world without artists is a world without visionaries, is a world without visions, and is a society without a future. Therefore, a great responsibility is put on the artist to communicate well and have a vision that will

---

[52] http://wespenre.com/great-initiation.htm, Section 3.

bring mankind forward, not backward. Words are symbols, and as such, they are powerful. Skilled linguists can manipulate people in any direction they want by using words as symbols. This is the reason why humanity is so split in their quest for the truth—there are too many con artists who are leading humanity astray. There are pros and cons with the Internet.

One thing the nano-second did was to implant symbols on gamma rays into the human body. As light equals symbols, we have certain symbols that are more important to the human evolution in its current state than others. Such symbols are, for example, the pyramid, the spiral, the parallel lines, the cube, the circle, and the Merkaba vehicle. The last one is what has to do with nano-travel. In the WPP, I wrote about many subjects, and some of them I mentioned briefly in order to *remind* the mind of its existence, but without overwhelming the mind by going too deep with it. It's only later, such as in this book that we need to go into detail on certain subjects that were more like afterthoughts at the time.

We hear about the Merkaba often when it comes to expanding consciousness, and much of it is disinformation. This is obvious because the AIF does not want us to be able to nano-travel and figure out who they are. Be aware of this, and be aware that although the Internet is excellent to use in order to wake people up, it's also a brilliant surveillance system. If you were the AIF, you would want to know where humanity is in their evolvement in consciousness—you would want to know how we think. What would be a better way to find out than to let our minds communicate freely within a global network that is highly monitored? People ask why truth-seekers are not taken out at a greater extent, but that's not the purpose. They don't fear individuals like me or others in the sense that they need to kill everyone who figures something out. No, they want to know how far we've come, so they can bombard us with counter-information. The Internet is an excellent tool to do so.

This is what the Pleiadians have to say about the Merkaba in the sense of nano-traveling:

> The five-sided figure represents the figure of the human being in its most unlimited state—the free human. Some of you know it as a symbolic structure called a Merkabah vehicle. It is the human design without any limitations. It is the human being able to fly, which is something that a large majority of you do not think you can do. This implant comes when you truly commit yourself to what was formerly not possible.
>
> [...]
>
> Those of your who are willing to believe that there are truly no limitations will be able to take the Merkabah structure and move yourself off the planet with it while you are still living on the planet. The desire to do this must exist in you if you are to be implanted with the Merkabah. Already some of you have attempted to travel with it, and you know how it can be used in your being. When you truly call the Merkabah to yourself, and you are willing to get the feeling of what that truly means—to be unlimited consciousness that travels with your body, without your body leaving the planet—that is when implant will occur. The Merkabah is not the highest implanting, as there are no highest or lowest implantings. Implanting comes when it will best suit your personal development. Once you have become implanted, there will be an unending process of new forms coming into your being.[53]

The Pleiadians go on with explaining that we do not consciously choose which symbols we want to download—it is determined by our everyday choices in life. What we mainly have our focus on will determine which symbols we will have

---

[53] ©1992, Barbara Marciniak, "Bringers of the Dawn", pp.182-83, op. cit.

access to. In other words, the areas we focus on will attract the symbols we need at the moment to go further in our development.

We all agree that certain symbols mean certain things—for example, an airplane is a symbol for traveling through air. However, although we may agree so far, we do not always agree on the airplane's safety. Some people think it's a perfect vehicle to travel relatively quickly from one place to another, while someone else thinks it's a deadly time bomb that can crash and kill you any time. Therefore, when two people look at the same object, what they think about it may be different. The other person may or may not know the other person's thoughts toward the object. Therefore, one particular symbol is charged with many different emotions, which makes the object powerful and can accomplish anything a mind is capable of imagining. Being aware of this, we can measure our own increase in awareness and consciousness by monitoring our thoughts and perceptions regarding a certain object.

Before you are born into a physical body, you carry only your internal images—your inner symbols. These are the symbols you have carried with you through your lifetimes and have been stored inside. These symbols can be accessed anytime through thoughts and emotions, which will activate the symbols/images and bring forth the memory. However, at the time of birth, when you open your eyes for the first time in the new body, you transfer the inner images to the outer world and synchronize them with each other in a way that is appropriate for a 3-D reality. The rest of the symbols will not be activated and remain dormant. A baby who is born into the same nationality twice in a row will learn the language much faster than a baby who isn't. As a baby, you often think in the language that you used in your past life until you learn the new language. This has everything to do with symbols.[54]

Sound is also a symbol, and thought is sound, although we humans can't hear it on our level of reality. However, in other dimensions, thoughts are audial, and can be heard by that form of consciousness. Thoughts, as well as spoken words, are not private, and in the larger scheme of things there is no privacy. This may sound scary to many people, but if you see this as a norm, your thoughts are not very different from other people's thoughts. No one will point fingers and say, "Listen to that individual! Can you believe what he's thinking about?" On that level of existence, manipulation and control over others is not a factor. This goes way beyond what we think of as telepathy. In a telepathic communication that is intended to be consciously shared between individuals, you will be able to control the access to your thoughts and only send off what you intend to communicate—not much different from using spoken words, except for the difference in speed and comprehension.

Using the Language of Light to Travel Within

As we now have a better understanding of what symbols, images, and the Language of Light are, there are some exercises related to this. I understand that we all lead busy lives, and it seems like we don't have time to do all these exercises, but there are ways. It's not that we need to do them all every day, but just pick the first one and practice it until you feel comfortable with it and then go to the next. Although everybody is different and there is no fixed order in which these exercises need to be done, for the majority of people, I have presented them in the correct order for optimal advancement. It's up to you how often you want to practice,

---

[54] Seth Speaks, p.151ff.

but of course, the more time you can spend on it, the faster the whole process goes. You don't need to master each exercise before you go to the next, but the point is that you need to experience firsthand how your own multidimensional body works. If some exercises don't seem to work for you, try the next one, but give each of them a fair chance because, optimally, they will all work and that's when you get the best results.

The first exercise requires direct sunlight. If the season is not right and sunlight is very scarce, you can wait until you get an opportunity, and in the meantime skip to the next. Just be sure to go back to this one because it's a very important one since you will be able to see some of these symbols for yourself.

For the optimal results, go outside for this exercise, but it also works if you're inside and can see the Sun directly and not just the light that's coming from her. Therefore, locate the Sun in the sky, say hello to her (she will literally know who you are—she is a sentient being) and thank her for bringing all her wonderful light and warmth to Earth in order to make life possible. Then, close your eyes and turn your head directly toward the Sun for approximately 10-15 seconds. Then turn your head in a slightly different direction to avoid direct sunlight in your eyes (which will happen even if your eyes are closed) and with your Third Eye [55], look at the inside of your eyelids (your head should still be turned toward the Sun, so that the sunlight hits the left or right side of your face. You need the brightness of the sunlight). You should now be able to see symbols floating around from side to side, while some of them may disappear outward and others are standing still. These symbols can have all different kinds of shapes and form, and it's of no significance what shapes and forms you are seeing as long as you see something. Observe them as they appear and establish what they look

---

[55] The *"Third Eye"* is your pineal gland, which is located in your brain, but you will perceive the Third Eye as being located inside your forehead.

like. Are there pyramids, lines, squares, rectangles, circles, black holes, or something else?

Sometimes you can continue observing symbols for quite a while before they eventually fade away. To avoid too much direct sunlight, doing this exercise once or twice in a row should be enough. If you want to do more, take a break and do something else for an hour or so and go back and do it again. After that, it's probably enough for one day.

This exercise is observation only. You may notice how some of the symbols interact, while others seem to move away from each other. Work on seeing patterns, if any, and try to establish which symbol or symbols are the most dominant. When you're quite sure which one, or which ones they are, research the Internet for Sacred Geometry sites and learn what your specific symbols signify. See how they can relate to you. The most dominant ones are probably the symbols that you downloaded to a large degree during the nano-second—*your symbol or symbols of choice*—albeit indirectly so—as we talked about earlier in this chapter. This is very interesting because these symbols can teach you a lot about yourself that you may not have been aware of, and if you are one of those who believe you are here on a mission but haven't figured out what that mission is, the symbols might tell you.

The next exercise also works best in direct sunlight. It is done in exactly the same manner as the previous one—except that this time you want to interact with the symbols. Here you may play around with them as you please and see what happens. Whatever happens is okay—there are no set rules for this. The highlight of this exercise—at least from my experience—is to locate black dots or circles in general, which will work as stargates or black holes into other realities. When you locate one of these amongst all the rest of the symbols, go inside of it with your Third Eye and follow it to wherever it will lead you. My own experience (which may or may not be the same as yours) is that this *black hole* often leads to a tunnel and a *white hole* on the other side. Depending on *which* dot or hole I choose to follow determines which reality I will land in. It has happened to me that I enter another part of the universe, and sometimes another planet that I can explore in *spirit form*. Other times it leads me to places that are beyond my comprehension at this time, but I do my best to explore them anyway. You can return back through the same hole whenever you want—all you need to do is to think yourself back into your head, if that's how you want to visualize it. You never have to worry about *being stuck* on the other side of the hole—that would be impossible. If you have a bad experience, entering a place you don't like, you can always go back and try another dot.

This exercise is extremely useful because what you are basically doing is that you nano-travel. Everything you experience *inside* is actually more real than what you experience *outside* because everything that's apparently outside of yourself is first created on the inside, but when it reaches the outside, it is always distorted to a larger or lesser degree. Hence, strange as it sounds, what you experience on the inside is a more undistorted reality. Hypothetically, with some practice, you can see these black holes even without sunlight—even when sitting in your living room. If these experiences I've just described that happen to me on occasion are not happening to you, it's of no consequence. The purpose of the exercise is to move within any objects that you see—regardless of the shape of the objects. What happens on top of that is beyond the scope of this exercise . However, the more often you repeat the exercise, the bigger are the chances to see the black holes and travel through them.

A more direct way to nano-travel is to just think yourself somewhere, and a part of your consciousness will go there immediately, taking the most direct route possible. Every time you think yourself somewhere, a part of yourself is actually going there. However, I believe that most readers think of nano-travel as being present at the other location in a similar manner as you are present here, and there are humans today, here on Earth, who are able to do this already. Many of them are working within the military. Remote Viewing also comes to mind, and that, too, is a form of nano-travel. The remote viewer travels in spirit to a place decided beforehand, be it on Earth, the moon, or on some other planet inside or outside the solar system. Because of the Quarantine, no one is supposed to be able to leave or enter the solar system without permission, but it still happens all the time, as the Quarantine, similar to the Grid, has holes in it. Therefore, not everything that enters and leaves will be caught. Of course, if you're a remote viewer working for the military, you know how to pass both the Grid and the Quarantine, whether you have permission or not.

Anyway, there are more sophisticated ways to nano-travel than remote viewing. Many star beings and star races use nano-travel to go instantly from place to place in time and space, but most of them use technology to be able to do so, unless they are non-physicals. In the case of non-physicals, nano-traveling is a way of living and no technology is necessary.

Humans, however, who still possess bodies in 3-D, will use their bodies to nano-travel, and they will do so by going within. By splitting our Divine Fire, we can *ride the Avatar* anywhere in the universe. When you do it the way you were designed to, you will experience it being just as real as it is sitting there reading this book—you will feel like you are there in spirit and will be able to experience the time and space you are traveling to just like a non-physical would. Just like you do on the astral plane between lives, you can then use an Avatar to manifest in any shape or form you want, and you can choose whether you want to be seen by other beings or not. Your personality is basically choosing a probable timeline to travel the stars and can therefore create whatever you want. You can even possess an alien body if you so wish, but you need to stay within the boundaries of what Universal Laws teach you. At the same time, you are still on Earth, doing whatever you're doing. I get the impression that it is like a light switch, where you can shift your attention between the two locations. Sounds like science-fiction, doesn't it? Still, science fiction is just telling us what is already possible because if someone can think it up, it *is* possible. Anyway, how does this work in more scientific terms? How can you be in two or more places simultaneously and experience them all as if you were there with your whole presence?

It's not as strange as it sounds, if we think about it. The reason why we may consider it impossible or mind-boggling is because we are thinking in linear time. When we're multidimensional, there is no such thing as linear time, unless we decide there is. Even if we decide that there is linear time for some practical reason, we can change our minds anytime and experience time differently. Therefore, if all time is simultaneous and non-linear, we can be in different locations at the same time and switch between them as we wish. Consequently, in 3-D thinking, some people may ponder whether time is *standing still* in the other location while they are experiencing life in one location. Again, we need to learn how *not* to think in terms of linear time. When we think multidimensional, it's easy to understand the concept of nano-travel.

However (and of course there is a caveat), at this point we are still working on becoming our true multidimensional selves again, and we need to take things in the order they come. I just want to have the reader visualize what nano-travel means, and this is what we all are going to be capable of in the future. It makes remote viewing look like child's play, doesn't it? Therefore, it will take some increase in consciousness and awareness before we can take the step fully and use our Divine Fire to travel across the universe and perhaps beyond. We need to take baby steps to get there, but rather than telling somebody that "oh well, all we need to do is to disagree with the AIF and their control system and we'll snap out of the trap," which is true but seems rather unobtainable, we need to do it in a way that is more in people's reality. This is where books such as this one are valuable because they explain the process from the beginning and can hopefully make the reader visualize the goal. Then, by doing the exercises, we learn how to go within and trust that our bodies take us where we want to go. Instead of pumping it full of beer and greasy hamburgers, we take care of it and use it for what it's meant to be used for. No one will be happier than the body itself—literally so.

Disclosure of the ET Phenomenon from a Multidimensional Perspective

> [The universe says]: Here are all the situations representing the beliefs you have.. These situations are given to you by the universe automatically to show you exactly what your beliefs are. They are not to prove you are stuck in anything, or to prove you have failed in anything, but to show you beyond the shadow of doubt that, 'Look, this is the reality you get because that's what you believe to be true. If you don't prefer it, then change the beliefs.'" – *Bashar, channeled through Darryl Anka.*

Many channeled entities and others say that the Multiverse is a friendly place, and that we don't have to fear. I agree that we should not fear, unless it's valid fear that can save your life or save you from something unpleasant. However, I'm more in line with Bashar in the quote above, that we create our own reality with our belief systems. The entities who say that the Multiverse is a friendly place—amen—simplify things, and a person may be shocked to see that it's not as friendly as they thought. I would bluntly change the statement and instead be honest about it. *The Multiverse is as friendly as you make it!* Yes, it is as simple as that. The reader probably understands by now that we do create our own reality and our own belief systems, and optimally, they are now, as we're getting more evolved, more fluid and changeable.

I'm not trying to sound pessimistic or negative, but it's imminent that we create the belief system we want to live by because the one we create *is* the one we have to face. Therefore, instead of us complaining about our situation, we just start with changing our belief systems instead, and importantly—don't get tricked into a belief system you don't like or fool yourself into one because of other people around you. You are the one who is evolving you, and Mary and David are evolving themselves and have the right to their own belief systems. However, you don't have to share theirs if they don't benefit you.

I am repeating this occasionally from different angles and with different allegories because it is so important. There are so many people who are evolving right now, studying spiritual and conspiratorial material, meditating and working on themselves, but no one has asked the questions: why are we doing this? Why do we have to evolve? Can't we just stay as 3-D beings forever? What are the benefits from evolving?

Well, you may say, one obvious reason is the trap we're sitting in. We are slaves, and who wants to be a slave? Others may say, to increase our consciousness and awareness, while a third category perhaps states that it's a normal part of the evolution—species do evolve! Yes, this is all true, and sitting in a trap is reason enough, but there are 3-D realities where the species are not trapped. Why do they evolve? The real answer is twofold: First, we need to be part of and aware of other cosmic beings and be able to communicate and interact with them, and second, we are here to explore the Multiverse, and if we don't evolve, we will stagnate.

For some time in the development of a species, we are meant to be left alone and do our thing and evolve to become something unique for our specific species without influence from others, but eventually, evolution means that it's time to interact with the cosmos—the time of isolation is over. This does *not* mean that saviors should come down from the skies and tell us how to evolve and how to make contact. The willingness to make contact must come from us humans! This is very important. We have now long since passed the point when we should have reached out in the cosmos as Homo sapiens, but due to the prison we're sitting in, unbeknownst to most people, we haven't done what we were meant to do. Instead, star races are bypassing us and trying to make contact with us, which is the wrong sequence. Although I just said that we should be ready by now, we're not. Our governments have made treaties with the wrong aliens and have made our situation here unbearable. That only shows that mankind was not ready for contact then, and we're not ready now. Most people are not even remotely close to becoming multidimensional, something that is required for ET contact.

Genetic engineering and manipulation of a species is one thing, and it can be done with good or bad intentions. Either way, we are designed to evolve—it is part of a universal code and common to all species in the cosmos.

Our situation is unique because of the hierarchal control system. We are like children who never were allowed to develop, so we are mentally and physically handicapped, compared to what we ought to be by now. Tell mentally or physically handicapped children to start troubleshooting computer networks or something of the sort. They would be overwhelmed. This is what now is required by mankind when UFOlogists and others scream for Disclosure. Some of us would love disclosure—open the files and confront all the crimes and treaties and what has been done to us in the name of National Security. However, it's a very touchy subject. I think the world should know what is going on behind the scenes—in that sense I'm for disclosure—even when it comes to the ET phenomenon. However, we need to think more than twice here. What would happen if the X-files were opened and the truth came out over a short period of time? People would be in total shock, and many couldn't handle it. Their belief systems would be shattered—many would go insane—others would be in denial—many would cry for justice and storm the government buildings and hang their representatives, one by one, whether they are guilty or not. We would see all kinds of chaos, and many, many people would die in the tumult that would follow. Of course, we can choose to go through that and *have it over and done with*. We should seriously consider that so we at least come out of it with the truth intact. However, would we?

Here is the dilemma. If the pressure on the governments would be so high that they believe they need to give us something (and we may come to that point soon), they will open certain files, but definitely not all of them. They would hang out some people and throw them to the wolves to make us satisfied, while the real criminals would get away with it. What the Disclosure supporters forget and sometimes are ignorant about is that we are controlled by the same ETs we want to expose. Do we think that they would give us more than what is absolutely necessary? When they give us some carrots, they also make sure they can gain from it as well.

Dr. Steven Greer just recently released a film, *The Sirius Project*, in which he demands a full disclosure with the emphasis on getting free energy. However, he presents all aliens as being friendly, which is a deadly deception. That makes the bad ones able to continue their work behind the scenes.

It's shocking enough to let the world population know that the ETs are here, but how do you explain to people that they are interdimensional and multidimensional? It's not even real to people—they have no idea what that is.

This is why I think it's too early. Mankind is far from prepared, and even if humanity would take the bull by the horn and accept the fact that there are beings from other planets here, there is plenty of room for deception. It could very well be an introduction to the Machine Kingdom, which I covered in detail in the *WPP*. Dr. Greer is constantly mentioning technology and is promoting the newest android phones etc.—making them mandatory in order for interested people to be able to see some features that the Greer team is presenting. Not a good sign.

Instead, we need to build our multidimensional abilities. The ET contact will come later, and most probably peer-to-peer —on a personal basis, or with a smaller group. The rest of mankind may fall for deceptive Disclosure programs, and there is not much we can do about it. The information is out there for everybody to learn the truth, and if you can do it, they should be able to as well, but they're not doing it. Can you force them? No. Again, it's a personal responsibility to find one's own truth.

It's in the light of what we've just discussed here that it's even more imperative that we stick to what we know is the *soulution* and continue doing our thing. With everything we know, there is no other way, and best of all—it's the way it's supposed to be.

The Feminine Side of Men

In the WPP, "The Second Level of Learning," I frequently referred to the Divine Feminine and that people need to balance themselves—the female needs to find her male side and the male his female side. This doesn't mean that women suddenly should express excessive masculine manners and vice versa or that one sex should dominate the other—it has nothing to do with that. First, everything in this reality needs to be as much in balance as possible to work the best. We were born with a certain sex, so that's the sex we have chosen for this lifetime, but it's been proven that the female has more Fire than the male—or at least has easier access to it. On one level, balance is needed in order to understand the other sex better, but men need to develop the feminine side of themselves, which is always there, regardless of how macho a man considers himself to be.

The first religion on Earth was the religion of the Divine Feminine, and that religion came directly from the stars and the original Creator Gods, the so-called Builders and their Helpers, the Founders. These *gods* were actually not masculine but feminine, and they brought down their religion here and taught their creation, early mankind, their wisdom. They taught the females how they could get access to their inner Fire and use it to heal, control the weather, talk to animals, shapeshift, but most important—the Fire kept mankind connected to the stars—to their origins. Thus, the first shamans were women, and through certain rituals, they could connect directly with the Goddess Universe and the Orion Empire. At that time, males had powers developed too. There were so-called *Men of Fire* as well, although it was harder to develop enough of their female side to be able to do what the female shamans were capable of naturally.

The reason males have a harder time is because we live in a feminine universe, where the feminine energy is the driving force. The male energy came later. How that happened is too much to go into here and could be a subject for a whole new book, but at this point, let's just say that the male energy eventually was required so that a species would not succumb. Before the male was present in the universe, the female was hermaphroditic, and her offspring was always female and a clone of the mother. This was billions of years ago. With time, it was noticed that to have more variety—a second sex was needed, and males were created. This created more randomness in the DNA, and the offspring were no longer a 100% copy of the mother. However, to be a male also meant that his DNA was altered from the original universal DNA, which contributed to him having more difficulty bringing about the female Fire strong enough to connect to the 96% Spirit Universe.

Unless a man is so fixated with being a man that he refuses to have anything feminine inside of him, most men know that they have a feminine side. However, in a male-dominated society, we men have learned to suppress this side of ourselves to a larger or lesser degree. Of course, the AIF, which is a male-dominated regime, wants the women with the strongest Fire for the AIF to take advantage of. These women become Priestesses in their secret societies. However, in society in general, women are usually degraded to a second-class citizen, whether it is overt, such as in the Middle East and Islamic countries, or covert, as it is here in the West.

Once we men, on an individual basis (and later on a more collective basis), have been willing to let our female side come out from her hiding place deep within, we will not only feel better and more balanced in general, but we will also notice that we have more psychic power

A Comparison between Physical and Non-Physical Beings

A big part of regaining our multidimensionality and reconnecting with the Spirit Universe is to practice Sacred Sex. Here on Earth everything is about sex—without sex, nothing would reproduce. This is the brilliance of the 3-D existence—no cloning needed and no constant genetic engineering or manipulation. Therefore, sex equals reproduction, but for us humans, it means more than that because we were given the Fire of the Goddess, which means that we can connect with Her universe via the female orgasm. However, before we go into that in some more details, let us first learn the difference between how it is to be a non-physical entity and a physical, third-dimensional being, such as ourselves. This helps us understand ourselves better as sexual beings. I'm going to take Seth as an example because he is giving us such wonderful comparisons, and I am going to paraphrase some of it. Some of it will be my personal thoughts as well.[56]

The body is only one of the differences between physical and non-physical entities. These entities have different experiences that are not shared between them. Seth, who once was a 3-D being, explains that as a non-physical he has more opportunities in many aspects, such as that of creativity. He says that his environment is more pleasurable (although he admits that his definition of *pleasurable* has changed since he walked the Earth) and provides opportunities for creative activities. He also says that his environment is at least as vivid, varied, and vital as the physical experience.

Being a non-physical is not a one-dimensional experience—you can travel between dimensions, similar to traveling from one country to another on Earth. Although Seth is not living in

---
[56] See *"Seth Speaks"*, Chapter 2.

a city or on a planet, such as we do, he is not living in empty space either. In fact, he looks at space different than we do—space, for him, is an environment he can use to fill with something. Hence, he uses his creativity to surround himself with an environment he likes. Therefore, his environment is a reality of existence that is created by him and others who are similar to him, and this represents the manifestation of their development.

Non-physicals are often drawn to each other, just like we humans are—like attracts alike. They create structures as we do—therefore, that's what they mean when they say that their dimensions are just as *physical* as ours. However, their structures are not permanent, and they can un-manifest them at-will in a matter of an instant. Similarly, 3-D beings are building structures that are first created in their minds, so in that sense it's no different, except that in our reality everything appears much more solid and takes time to create, and once you have created something, it requires more work to undo it.

The soul is feminine in nature, but of course, no sexual activity as we know it is possible in the non-physical world, so there is no offspring. Non-physicals can manifest as males or females, and they can have *artificial sex,* which remotely can be compared with the characters in a video game having sex. The non-physical can transfer some of her essence into the manifestation and experience some kind of sensation, but it is not nearly as pleasurable as on a 3-D planet. Hence, many of them, who have experienced 3-D realities in the past, where sex is the way to reproduce (in some worlds it's cloning and genetic manipulation), often want to go back after having spent some time as non-physicals, and those who never have experienced sex are curious and also want to take a body, eventually, to see how it is.

Food is another issue. Non-physicals don't need to eat like we do because they don't have to feed a body to survive. This has advantages and disadvantages, according to the non-physicals themselves. It is nice not to think all the time about having to feed a body and instead being able to concentrate on other things, but then again, after a while, they miss the tastes and smell of good food. I can somehow relate to this as an American immigrant. If there is anything I miss at all from my old home country it is the food—I miss the smell and the taste.

In addition, Seth says that non-physicals often manifest themselves in some kind of form to show their uniqueness to others. Most non-physicals change their form occasionally in order to be true to their inner experiences. We here in 3-D do the same, but it's much more subtle. Often, if we are to look ourselves in the mirror every day, we don't look exactly the same every day, and we comment on it. We may stand before the mirror in the morning and say, "I look old today," "Today I look good," "My eyes seem bluer today than they were yesterday," and these observations are real. While we're still talking about form, the non-physicals can create several forms of themselves and travel with them simultaneously to wherever they want to go, but we humans do the same thing. We may be sleeping on the couch, while a part of ourselves leaves the body and appears in a friend's room on the other side of town. We usually don't do this consciously—what we create is another thought form of ourselves that then can appear elsewhere. Therefore, we are not limited to creating one thought form at the time, something we've discussed before and something essential in nano-traveling.

Non-physicals communicate telepathically because they of course don't have vocal chords and don't need any. However, the term *telepathic* still doesn't give justice to the method of communication they are using. When we think about telepathy we often think of thoughts being transferred between individuals instead of spoken words. This form of telepathy is quite primitive, and instead many non-physicals communicate with thermal and electromagnetic images, which can support much more data and meaning in one *sequence* of transmission. The speed of the transmission depends on the present emotions of the transmitter, although they don't have emotions in the same way we humans do, something well worth mentioning because it's very important.

My perception is that Seth is transmitting to his vehicle, Jane Roberts, from the KHAA (or the 96% Spirit Universe) because this is what he has to say about his own emotions and those of his friends:

> We do feel an equivalent of what you call emotions, though these are not the love or hate or anger that you know. Your feelings can best be described as the three-dimensional materializations of far greater psychological events and experiences that are related to the "inner senses".
>
> I will explain these inner senses to you later, at the end of this chapter. Suffice it here to say that we have strong emotional experience, although it differs in a large measure from your own. It is far less limited and far more expansive in that we are also aware and responsive to the emotional "climate" as a whole. We are much freer to feel and experience because we are not so afraid of being swept away by feeling.
>
> Our identities do not feel threatened, for example, by the strong emotions of another. We are able to travel through emotions in a way that is not now natural to you, and to translate them into other facets of creativity than those with which you are familiar. We do not feel the need to conceal emotions, for we know it is basically impossible and undesirable. Within your system they can appear troublesome because you have not yet learned how

to use them. We are only now learning their full potential, and the powers of creativity with which they are connected.[57]

This statement may sound quite comforting and relieving for a human studying metaphysics in-depth because of the usual experiences we have—unfortunately, from our perspective, star beings are quite limited in the range of emotions. Of course, on Earth, we are often contacted by future versions of humans, who are choosing to become more like cyborgs than biological entities in our future, which can explain the lack of emotions, but I've personally heard from more than one independent source that the range of human emotions is quite unique. Star races don't have those emotions because they don't have the Fire of the Goddess in such a direct form as we do. Thus, star beings who contact us may seem more *insensitive* than we are and may express themselves in ways that are more direct, without having any second thoughts about whether the other person may be hurt because of their insensitivity. ETs are *more to the point* and not at all as emotional as we are. This can sometimes create a problem when the human doesn't understand this concept. It doesn't necessarily mean that the star being is rude or insensitive from their perspective, although they sometimes may come across as harsh. I think this is a learning lesson for us, which can be tough, especially if we are overly sensitive humans. I hear comments repeatedly from star beings that humans are unique with their range of emotions and that this is what makes us human in the first place.

When we leave our physical bodies and go to the astral plane between lives, we still keep our emotional body as well as our astral body and other metaphysical versions of it—therefore, we do keep our emotions in the astral and, most probably, if we go into higher dimensions as well. If we retain our emotions

---
[57] Seth Speaks, p.11, op. cit.

(and all indicators point in that direction), we have some adjustments to make because other species and non-physicals out there may not have our range of emotions, which can be a shock for us in the beginning. This, in my opinion, doesn't mean that we should work on getting rid of our wide range of emotions or keep them under strict restraints because then we're not human anymore, but I do suggest for those who believe that they are oversensitive to work on *toughening up,* or you will probably believe that you are *run over* by ETs with much stronger intentions and energies in general. Star beings don't hold back, from what I have come to understand—it's only humans who hold their emotions back. This means that we are indeed very powerful if we want to be, and this is probably the whole reason why we hold back in the first place—we don't want to hurt others—and the fact that we never had the chance to develop on our own created something similar to a traumatized child, making it hard to come to terms with so many feelings.

The AIF, when they arrived here on Earth ½ million years ago and started creating Homo sapiens from what was left of earlier versions of humans after an alien war on our planet, also tried to restrict our emotions and especially eradicate our *love emotions.* All they wanted was obedient workers, and love had nothing to do with that. However, as it were, the love emotions were deeply embedded even in the previous versions of mankind, and were part of our essence, so the AIF didn't manage to eradicate them, and this is the only reason we still can feel love.[58]

However, if we have a tendency to overreact and take things too personal occasionally, we need to work on that, or we'll have problems. The reader may think that this can wait until later because we are not going to meet with aliens anytime soon, but I would say that we shouldn't be so sure about that. In the next chapter, it will be evident that within a few years,

---

[58] Pleiadian Lecture and Workshop, San Francisco, California, May 18-19, 2013.

many humans who never thought they would get in contact with star beings at all suddenly find themselves experiencing just that. Therefore, it's never too early to start working on this. Suffice it to say, it's never a bad idea to work on this because overreactions and oversensitivity always stem from trauma and need to be addressed anyway, with or without star beings involved.

Still, being a disembodied human in the 4% universe may be a challenge because we *are* different from other star beings. Not that other star beings are all the same—far from it because they have personalities just like we do—but no one is like us because we are a special experiment. We were meant to evolve on Earth, and once we are done evolving, we could choose whether we wanted to stay as Guardians of the Living Library or return to the 96% Spirit Universe, from which many of us basically came. Well, we do have a third option as well, which would be to leave Mother Earth and explore and find a home somewhere else in the 4% universe (the visible universe), but then we have to learn how to deal with our emotions while we're out there.

The second option, which involved returning to the 96% universe, the Universe of Spirit, there is no such thing as solid bodies, however, but you can create freely whatever you want, including bodies that are more transparent, and you always have your Avatar. Regarding emotions, it is my understanding that the universe of Spirit is also the Universe of Love in its highest form, and emotions will blend with that.

Non-physicals, of course, don't know the term *death*. They can move into many different environments and dimensions and follow the rules and physical laws applicable to the dimension they are in. However, regardless of where they reside, time as we know it doesn't exist. There is of course nothing like 4 o'clock and 9 o'clock in the reality of non-physicals. They live in a never-ending present moment, and although they can create pasts and futures if they like, they always do so from the reference point of an everlasting present. In that present, all probabilities are explored, all thoughts are evaluated, and all feelings are entertained. Because time is irrelevant for such a being, doing so is not *time consuming*, as we think it would be. This can be very hard to comprehend for the human neurological system. For example, if a non-physical would think about me, she would not only think of me as I am in this present moment, but would perceive my entire past and my entire future instantaneously, just as natural as if you would think of me sitting here typing on my keyboard on an early Wednesday morning. Now, perhaps, the reader may understand why we need to evolve in sequence and not learn all at once—our neurological systems would be fried in no time, and we would be so overwhelmed that total insanity would be the only term we can describe it with. Schizophrenic people experience this to a certain degree but don't come close to how well developed these attributes are in a non-physical being.

In our own, from the above perspective, limited abilities in the 3-D world, our physical reality constantly changes, although we do our best to ignore it. We are working very hard, without being aware of it, to maintain physicality, and it takes a lot of our energy to do it, while the non-physical being has an abundance of energy to play with. It is in our dream state that we humans *get a break* and are able to enjoy the freedom of limitless creation.

Albeit, non-physicals can travel between densities and dimensions, they are not able to experience everything there is within these dimensions. As Seth says, there is much more variety in the non-physical existence than there is in the physical, and there are many camouflaged systems where consciousness lives, to which Seth does not have access. He continues by saying that not all personalities have once been physical—some have developed along different lines, which would be very alien to us. Then he says something I find quite interesting. He is telling us that consciousness is, of course, not physical and must, therefore, present itself in a different form, and it can do so in many different ways. In some of the more extreme ways, from a human perspective, consciousness expresses itself as highly mathematical and musical patterns that are themselves stimuli for other universal systems.

If a non-physical on Seth's level would visit our living room, the first thing he would see would not be material furniture, but instead a phosphorescent-like glow, the aura of electromagnetic structures that compose the molecules themselves. If he were in a play mode, he could shrink himself to the size thousands of times smaller than a molecule, land on it and pretend this molecule was your world, and thus see the living room as your cosmos—your universe. This is possible and not at all as strange as it sounds. After all, what is nano-travel? Some nano-travelers may be 100% aware of the mechanics around their travel, while others simply know how to do it.

Seth admits that he is experiencing some kind of time, but when he starts explaining how it works, it sounds strange to us humans. He says that their psychological time could be compared in terms of environments to the walls in a room, but in his case, the walls would constantly change their color, size, height, depth, and width. It sounds like a psychedelic trip! However, to them it's normal. We may think now that we don't want to live in an environment like that, but if we came to that point, we would simply experience it differently and see the beauty and the logic in it.

Our physical senses create the reality that they perceive. A tree is very different from a bird, a spider, or a microbe. It doesn't only *appear* to be different—it *is* different. We humans have our highly developed senses through which we perceive the tree, and the molecular structure of the tree we can tell is different from that of the bird. However, our senses are very specialized to function within the human system, but if an ant or a bird would experience the same tree, they would see it different than you see it, even though you are all in the same reality in the sense that you can see each other. Still, the only validity with which you can perceive that tree is your own—it's even different from other humans, but much more similar than compared with an ant. You would be able to see three dimensions of that tree, in general, while the ant, being so close to the tree if it climbs up its trunk, can explore many more dimensions and densities of that tree. We don't think in those terms, but if you do, and you do it right, it should give you new insights. A tree is not just a tree seen from a human perspective—that tree can be perceived in millions upon millions of different ways, depending on whom or what is watching and experiencing it! When you are out in real nature next time, away from cars, pollution, and the city chaos, think about these things—experience nature close up. Study it, acknowledge its awesomeness, perceive its wonder, and then thank Mother Earth for having the grace to host us. Many of us have realized how privileged we are to be children of Nature. Once we have cleaned house and can experience it the way it was supposed to be, nothing in the universe could be more awesome!

I have many times asked the reader to aim for clarity of mind. Your thoughts need to be clear, and what comes out from your mouth needs to be well thought over. In a time where we are forced to multitask and the stress level is barely sustainable, it's hard to keep our thoughts clear. Particularly during the nano-second, when time sped up a million times or more at the end of the cycle. Everything had to be done at super-speed. When this book was written it was early in 2013, and I think most people think that things (including time) are significantly slowing down, and we think we can catch our breath again. One of the tasks we had at hand during the nano-second was to be able to be clear even under those harsh circumstances. There was a very specific reason for this. Without clarity of mind, we cannot create the future we want. If our thoughts are spinning, wandering from subject to subject without being completed, we create unfinished timelines upon unfinished timelines that we then will catch our attention and confuse us, and we will eventually end up in the asylum. All of us have probably at one time or another met someone who is talking constantly, trying to tell you something, and then in the middle of a sentence starts talking about something else. Then they repeat this pattern over and over until you feel like you want to scream and run out of there. These people have a huge issue with clarity, and I advise you to stay away from such people until they have managed to pull themselves together—you don't need that kind of confusion in your life.

The reason for having a super-clear mind is because you will need it in the New Era and the New World. If you don't know what you want to create and stick to it, you will never get anywhere, and soon enough more and more of us will get ET contact, and they will not contact people who are confused—I can promise you that. If there is something they avoid, it's exactly that. Communication with humans will more often than not be telepathic—at least in the beginning—and then it's important that the human and the ET understand each other. Therefore, if you think that you have an issue in this department, start using breathing exercises, meditate, and reorganize your life so you don't have to feel the stress and anxiety that leads to an unclear state of mind. Please don't tell me it's impossible for one reason or another because if that seems to be the case, you need to change your belief system that tells you it's impossible. It's important enough to take me seriously on this. The year 2012 is over, and now we live in a small window of peacefulness and a slowed down environment, compared to how it was. If we continue with the same speed now as we had during the nano-second, we will crash. The energies right now don't support that kind of stress. Everything is slowly calming down. It will not last forever...

Now, let's discuss the concepts of space and time. We humans think we have it all figured out—all we need to do is to look into these enormous telescopes in the observatories or look at NASA pictures in books and newspapers and we know what's *out there*. Not so. No more than the table and chairs in your room are solid, no more real are our perceptions of the universe around Earth. As Seth explains it—there is no space between his own reality and ours. Our planetary systems exist at once—simultaneously—both in time and in space. What we see appears to consist of galaxies, stars, planets, nebulae, space, and time. These seem to be at certain distances from each other. This is an illusion! As third-dimensional beings, we are heavily programmed to see the universe this way, and nothing else would feel real to us. What we perceive is mental, however, and is not physical at all. This doesn't mean that we can't potentially travel between star systems, just like we can walk from house to house and travel from town to town here on Earth, but it doesn't make the universe solid, and it doesn't make the seemingly long distances real. Seth says that when he enters our system, he moves through a series of mental and psychic events. We humans would interpret these events as space and time, and Seth uses these terms when communicating with us because his own language, when describing the events, would make no sense to us at this moment.

We take for granted that our physical universe is there and will probably always be there. We look for some outside source who is creating it all the time or created it once upon a time, when in fact, we humans are primarily the ones who create the physical reality. If a star being from another dimension would travel our way (in our way of thinking), and wasn't tuned into our frequency of matter, the star being would just travel right through it without even noticing there was something there. In their reality, there is indeed nothing there, and they can prove it. However, when they tune into our little tiny frequency that is 3-D, a reality of matter slowly starts being visible where there previously was nothing. Suddenly there is a whole universe of matter materializing before their very being! This is how it works!

Every second of the day, an enormous quantity of dark energy and matter travel through our bodies. All this dark matter and energy is the 96% universe, which we can't perceive in our normal 3-D reality. Still, the 96%, just as the 4%, universe is teeming with life, and life forms of all kinds are passing through our planet and our physical bodies every second without us knowing it. These beings can, if they wish, tune into our frequency and thus perceive us. More likely, they would in that case go to a frequency very close to ours not to appear out of thin air and scare us all into heart attacks. Still, people constantly see *bleed-throughs* from these other dimensions where beings are purposely tuning in to a frequency very close to ours to observe us. That's when we for example see UFOs appear and disappear, in and out of our reality.

However, we are the ones who create matter. Each of us humans acts as transformers, automatically transforming highly sophisticated, electromagnetic units into physical objects, and we are not even aware that we are doing it! In addition, we are surrounded by *weaker* matter—however, its vibration is not low enough to be materialized in 3-D. Therefore, our physical reality is only a reflection of our inner reality, which we keep alive as an illusion outside of ourselves by renewing it in every blink of an eye. At any time, we can decide to not renew it, if we all understood how we keep it in position in the first place. The 3-D universe would disappear for us. However, there are other beings on other worlds who keep this same frequency going, and for them 3-D would still exist, but not for us.

Sacred Sex and the Divine Blood of the Goddess

Sex is one of the most important gifts mankind received from the Goddess, and it has been grossly misunderstood over the eons. Of course, everybody understands that without sex we can't reproduce in a natural way, and the species would soon die out.

However, not only humankind uses sex to reproduce—sex is what keeps the Living Library going. Plants do it, too, and so do animals. It is quite brilliant if you think about it. No one needs to be here and overlook the Experiments 24 hours a day—the Experiment takes care of itself! No cloning, no constant genetic manipulation—well, theoretically, at least, because this is the way it was planned and supposed to be. No one had taken into consideration that an alien invader force would take over the planet and use us as slave labor. This is where sexuality went wrong as well. The invaders came here with a patriarchal mindset, where sex was nothing but pleasure and, perhaps, a reward for a successful male, who had won many battles and was strong and able to protect the *weak female.* That's how they looked at it, although the female always is the strongest sex because she is the one who carries and gives birth to the child.

Before the AIF came into the picture, the early humans knew what Sacred Sex was and how important it was. Female shamans, who had learned their practices from the original Creator Gods, expressed their sexuality in their ritual, but not necessarily to have physical sex with a male during the shamanic process (although this happened in a later, slightly distorted version of shamanism). Instead, the shaman held on to her sexual energies and delegated them to the 12 different chakras—7 within the body and 5 outside the body. Her sexual energy and the intense rituals gave her maximal ecstasy, which would light the Flame of her Fire inside, and that could make her reach out to the cosmos and project the energy like a laser beam right into the 96% universe. This way, the tribe, via its shaman or shamans, could be in communication with the stars—particularly the stars of origin in the Orion Empire.

The earlier human experiments were multidimensional and could nano-travel through space. This applies to both the Neanderthals and Cro Magnon[59], and other varieties of humans, such as the Namlú'u.[60] Many of these tribes could, via their shamans, travel the universe together during their rituals, as well as bring good energies to their crops and create conditions for a good hunt.

These days, most people think that the early humans, before Homo sapiens, were quite primitive, and all they were good for was to hunt and bring home meat to the family or the tribe. Indeed, before they were manipulated with, they were much more than this. The *primitive* humans were multidimensional and knew about sacred sex because they've learned it directly from the original Creator Goddesses, who were dragons, reptilians, and humanoid in nature[61]. When a male and a female had sex, it was not just to release sexual tension, but to connect with the stars and communicate with the Multiverse, including the

---

[59] Pleiadian Lecture, early 2013.
[60] See *The Wes Penre Papers*, Levels II and III.
[61] Someone very dear to me was recently attending a Pleiadian Lecture, where the Pleiadians said that not only the Gray template can withstand radiation and harsh conditions in space—the Reptilian body can as well (and we may assume with quite some certainty, the Dragons, too). Humans can't. We are meant to be earthbound and travel inside. This is what makes us human.

96% and the Spirit Energy therein. You could say that humanity was only an orgasm away from the Goddess.

Since the AIF came into the picture, shamanism has been ridiculed, discarded as something primitive and superstitious and even banned in many places. Still, the Elite have always used shamans for their own purposes behind the scenes, unknown to the rest of humanity. In modern times, sex has become very superficial, and mainly to release sexual energies. Often, it is pleasurable and feels very good, but not always afterward—especially if there is no love between the partners. Today, teenagers have sex with their friends just to *do them a favor*. Then the whole idea for sex has been lost.

I am not going to go into too much about shamanism here, but rather concentrate on the relationship between us humans in daily life, and how we can reach higher realms by having Sacred Sex.

I wrote about this in the *WPP*, "The Second Level of Learning," but will repeat it here since it is very relevant and important to understand on our multidimensional journey. What we have (and which I have brought up several times in this book) that most other beings in the 4% universe don't have is the Divine Fire, but there is another thing we are quite unique with as well, and that is our Divine Blood! Those who have researched black magic know that the magicians often drink human blood in order to accomplish the goals of the ritual. The most powerful blood is that of women (especially menstrual blood) and the blood of innocent children. It's never been quite clear for people who are not High Priests or High Priestesses in the black magic secret society why it's so important to use certain kinds of blood, but that is the answer.

The menstrual blood is a gift from the Goddess, and the menstrual periods were something She wanted the females to go through as something sacred. On the battlefield or when people are getting wounded, they bleed, but that blood is often associated with trauma and is therefore in that sense *contaminated*. The menstrual blood, however, is not. Though women may have cramps and different levels of menstrual pain connected with their periods, it is not, in general, connected with traumatic circumstances—hence, the menses are *clean*.

The Goddess gave us an incredible gift, which is the ability to have Sacred Sex, and thus eat the fruits from the Tree of Knowledge. However, it is through the blood that runs through our veins, combined with Sex Magic, that makes us able to connect to the Inner Sanctuaries of the KHAA. We humans can achieve this by having sex during the menstrual cycle.

All blood, in all beings, is the life force of the Goddess, but the Goddess can make the blood purer or more diluted as She wishes. Humans have the key to the Living Library, and through our pure blood connection with the Goddess, we can enter the KHAA unconditionally—no strings attached! Normally, this is something a star being (or soul group) accomplishes by showing their ability to express compassion and Divine Love.

Much has been written about Sacred Sex, and it has been made complicated, which is done on purpose. The AIF complicated the matter so that humans forgot how to accomplish the goal! Today, hardly anybody knows how to do it. However, if two people truly feel tremendous love for each other, they may do it correctly without even knowing anything about the story behind it. However, even if true, they normally don't know that they need to set distinct goals or their sexual energy will be hijacked. By hijacking these energies from two lovers, the AIF can accumulate it in their own system and potentially use it in a future attack on the Orion Empire and the Spirit Universe. Therefore, from their perspective, as usual, it's best to keep mankind ignorant.

For the goals of Sacred Sex to be achieved, two human beings must not only love each other, truly and honestly, but also know each other very well (Sacred Sex would work between two women as well). They also need to be very honest in their relationship. When this is accomplished, and these two people have sex (especially during the menstruation period) magical things can happen. The eyes are the mirrors of the soul, so both people will gain so much more if they keep eye contact during the act. By doing so, they can see the emotions and the ecstasy in each other's eyes, and the two lovers blend together and become as one. Although this works between two women as well, the male sperm has its own magic, which adds to the process. The woman giving away her most inner secrets by sharing her blood with her lover is the ultimate gift she can give a man. During the act, the man also has the opportunity to drink from the fountain of the Goddess, and both the male and the female get electrified.

When the orgasm comes, the explosion this creates in the 4% Universe as well as in the KHAA is a merge with the Goddess herself. The power in this, as well as in the sexual act all together, is enormous. Therefore, it is extremely important to set a goal before you have Sacred Sex. What do you want this powerful act to accomplish? It could be anything from empowering yourself so you can use this extended power to create good for yourself, your family, and your friends or to extend the effects to include the whole planet in a positive way. Anything in between is great as well. Sometimes, when something needs to be healed and repaired in one's own life, it is perfectly okay to let the energies go in that direction. What the goals are is your personal choice and something no one else has any say in, but it's very important to set the goals so that the energies are not hijacked by negative beings in the astral. Earth, seen from the astral, is a planet full of explosions, like erupting volcanoes shooting their lava up into the atmosphere or like lighthouses turning their lights on and off in a blinking manner. These are the energies of people having sex and orgasms down here on the planet. It's simple for the AIF, waiting in the astral, to suck these energies in as much as they want, and nothing (or very little) reaches the KHAA. Thus, the whole intention for having sex (besides making babies) is lost.

As I'm sure the reader understands, much has been done to suppress this knowledge, and the bleeding cycle of women has been degraded to something dirty and messy, when in fact it is the ultimate share. This doesn't mean, of course, that a man and a woman should only have sex during the menstruation periods. Sacred Sex can be done anytime if the right love connection is there between two people. They can still achieve goals that are very powerful without the blood connection by just sharing their emotions and by looking into each other's eyes during intercourse. This way, it's not only the second chakra that's involved in the sex act, but all the upper chakras as well, and it even opens up the eighth to twelfth chakras outside of the body, which are normally quite closed as long as we are imprisoned here in 3-D.

No ETs can accomplish what two humans in love can do, even if they seduce a woman to such a degree that she is fooled into loving him dearly (which happens—they can be extremely seductive). The problem is that he can't love her back the way that she loves him—it's not in their system to be able to feel that much love. The only true love they can feel is the love for power and technology. That's where they want humans to end up as well, and we will, unless we change our ways. As alarming as it sounds, we humans are the only beings in the 4% universe with our range of emotions! There are apparently no other beings out there who can feel as strongly as we do—there are even star races out there, as we know, who almost lack emotions.[62][63][64][65]. We need to remember that the 4% universe is a universe of force. If we want to experience the *real* universe, which still is under the Goddess' control, we need to aim for the 96%, which is the universe of love, compassion, knowledge, art, and creation.

A few hundred years ago, when a woman's menses stopped, it was believed that she was to be feared because she could hold the blood and keep all the power to herself. In reality, when a woman goes through this period of less and less menses, or a longer period of time between them (although, it's not uncommon that women bleed more during menopause than they did before), she literally experiences a pause. If she is aware of this and doesn't feel guilt, shame, or sadness during this time period, she is actually transforming something inside, and she is landing in a place of more wisdom. Instead of absorbing this wisdom, most women are taught that they are less attractive and are getting closer to death, and they learn to hate and curse their bodies, and in other, perhaps less extreme ways, learn to dislike them. This puts the body off balance, and it can react in the most unpredictable ways, which then is being erroneously connected to menopause. Other women (who may not feel these negative emotions and instead continue loving their body) often don't have any particular problems during menopause. I know women (my mother included) who had their menses as usual, and one day they just stopped. They didn't feel anything unusual with their bodies during the whole menopause process. Now,

---

[62] Pleiadian lecture, 1991 (http://www.bibliotecapleyades.net/pleyades/pleiadiansbook/pleiadiansbook_contents.htm#contents).
[63] Anonymous ET source.
[64] Bashar, channeled by Darryl Anka.
[65] The Cassiopaeans, channeled by Laura Knight-Jadczyk + miscellaneous channeled material.

I'm not saying that all women who have problems during menopause hate their bodies, but I am suggesting that if women washed away all these patriarchal ideas added to the menopause process, women in general would be able to go through the experience as something quite positive.

Our thoughts are recorded by our blood. They are imprinted together with our feelings and radiated outward so that everyone who wants to can read them. We are the sum of ourselves in the physical form because of our blood. This is why having a blood transfusion is a very critical thing to do, and this is also the reason why certain religious groups refuse to have one and prefer to die (they even let their children die rather than having them go through a transfusion). What happens when we get someone else's blood in our veins is that we also adopt that person's personality, emotions, and memories to a certain extent—i.e. our personality may change afterward. These same religious groups believe that their personality (and the reason for their lives) disappears during such interference.

The blood is produced within our bone caverns that serve as our skeletal structure. This is why shamans and others use the bones of their ancestors in their rituals—they believe that the memories of the deceased are stored in the bones. This is actually quite correct because the memories are stored in the blood, and the blood is created in our bones.

When we align our consciousness and become more aware, we also automatically purify our blood, and our blood becomes something very, very sacred.[66] The red blood cells are manufactured in the bone marrow, and when we realign the bone, the bone purifies the blood and sorts out the inner secrets of identity. This is why bodywork changes the structure of our blood.

---

[66] Barbara Marciniak, ©1994, "Earth—Pleiadian Keys to the Living Library", p.95ff.

What women have forgotten is that the blood is the source of their power.[67] The Pleiadians say:

> The blood carries the genetic code, and because the Mother Goddess is the source of all things, this is where the code comes from. It is where the story is hidden. Menstrual blood can be used to nurture plant life, to mark Earth, and to let Earth know that the Goddess lives again. In general, women don't bleed into Earth anymore. Doing so is a direct transference of the energy of the Goddess.[68]

By letting the menstrual blood touch the Earth, women nurture her. Therefore, in a society where we spend most of our time indoors and we have clothes on, I think it may be a good idea to let some of the menses be spread out over the property to nurture Mother Earth. The Pleiadians relay a message to all women so that you understand that your menstrual blood is the source of your power and your deepest inner knowledge. In the bleeding process lie many of the keys to bringing the Goddess back onto a planet, which is so energetically altered toward male dominance and negative power.

Furthermore, the Pleiadians tell us that if we are not interested in the Goddess energy and the mysteries of the blood, we miss out on an integral part of life and will not understand what is occurring on our planet. Men need to learn how to honor the blood (especially the pure menstrual blood), and women must do the same thing, and if these things turn us off, or we think it's not important, we are completely missing the point. The Pleiadians say that this is the most powerful teachings they can give us right now to help us understand what is coming. They

---

[67] Ibid.
[68] Ibid, p.95, op. cit.

emphasize that we need to honor the Goddess vibration that comes through our hearts and helps our hearts open.[69]

Menstrual blood is highly oxygenated, and the purest of all blood, and in humans, it carries the decoded DNA. The Pleiadians tell us it's the oxygen that decodes those strands and allows the restructuring of the data.

As an aside, perhaps, I keep stumbling upon information from everywhere about the moon. Even the Pleiadians in their material talk about it as a construct, and that it highly affects humans and all life on Earth (which is quite commonly known), and especially the menstruation cycles. The Pleiadians say the moon is a very powerful electromagnetic computer.[70]

As we know, men don't bleed. Therefore, the only way for men to, in an appropriate way, take the power of blood inside them is for a woman to gift him with her blood—to share her sacred elixir. It can be done through oral sex, or to eat fruit and vegetables that have been grown in the soil where a woman has spread her menses, or a man can be marked on the back of his neck or the soles of his feet with the blood from a woman. His body will absorb the knowledge.

Unfortunately, having sex during menstruation has had such a deep negative imprint on the human mind that many people think it's repelling. If the reader (whether a man or a woman) enjoys having sex during the bleeding period, you have overcome a deep imprint. This is a very ancient ritual that stems from the time when the Matriarchs were dominant on our planet, before the Patriarchal Regime took over. It was very powerful and kept the inhabitants in connection with the Goddess.

The men's equivalence to menstruation is the sperm. The sperm is the Goddess' story encoded in the male vibration, and

---

[69] "Earth—Pleiadian Keys to the Living Library", p.97.
[70] Ibid, p.98.

contains the interpretation of how the male remembers that story.[71] Here is the interesting thing for us men: when we have sex with a woman during her period, our sperms can act as explorers and telepath back to us the power and knowledge of the woman. A man can, under these circumstances, get access to the woman's full identity. This is why it's so important that the partners are very honest with each other and don't mind sharing all the secrets because if the woman is willing to share her menses with a man during the sexual act, he will get access to her inner sanctum. Her inner sanctum is the heart of the KHAA.

The Fire of the Goddess, which we received as a gift from her, is in the human body directly connected with the blood.

The Tree of Knowledge has to do with Sacred Sex, and the Tree of Life has to do with blood. We know that blood is red and sperm is white. These two, mixed together, is the key to longevity and *eternal life.* In secret societies, this is well known (especially at the upper levels), and men, especially, who had this knowledge, went crazy about mixing semen and blood and drinking it. Conspiracy writers (more often so in earlier years than now, unless they are Christian) curse everything that has to do with mixing these fluids, when indeed it is something extremely important for us to understand and even practice. It's the distorted aspect of it that has given it a bad reputation, plus the fact that the AIF and their Global Elite bloodlines have always wanted to keep us ignorant on this subject. It is therefore quite important that we stop having sex just for our own egotistical pleasure and start setting goals for our sexual acts. They can be the same goals repeatedly, and don't have to be changed every time we have sex. However, we need to set them in our thoughts before we start being intimate, or our sexual energies *will be* hijacked. If you feel fatigue or extreme tiredness after you've had sex, when you're otherwise healthy and energetic,

---

[71] "Earth—Pleiadian Keys to the Living Library", p.103, op. cit.

it's very possibly a sign that someone stole your energies during the intimacy.[72]

The Six Heart Virtues—Making Use of the Fourth Body Chakra

The human body is made up of seven chakras, or body centers, from which energy flows in both directions. This is what most esoteric teachings are telling you and shouldn't come as a surprise to anybody. What most people don't know, however (unless they have read my papers) is that there are also five chakras outside of the body, which make us connect with the *Outer Universe*. For those who are not familiar with the chakra system, I will list the 12 chakras here:

1. The Root Chakra (or the Red Chakra) is located at the base of the spine, in the *coccygeal* region (the 3-5 separate or fused vertebrae below the sacrum, which is the large, triangular bone at the base of the spine). The first three chakras are the "Survival Chakras," and this particular one has to do with *fight-or-flight*, when survival of the body is threatened. It is related to instinct, security, and survival, but also to sexuality. It also has a relation to the sense of smell (something that usually diminishes with age—more so in men than in women).

2. The Sacral Chakra (or the Orange Chakra) is located in the *sacrum*, which is the large, triangular bone at the base of the spine and the upper back part of the pelvic cavity. It corresponds with the testes and the ovaries that produce the various sex hormones involved in the reproduction cycle. It is also generally connected to the

---

[72] A major part of this *"Sacred Sex"* section is taken directly or indirectly from my previous paper of November 3, 2012: *"Humanity's Future, Paper #3: Life after the Nano-Second, Part 3—The New Mind"*.

genitourinary system and the adrenals and is associated with relationships, violence, addictions, basic emotional needs, and pleasure. On a physical level, it corresponds to reproduction, on the mental level, it has to do with creativity, and on the spiritual level, it governs enthusiasm.

3. <u>The Solar Plexus Chakra</u> (or the Yellow Chakra). This chakra is related to the metabolic and digestive systems. It plays a major role in converting food matter into energy, and digestive problems often stem from blockages in this chakra. It also governs issues of personal power, fear, anxiety, opinion-formation, and introversion.

4. <u>The Heart Chakra</u> (or the Green Chakra, also sometimes the Pink Chakra) is the most important chakra for us humans now when we are evolving. Although we want to open all chakras eventually and be able to be in charge of them, the Fourth Chakra, *The Heart Chakra* is what we always need to pay attention to. One of its symbols is the hexagram, or the six-pointed star, which basically is two triangles, put together—one pointing up and the other pointing down. On this level, it signifies the male and the female polarities, and the union thereof.

The Heart Chakra is related to the thymus, located in the chest. It has to do with the immune system as well as being part of the endocrine system. This chakra is involved when fighting off disease and can be adversely affected by stress. The Heart Chakra involves complex emotions, compassion, tenderness, unconditional love, equilibrium, rejection, and well-being. Physically, it governs circulation—emotionally, it governs unconditional love for the self and others—mentally, it governs passion—and spiritually it governs devotion.

5. <u>The Throat Chakra</u> (or the Blue/Turquoise Chakra) is parallel to the thyroid and responsible for growth and maturation and clarity of speech, stemming from fluent thoughts and clarity of mind. It governs communication, independence, and security. In *Dream Yoga,* it plays a dominant role in *lucid (conscious) dreaming.*
6. <u>The Brow Chakra/The Third Eye</u> corresponds to the colors violet, indigo, and deep blue and is linked to the *pineal gland,* which has to do with envisioning. The pineal gland produces melatonin, which regulates the sleep cycle and when to wake up. This chakra is balancing the Higher and Lower Selves and trusting inner guidance. It also has to do with intuition.
7. <u>The Crown Chakra</u> (or the Multicolored Chakra) is generally considered the chakra of pure consciousness and is located either on the crown of the head or just above the crown of the head. It also symbolizes wisdom and the death of the body. Its inner aspect deals with the release of karma, the physical action with meditation, the mental action with universal consciousness and unity, and the emotional action with *beingness.* However because most teaching orders let the chakra system stop here, this chakra is thus the highest, but there are an additional 5 chakras, adding up to 12 chakras all together (we live in a universe of 12+1, where the number 13 is reserved for the Goddess). Hence, the Crown Chakra is also a connecting point to the upper, *out of body* chakras that follow. The ninth through twelfth chakras are relatively undeveloped in most humans at this point and are truly multidimensional. Not until we become more in tune with our own multidimensional selves will these chakras leave their *cocoons,*

open like flowers in spring, and expand outward toward the point where they are supposed to be located.

8. The 8th Chakra (color unknown) is within our realm of activity. It hovers 12 inches or more above our heads. Most people keep their eighth chakra close to their physical body.
9. The 9th Chakra (color unknown) is also quite close to the body, within a few feet from it. When these nine chakras are more developed, this chakra will move out into the atmosphere of Earth to become more of an Earth chakra, connecting into the gridwork. It's a link.
10. The 10th Chakra (color unknown) is much further out, as are the 11th and 12th chakras. The 10th Chakra, once it is in line and plugged in, will be in your solar system.
11. The 11th Chakra (color unknown) will move out into our galactic system.
12. The 12th Chakra (color unknown) will be located and anchored some place in this universe.[73]

The chakra that we will automatically concentrate most on as we are evolving is the 4th—the Heart Chakra, which has a lot to do with compassion but also other emotions that are important for us in order for us to become multidimensional. Mahu Nahi, who wrote down the teaching from the Wing-Makers[74], talks about the Six Heart Virtues, which we would gain a lot from practicing in our everyday life. When something happens that we have some problems with handling—whether it has to do with people or situations in general—he suggests that we take a look at the following six virtues, see which one (or which ones) apply, and then simply apply them to the situation. The Six Heart Virtues are (in alphabetical order):

---

[73] Chakras 8–12 taken from Barbara Marciniak, ©1992, *"Bringers of the Dawn"*, pp.55-56.
[74] http://wingmakers.com/

Appreciation
Compassion
Forgiveness
Humility
Understanding
Valor

If we just memorize these six virtues so that we quickly can go through them in our heads, we can then easily see which ones apply to the situation we are in. In the beginning, if it's easier, write them down on a sticky note that you bring with you in your pocket or in your purse. After a while, we'll notice that we don't need to dig into every situation deeply and thoroughly and get lost in the complexity of it. Instead, by applying the above, many otherwise seemingly unresolvable situations can be dealt with within seconds.

I have the free pdf file Mahu Nahi offers online, called "Living from the Heart" available for download on my website, so I suggest you click here, http://wespenre.com/pdf/living-from-the-heart.pdf, and read it through. It tells you more about how to use the Six Heart Virtues.

Our Breath—The Physical Body's Connection with the Quantum Field

When people come to me and tell me that they are either fearful, anxious, depressed, or feeling powerless, I tell them to breathe. If they haven't heard of this before, first, they look at me as if I were weird. Then I tell them, of course, what I mean by this—different explanations depending on how high their level of knowledge is—and to many, it at least makes sense enough for them to try it out.

In fact, breathing exercises connect us with the quantum and subquantum fields—the universe of the smallest particles known to man, where everything is connected and that also *is* the All That Is—the Spirit World and the Goddess. If we feel out of touch with ourselves, our fellow man, our work situation, or our love relationship etc., or if we feel fearful or have any other kind of unwanted emotion or condition to deal with, we have a tendency to try to deal with it in the physical universe and think we can solve it that way, when the source of the problem is not in the physical universe. The reason we have any of the above issues (or other issues not described here), is because we are disconnected from the quantum field, which gives the cells in our body life and energy and make them spark and ignite. The most common indicator that you need to *plug yourself in* is if you feel out of energy or fatigued.

We humans have a tendency to go on with life, trying to do the best we can to handle what we think we need to handle in a day. We perceive it as if we have next to zero time to tune in to anything spiritual, so we even forget that we are spiritual beings. Instead we make ourselves vulnerable for attacks—both from humans and the spirit world because we ourselves are disconnected. Then we wonder why we are not feeling good.

Another thing that seems typical for us humans is that even if we know the remedy to something, we don't practice it when we need it the most. A depressed person, for example, doesn't want any solutions as long as he or she is depressed. A friend may come up with ideas and solutions for the depressed person, who doesn't want to hear about it and rejects every idea, regardless if the ideas are good or bad.

Breathing exercises *are* the remedy, and it's so easy to prove. Do one and you'll notice for yourself. Then, of course, it's your responsibility to do it on a continuous basis and apply it when you feel disconnected from the Divine Feminine. I have mentioned the importance of breathing so many times in my writings that the reader who has read them all may be quite tired of hearing about it by now. However, sometimes I wish I could write a book with only one chapter, talking about breathing exercises, and then repeat that chapter seven or eight times to make it a whole book. No one would read more than the first chapter, but perhaps they would think that "Hmm, maybe Wes thinks this is important!" If true, the reader would have hit the nail on the head.

There are many different breathing exercises you can learn, but I want to once again recommend something from the WingMakers. You or I may think what we want about their teachings in general, but it's always a matter of sorting out the wheat from the chaff, and both the Six Heart Virtues and the *Quantum Pause*, which I will now introduce to you, are exceptionally great stuff. Therefore, I advise you to explore the Quantum Pause for yourself and start practicing it—it will certainly pay off. I have that one as well on my website, and you can download the whole Quantum Pause section here, http://wespenre.com/pdf/Appendix-cognitive-section-quantum-pause-breathing-exercise.pdf.

This should conclude what I wanted to share in this book for practices that get us closer to our natural state of multidimensionality. If you do the exercises and consider taking what I've written here to heart, you will notice after a while that you will change drastically, and then, when you look back to whom you were *before* you started reading this handbook and compare it with whom you will be after have used it for a while, you will probably be quite amazed. You will possibly also notice that you will find your own versions of what I've taught you, and even new exercises that you can use on yourself.

The last chapter will discuss what it will be like when we once again become the Guardians of the Living Library as multidimensional beings in a human body, free from suppression and outside manipulation. We will discuss a Paradise on Earth—Homo Nova, the New Human!

CHAPTER 7: HOMO NOVA—THE NEW GUARDIANS OF THE LIVING LIBRARY

A Voluntary Mission and the Year 1 AN

Many who read this book will feel excited about the Splitting of the Worlds, I'm sure, and will be more than happy to start working on this now—the sooner the better—so when they reincarnate the next time, the world is a better place to live. Then, born into a body that is matching the new energies better than the one they currently inhabit and being more multidimensional, they can accomplish more together with others in the same situation.

Others, on the other hand, have had enough and believe that they want to leave this solar system altogether and continue to grow somewhere else. Both options are absolutely possible, but for those who want to leave, is it okay to *abandon* the fellow human, or do we actually need to stay and help?

You who read this book within a generation after this handbook came out have been what some call *System Busters*, which means *Forerunners* in this case. You were one of the brave ones who decided to go against the current tendency and raise your vibration in order to increase your own consciousness and awareness, but also so others could be inspired and jump on the bandwagon. You will be surprised how many young people—anyone from 14 years old to 25—suddenly come out and know just as much, if not even more, than you learned in 25 years.

They picked it up in no time! This has already started to happen because I am getting very profound letters from young teenagers who discuss the deepest and most difficult information I have shared with the world. Don't be jealous and think you spent all these sweat and tears finding it out, when they just seem to *get it*! It's natural and was expected. When these children contact you, you are talking to a member of the new Homo Nova species, and that is very good news! These children were born during the nano-second, and they were born in higher frequency bodies. They are still working on finding out, but they are way ahead of their schoolmates, who can't keep their eyes off their Android phone.

These spiritually evolved and very knowledgeable children are our new generation, who is taking over after us. We were the Forerunners who had to set the protocol, and I'll tell you—we did, and we did a good job!

Now is the time to make a choice. We are currently living in what the Pleiadians (the same beings who coined the expression, *nano-second*) call the *post-nano*—a new term they have coined, so we'd better get used to it. Perhaps in the near future, when the New World is established, the year 2013 will actually be renamed the year 1 AN, which means *After Nano*—who knows? That would actually be nice, so we can leave the suppressive system behind us and start anew. That, however, is something we need to vote on later. I will, in my writings from now on, call this year 1 AN, anyway, until we can either establish this, or vote it down. It gives people some time to think about it. Remember, in the After Nano, after the planets have split for real, there will be no huge government bodies that will decide this or that—it will be up to *We the People* until we have established the kind of system we want to endorse.

Anyway, back to our choice. Many people are now mighty tired and think that they have had enough of Earth for a while.

No one needs to feel ashamed when thinking this way—anybody who has come as far as to read this handbook has done more than is expected of them to raise the frequency of this planet and has the right to move on if he or she wishes to. If you are one of them, you can rest assured that the world is in good hands, and the Splitting of the Worlds *will* take place!

There are many benevolent star races that have observed us and applauded us during the nano-second, and I'm sure celebrated when it was over, thinking we, overall, did a good job. Against all odds, a certain percentage of mankind did not fall into the trap of craving a technological society to become copies of the gods, only that they never became *gods* themselves because they never even realized that they were slaves, and those who did, didn't care. Just like the old star race, here called the AIF, the majority of mankind has deliberately chosen to become like them, where they measure progress, not in frequency, but in technological advancement. This is their free choice in a Free Will Universe, and we are not in a position to judge them, as little as they should judge us. There is no right and wrong, only choices and consequences.

We have discussed earlier how this Earth was limited and set to a certain range of frequency, in which everything on this planet needs to vibrate to be part of the prison. However, when a being starts vibrating higher than this range of frequency, he or she grows out of the prison and begins to stick his or her head out on the other side and notice what is out there. It can be compared with the bars in a physical earthly prison. The bars are of a certain thickness to keep the prisoner in. However, if the prisoner gets much stronger, and eventually gets strong enough to break the bars enough to escape, the prisoner is free. This is similar to how it is for us.

We can't move backward. Once we have achieved a certain frequency, there is no way back. Hence, we may think that we have not only grown out of the version of Earth we're still dwelling in, but we also think that we have outgrown our bodies, and it can sometimes feel uncomfortable in different ways. In worst cases, the body can even get sick, but more common is unexplainable pain, neurological problems, fatigue and tiredness, and headaches that come and go (there may be a lot of other phenomena as well). If you go to the doctor, he or she may just scratch his or her head, not knowing what's going on because the lab tests show excellent results! Beware that the doctor does not medicate you when no medication is necessary in order to get rid of you. You can still train this higher frequency body to become more multidimensional, and it's a good idea to do that, and if you are persistent, the discomfort may very well disappear. Still, if you decide to reincarnate again to prepare for a better world, there is no possible way to incarnate in this version of Earth because the vibration of your spiritual body is so much higher than of those people who live here now. Hence, you will automatically incarnate in a body on a version of Earth that fits your current frequency. If you could jump back and forth between these two realities right now, you could clearly notice the difference.

I know there may be quite a few people who have evolved during the last 25 years who used to have a lot of friends they could share things with and have fun with before the nano-second. You may be one of those I'm talking about. Then, the more your frequency increased, the lonelier you felt because suddenly there was no one you could share your thoughts with. You had outgrown all your friends. Perhaps at times, you even feel depressed and are longing for love that you no longer seem to be able to find. If this is the case, you are not alone—it's actually quite common. Remember, though, that this is only temporary, and you are heading toward a new world where love and compassion will be the norm. In the meantime, it could be a good idea to maybe move to a community where you can meet with the like-minded and not just e-mail them on a computer. Still, due to job situations etc. it might not be so easy.

First, you will feel so much better and so much healthier and happier in the next incarnation. Also, you will see that you have much more freedom and will be left alone by suppressive elements to a much greater extent than you are now. You will also notice that there are many like-minded people incarnated simultaneously with you, or within a few years difference. Also, the longevity of the new, more vital bodies will be much higher. There shouldn't be any problems living until you are 250 years old and even longer than that a few generations down the line until death becomes obsolete. If your body is in a fatal accident, or it can't serve the purpose, you can take a new one without losing your memories. It's not going to be much more inconvenient than it is now to switch cars. For a few generations, the Machine Kingdom will be built alongside your own reality, but you and those who are vibrating on your level will not mingle with them. It's like now—we know that there is a culture in the Middle East that is different from ours, and we hear about it, but we don't go there and hang out. We let them do their thing and we do ours. However, no heavy version of the Machine Kingdom and no heavy version of the Global Elite influence are going to be able to exist side by side with you even in the next incarnation because the vibrations are so different from each other. In other words, the heavy duty Machine Kingdom is built as we speak, but a first splitting of worlds occurred already in the last quarter of 2012, so you and I will never experience that version. I don't know if you have noticed, but I have had bleed-throughs, or *flashes* of the heavy duty version of the Kingdom in my awakened state, and those flashes have lasted for maybe a few seconds. This short amount of time still gave me a lot of information, and it was quite horrifying. That's when I realized that I made it to the *right side* of the split. There are still going to be some difficulties ahead, but for most of us, the worst is behind us. The difficulties I'm talking about will be discussed in the next subsection to this chapter.

When we reincarnate the next time into a more spiritually advanced version of Earth, we will most likely do so without amnesia, and that means that we are multidimensional by default. Still, we are like nestlings who are trying their wings for the first time—there is a risk of falling out of the nest and being prey for someone waiting either on the ground or in the air—only because we were too eager and jumped out too soon. We weren't ready for the big adventure, and there are those who may be able to take advantage of that. This is why I believe it's so important to prepare ourselves how it is to be a multidimensional being in a solid body, just like we do with handbooks such as this one. We don't need to be perfect, but we need to disagree with the current regime and be willing to go our own way, and it's necessary in order to smoothly be able to take the leap into the next lifetime to practice how to be multidimensional. You will not regret it when that day comes!

Many of us are old Namlú'u[75] souls trapped in AIF manipulated Homo sapiens bodies, but not all of us are. The Namlú'u souls have already gotten accustomed to what it means to be multidimensional and have an easier time grasping the whole concept on a higher level than those who were new souls at the

---

[75] The Namlú'u were the multidimensional androgynous human species who lived on Earth before the AIF came. They were the Guardians of the Library, but were seduced by the AIF to enter the genetically manipulated bodies the AIF had prepared for them and have been stuck since then. Read much more about the Namlú'u in the WPP, *"The Second Level of Learning"*.

time when the AIF trapped humanity in the 3-D, but even the old Namlú'u souls are *rusty* and need to practice their old skills.

We humans are so lucky. If all people on this Earth knew what a privilege they have, they would jump on the train right away. What I mean is that there are two types of multidimensional beings. It's us, who can train ourselves to be able to travel everywhere (with a few exceptions) and explore the full Multiverse, and then there are those who are also multidimensional, but can only explore the eight dimensions of the 4% universe—six physical dimensions and two non-physical. The channeled entities who fancy themselves with being multidimensional can still not enter the KHAA, and that's the whole point. They want the code in our DNA which gives us humans access to the 96% Spirit Universe, and they know it's somewhere in our blood, but they can't figure it out. Well, I can tell them right now—it's because they can't feel the range of emotions necessary to be accepted into the KHAA—they can't feel strong love! That's why many come here and do genetic experiments with us by abducting us. However, will they ever figure out how to get through the gates that lead into the 96%? I honestly don't know. There are sources who tell me that they probably won't. If true, all they will have access to as long as it's still there, is the universe we can perceive in our 3-D state, including all the solar systems and galaxies out there and the other five dimensions that are available in the 4% universe.

Remember—you never lose what you've learned. While being trapped here in 3-D, and even in the 4%, it is quite difficult to get in touch with our Higher Self, the *Oversoul*, and it's now, when we are expanding our consciousness, that we have started getting communication from that direction more frequently. The Oversoul is storing everything you experience and relays it to the Goddess (in very simple terms), and the Oversoul can also give you advice and help you when you ask for it. The help may not always be the way you had expected—you don't always get what you want, but you get what you need, similar to what that old Rolling Stones song says[76].

Wendy Kennedy is another channeler of the Pleiadians, although Marciniak's group says that Barbara Marciniak is the only one who is channeling *their* particular group, which means that Kennedy is channeling another Pleiadian collective. This collective says:

> The more frequently you access the higher records and hold these expanded states of consciousness in your third dimensional body, the more your body begins to reflect these vibrations. Remember, your body is created from an energetic template. As you alter the template, your body too must alter. This is what you call Ascension. The cells begin to vibrate at a higher rate, so much so that they cross over into a new dimension. This is how you will all generate your new form for the coming transition.[77]

Those who still wish to move on and not be part of the New Earth will already know how to do that once they leave this current body. If you're curious about how to do it in your awake state, you can rest assured that you have explored your options in the dream state to an extent that when you leave your body for the next adventure, you know exactly how to crisscross your way out in the universe and how to get to the KHAA, if that is what you want to do. Therefore, feel no fear because there is no reason. Whatever you want to do after you die, it's going to be fun for you because now you're in charge of what you want to do! Ponder this and you will understand why this no longer is a problem.

---

[76] Jagger/Richards, "You Can't Always Get What You Want (but you get what you need).

[77] Wendy Kennedy, July 5, 2009, "Fear of Choice—Ramshi, 12th Dimensional Master Geneticist/Universal Architect", op. cit.

The Three Important Post-Nano Phases Discussed

Just like the nano-second was split up in three different phases related to how fast time was accelerating, the post-nano world also has three phases, more or less related to how fast time is decelerating, although there is more to it than that.

This chapter was written in May, 1 AN, and by that time I could definitely feel how time had slowed down quite noticeably. It's funny because even when I talk to people who have no idea about nano-seconds and post-nano they say that time has slowed down in comparison to 2012 and the years before that. Therefore, it's definitely not just imagination.

When the Pleiadians talked about the nano-second, they added that the years 1987 through 2012 were the approximate time frame for the nano-second. It showed, however, that they were quite to the point. Personally, like I've mentioned elsewhere, I started feeling a deceleration sometime in October, 2012, instead of January of the year 1. Therefore, their prediction was close—at least in my case.

Anyway, the post-nano is considered to have started in January, 1 AN. The first phase is going to be between 1-5 AN (2013-2017), while phase two is marked down at anno 6-15 (2018-2027), and phase three will be anno 16 (2028) with an open ending. This section will paint a broad picture of what we can expect to happen during these phases. Normally I don't like predictions because if they don't come true, the author will be discredited, so I want to add here that these predictions are based upon astrological aspects as well as probable realities. What I am bringing up here seems to be the most probable reality for us humans in the near future, but as we and all ETs know, humans can be very unpredictable and we change our minds constantly and go in a different direction, which can be hard to predict. Therefore, let's just do our best here.

Phase 1 (Anno 1-5, or 2013-2017)

The first thing that happened we have already discussed, and that's the deceleration of time. We are still not down to a normal time rate, however, because that would have been the equivalent to standing on the breaks. If that would have happened, it would have been like if we stop a train at full speed—many people would have gotten hurt and many others would have died. Instead, it happens gradually, and we will probably see normalization by the end of Phase 1. This is definitely the time, however, when we can sit back a little bit and relax and ponder over what has happened during the last 25 years. How well did we do? How would we grade ourselves, individually and as a collective? Were we able to take care of business—i.e. get our debts paid and our major issues handled? Are we living in a place where we may consider living for many years ahead? Does it feel relatively safe in our local universe? Do we feel tremendously more enlightened, calm, and on track now than we did in 1987? If we can answer yes to these questions, we did great and are ready for what's coming next. If we feel that some or much of the above is still missing in our lives, we're past due and need to wrap it up immediately, but without starting to rush around again. However, if you're still walking around being afraid and anxious, you didn't work on your main issues during the nano-second, and you will be facing big trouble in the future unless you take care of these emotions right away. This is extremely important. If you still hesitate, I can't help but saying that in the future you will tell yourself, "Dang it, Wes Penre was right!" This is one thing I don't want to be right about in your case, if you are one of these people.

Still, these next five years are not going to be friction-free. The economy is still a major disaster, and there is minimal hope that the dollar is going to recover. As of this writing, the economy is on its way up, but that's just an illusion, as Bernanke and his criminal bankers are printing money in desperation to get business going and interest rates down, and none of these dollar bills has anything to back it up with! These days, even a fool can see what is about to come down. Therefore, make sure to invest in something of value and don't just keep money in the bank and think that's safe. If your money will be worthless, you may just as well deposit printing papers from your computer—they will be worth more than your dollars (or whatever currency you are using—it's probably going to be a global crash eventually). You may ask what to invest in, and that is a tough question because it's hard to say what exactly is going to keep its value. If you have a home, make sure to pay it off so you have a roof over your head—that's most important. Invest in food that can keep you alive for a few months (yes, I know that this is a charged-up subject, after Y2K etc. but see that as a dress rehearsal). What you invest in, in addition to the above, is your call, but you will need somewhere to live and something to eat and drink. If you have that, you have much better chances to survive if worse comes to worse—it's much better to be safe than sorry. I know that we basically don't own the land our property stands on, regardless of what papers you've signed, but at this stage, the government will most possibly not confiscate the land your house sits on if you've paid the house off. They will have other things to take care of.

This may sound like a contradiction—first I am saying that we can sit down and relax, and then I bring up the economy. I know, I know...still, we are talking about probabilities here. Remember that we *do* create our own reality, and I have talked about conditioning our own space and our local universe. If we do this successfully, we can handle whatever comes down. We can always go back to bartering for a while until things stabilize (which it will). If we need to barter, it's very good to live in a neighborhood where people know each other and mainly like each other. Then, the survival potential is so much higher. Therefore, keep yourself on good terms with your neighbors and help each other out when needed and asked for. Think about what your skills are and what you can do for others in case of a disaster and strengthen that. If you have a skill that's needed, which not many other people have (such as nursing skills) you are quite well off—it will be highly rated under such circumstances.

Now we'll turn this around again. There is also a chance it will not go as far as to when we have to barter and our money will be worthless. First, there are good people working behind the scenes right now to get things straight, and even though they can't save a destroyed economy, there are ways to make the transition easier. This first phase of the post-nano world—especially the last part of it—will be the time for exposure of corruption and crimes amongst politicians, businessmen, bankers, and other authoritarian people. As we know, it has already started, and even the Pope had to resign. There will most likely be more pedophilia scandals because raping children is a big thing in High Places. It goes back to the blood rituals we discussed earlier, black magic, feeding off fear, and worse. The corruption behind the scenes is so enormous that there is no one amongst the general public who can even start imagining what is going on. Much (but not all) of that will be revealed. People are already getting annoyed over the scandals of their Representatives, and many start realizing how naïve they have been and why the Founding Fathers sometimes said and did certain things in order to not be repeating old habits. Unfortunately, not even they could predict the inactivity and naivety of the population and how easily those in power could be corrupted and, in turn, corrupt others.

So what will happen when all this is revealed? Every week, there is always some new scandals being reported in the media, but what about if the newspapers were full of them? These are the times when secrets can't be kept anymore—especially not dark secrets. It's just the signs of the times. Consciousness is cleaning house! Many people will probably be very furious over the betrayals, and as George Bush Sr. said back in the 1980s: "If people knew what we have done, they would run us down the street and lynch us!"[78] There is a chance there is going to be tumultuous times, and they will transfer over to Phase 2. Whatever you do, *don't get involved in the tumult!* Nothing good is going to come out of that. We can't fight the Global Elite in a physical confrontation regardless of how convincing some people may be when they explain why we can. It's only going to lead to people are getting hurt and killed when the military will be commanded out on the streets. As usual, we need to handle these things from inside.

This is going to be a process that can take quite a few years, but sooner or later a substantial portion of the Global Elite will be exposed and people will demand a change. This time it will be harder for the Elite to get away by applying their standard formula, *problem-reaction-solution,*[79] because they did not instigate this exposure—the increase in consciousness did.

Now, this sounds good in certain ways because it looks like the public will finally understand some of the width of the corruption, but there is one thing that is not taken into

---

[78] Source: Cathy O'Brien and Mark Phillips, ©1988: *"Trance Formation of America"*

[79] *Problem-Reaction-Solution* is a formula the Global Elite is following to manipulate the public. If they want to change something that they know the public doesn't want, they create a *problem* that is big enough to start a *reaction* from the public to "do something about it". Then the Global Elite comes up with the solution to the problem they instigated in the first place. The solution is always the change that they wanted. For example, they want more surveillance, so they let an event such as 9/11 happen. People scream for a solution, and the solution is the increased surveillance they wanted in the first place. People don't see through the manipulation and now feel safe and happier.

consideration and that is the invasion, which has already to a large degree taken place within governments and other authoritarian organizations, banking, and businesses. The invasion was silent, as I mentioned in the *WPP*, where the AIF, returning in great numbers to Earth after just having had a skeleton crew here, did *walk-ins* on people they have personally bred and genetically manipulated so the invaders can feel comfortable mingling with humans. This means that a politician you see in a TV interview may very well be an ET—there would be no way to tell, except for his or her exceptional intelligence, which they can hide if they feel the need to do so.

My case in point here is that the AIF most possibly already know that this exposure is going to happen (since it has already begun), and they are ready to counteract it. It's my own belief that they understand that they have to deal with increased consciousness for a while until the Earth splits—therefore, they are ready to make sacrifices to satisfy the public. They know that the public is too confused and too manipulated to know what to do if all hell breaks loose, and they already have plans at work to restore order when the worst is over. Even if they have to sacrifice a few of their own, they won't mind. For them, a body means very little. If one of them would be sentenced to a life in prison, he or she simply would commit suicide and occupy another body.

This is one reason why it's impossible to fight this—it's too big, and there are plans within plans that we can only begin to understand. Therefore, the soulution, once again, is to ignore it as much as possible and strengthen our own local universes and restate our goals. Only those who understand this and can do it will survive the terror in the long term and be part of the New World.

Then we have the ET issue. It's not only the AIF we have to deal with—there were literally billions of star beings around our planet during the nano-second. Some of them were fighting for human bodies, so they could live on Earth during this important time period. Most of them wanted bodies because the learning curve was so steep. You could learn in 25 years what it normally takes millions of years to learn otherwise. Who wouldn't want to invest in that for a few years, even if they would be under suppression at the same time? Now, on the other hand, when the nano-second is over, many of them have left or are about to leave. "The party is over!" Left are those who are either hostile to us (The AIF) or those who want to see us succeed. The latter are the ones who want to make themselves known, but the former want to interfere, pretending to be the latter in order to once again confuse the matter. For them, it's business as usual.

We must understand that we have mainly two forces at play here—one is the AIF, whose purpose is ultimate control and the building of a Machine Kingdom. They do *not* want us to evolve and raise our frequency. Then we have the other force, such as the Pleiadians, who are basically a faction of the same AIF that is controlling us negatively right now. The difference between the two is that the Pleiadians, who sit in their own mess in the Pleiadian star system, have realized that in order for them to free themselves from *their* tyranny, they need us humans to evolve *without technology!* In other words, they need us to evolve the way we were supposed to in the first place. Thus, the two intentions clash! Lord ENKI, whom we also call Lucifer, is in charge of the AIF, and he knows that he will lose some humans to the Pleiadian Agenda. If we look at the evidence, it seems likely he is willing to let go of the faction of humanity who is ready to evolve and keep the majority for his own purposes. Besides, we do not know if ENKI and the Pleiadians have made an agreement behind our backs, so that the Pleiadians leave the majority who are ripe for the Machine Kingdom alone, if ENKI leaves the evolving humans alone. Eventually, the two main factions of mankind will split anyway, so it's not a big deal for ENKI. This is possibly why he and the AIF are leaving us relatively alone or as an anonymous source once told me: "In their eyes you guys are only humans, so they don't care!" What this means is that ENKI and his cohorts don't think very highly of us, and they don't fear us, or what we're trying to do. If we would try to start a war against him, on the other hand, ENKI would probably eradicate us just to *get rid of the annoying flies*. Thus, we need to be smart enough to know where our strength is and what we shouldn't put our nose in. We do have a responsibility, as I see it, to let mankind survive, and the only way to do that is to evolve. Those who choose the Machine Kingdom are doomed because they will not survive as a human species.

Phase 2 (Anno 6-15 or 2018-2027)

This phase is going to force the fence-sitters to make up their minds. It will be clear for many people that there are two main choices. Of course, the so-called *Machine Riders,* who are those young children who have incarnated here (and will continue to incarnate here) in these times to dig deeply into technology and make that the main priority in their lives, will just ignore and laugh at those who refuse to have anything to do with moving into Smart Cities and use *smart* products. It will be a hard choice for some young people, though, to go against the current trend when most of their friends are into these tiny devices that can do so much, and this is all they talk about. The ones we're discussing now are those who are young today and those to come within the next few decades.

During these ten years of Phase 2, the frequencies within the mass consciousness are going to clash in such a dramatic way that the Earth on a metaphysical level is going to take the full step toward realities where she can host the New Human.

Phase 3 (Anno 16 and onward or 2028 and on)

This future phase is when the Machine Kingdom is going to be well-situated in the making of some realities, while the New Era on the New Earth (or the New Earths) will become a fact. I use multidimensional terms here rather than linear, which means there will be more than one version of Earth that will house the Machine Kingdom as well as there will be more than one Earth that will house those who are going back to nature. In some versions, there will be people who will live like savages lived thousands of years ago, banishing all kind of technology and go back to making up fires in the wild and living either in tents or in small shacks, side by side with others who live in smaller cities, but only use the most basic technology, which will assist them in their daily life. In other versions there will only be those who live in small villages or towns, but the more extreme versions will be very rare. If we look at it from a multidimensional perspective we will be able to imagine all kinds of Earths because the versions are as many as there are humans and as many as there are thoughts thinking up future worlds. You need to have a multidimensional mind to be able to fully grasp this because it can be quite mind-stretching.

Living in the Living Library—Guardians of the New World

Now, can we be sure that once we have established our New Earth, we are not going to fall back into old patterns again? Of course, there is a small chance that even enlightened beings get fooled and manipulated—we already know that because that's how we got into this mess in the first place. However, there is a big difference between then and now. At that time, millions of years ago, humanity was naïve, even though we were multidimensional. We were playful, happy, friendly, and yes—naïve. It was not that we didn't know there were bad apples out there in the universe—some of them had visited Earth while the Namlú'u walked over the savannahs, and the Namlú'u's high vibration and integral manner were always winning attitudes. Besides, we were rarely alone here on Earth—there were other star beings here as well, such as the Titans and the Dragons. We had a lot of fun, letting our Fire swarming and swirling freely over the mountains and valleys and even out in the universe.

Therefore, if this was the case, how could we be so trapped? Well, we were trapped because of our naivety and innocence. We didn't know much about manipulation, and this was our weakness. Lucifer and his Fallen Angels noticed this, and Lucifer (Prince EA or Lord ENKI—same being) figured out exactly how to trap human souls. If we were innocent and enjoyed having fun, and more important, we also were extremely curious, it was simple to seduce us into taking bodies from which we couldn't escape. Once we entered them, we were trapped in a very sophisticated control system, which included life, death, and afterlife—there was no way out. It didn't help, either, that Lucifer won the war against the Orion star beings who were here at the time. Once the war was won, the Earth was Lucifer's.

Now, however, we are much wiser. I am not talking about the entire human population —I mean those of us who are awake and are heading back to where the Namlú'u once were. We still may have some way to go before we are as free as the Namlú'u were before the AIF came, but when we're there, we are so much wiser. Also, we will not be able to hide anything from each other. Not only will we be telepathic and psychic, but we will also be experts in reading energy fields. However, there is one thing here we should be aware of, and that is that the Namlú'u had better genetics than we do—we have *watered-down* genes from other star races as well as their genes. I don't know where we stand in comparison, but I know that we will be able to do more or less the same things that our ancestors did.

There are certain guidelines we need to set for ourselves. In my opinion, there are four main ones, built on ancient South American traits, that I think are worth implementing on ourselves, starting now. They are as follows:

1. Don't cheat
2. Don't lie
3. Don't steal
4. Don't kill

I think that covers it.

Another thing we need to practice if we want to become the Guardian of the Living Library is to go out in nature and *become nature*. For example, if you want to know how an ant lives and works, what is better than becoming an ant? Therefore, then the question is, how do you become an ant?

I don't know about you, but when I was little, I used to go out in the woods every now and then and study what was there. I could lie down on the ground so I could see the world from the perspective of the small creatures, such as the ants, the beetles, etc. I used to imagine how it was to be so tiny. Every little straw of grass was like a tree to them—they all lived in a microworld, I realized. Then I saw how the ants actually had paths and roads on which they traveled when they went out to grab little straws and other practical things they needed to improve the ant house. They always seemed so busy—they were hardly ever still—and I was thinking that they never seemed to get a chance to lie and relax like I did when I watched them. I also saw how loyal they were to each other. If an ant was killed or wounded, another ant that came its way immediately left what it carried and instead started carrying his ant-friend back toward the ant house. I also noticed that when two ants met each other on the road, they used their antennas to *feel* each other out—perhaps to see if the other one was from the same ant tribe.

I often used to do things like that, and I could fantasize how it was to be one of those ants, thinking of it as *a day in the life of an ant.* By fantasizing about it, I simply split my fire and inserted it in a tiny ant without understanding that this is what I actually did. I became that ant and could experience how it is to be one.

I also loved to communicate with the trees. We had a deep forest just outside our house when I was little, and when I grew up, no one was afraid of crazy people kidnapping children or raping them. In my neighborhood, that was unheard of, and our parents let us run free wherever we wanted as long as we were back for lunch and dinner. It was a wonderful time for us children! Today, no one dares to let their children do that anymore. Anyway, I could stand in the middle of a glade and watch the old trees very carefully. For some reason, I usually didn't have a problem with tuning into their frequency, and they told me old stories about what had happened in their part of the woods and even in other places, farther away. Even though they were all rooted and couldn't go anywhere, they all seemed to be aware of each other and knew what was happening in all parts of the forest. I was little then and didn't understand how that was possible when they couldn't move, but of course, they were connected via the root system and the earth. I didn't find it strange to be able to communicate with the trees because no one had told me that you couldn't. This is why it's so important never to tell our children that this or that is impossible. Nothing is impossible! The more the children are allowed to stretch their minds, the better. This will be very normal in the New Era, once we are well situated.

Communicating with nature and being able to *be* what you communicate with is very important if we want to become

Guardians of the Living Library. I strongly advise you to go out in the forest—drive to one if you can or if you don't have one close by—and start observing what is there. Once you are able to focus your thoughts on what is there in front of you, you will realize that nothing is what you thought it was—it's so much more! Still, being in communication with nature is not only to talk with plants, rocks, and animals, but to become one with all of it. This is what being a *creature of nature* means. Once we can do this, the love we will feel for Mother Earth will be greater than anyone can perceive at this time. That's part of being truly multidimensional—you become the dimensions, and you create them as you wish!

On a one-on-one basis, and sometimes within a group, many of us will soon be able to perceive and communicate with interdimensionals. As our frequencies increase, we will start seeing things that do not belong to the 3-D reality. Some of us have already started to do that. However, once we've reclaimed our positions as Guardians, ET contact will be as normal as anything else in our lives. Many are coming to visit, wanting something from the Living Library, and we will decide whether that is appropriate or not by reading a being's energies and looking at its history. We are also going to be teachers. We won't need to go to a class to learn about these things because we will just *know,* because we are integrated with nature. We will intuitively know which plants will heal certain beings, and which part of the Living Library will teach the visitor whatever they want to know. It will be a very rewarding and exciting existence. Upon all that, we will be able to nano-travel the universe without any need for spacecraft. We will be able to travel with our thoughts.

What people have the hardest time with before they *get it* and start thinking more multidimensional is that in reality nothing is *linear.* The analytical mind always wants to understand things in a linear manner, and if it doesn't make sense that way, it doesn't accept it. Still, most people accept that their dreams are not linear and make little sense to the analytical mind. If they could only comprehend that the dream state is more real than the awakened state, things would start to make sense. Or like Seth said:

> Your next question is easy to anticipate, of course, for you will want to know the origin of that 'interior universe' from which I have said the exterior one ever emerges—and here we must part company with treasured objectivity, and enter instead a mental domain, in which it is seen that contradictions are not errors—an inner domain large enough to contain contradictions at one level, for at another level they are seen to be no contradictions at all.[80]

This is something worth carrying with us. If there are two answers to the same problem, and they both seem to make sense when looked at one by one, but are different from each other, you have a contradiction. Hence, you may think that you haven't solved the problem. Instead, you may indeed have solved it in a more thorough way than you thought you ever could—you just solved the problem on two different levels of consciousness simultaneously. You can disregard them or accept them because they are contradictions to the analytical mind, but just remember that on another level of consciousness, contradictions stop being contradictions.

With this I am going to end this handbook on how to become more multidimensional in the New Era. I hope these pages have been a help to some, and perhaps, there are a few things you can carry with you to the next level of awareness.

We live in extraordinary times, indeed, and I, for one, am happy that I was able to get a body this particular lifetime—

---

[80] Jane Roberts, "Seth on the Creation Myth", op. cit.

perhaps the most important life I've been living in a physical reality. Never before, since we entered the 3-D reality, has the future looked this bright. We are about to do something that goes against all odds, and humanity's future literally lies in our hands.

Thank you for letting me share my thoughts with you, and I wish you a wonderful journey into a multidimensional reality in a Multiverse that is unique for you.

Your love and your knowledge will protect you—always!

Printed in Great Britain
by Amazon